Sam B. Hall Jr.:

Whatever is Right

By Jerry L. Summers

ISBN: 1-878096-77-X

First Printing, 2005

East Texas Baptist University
1209 N. Grove Street
Marshall, Texas 75670-1498

Table of Contents

Representative Hall on the Capitol steps.

Preface

This book is the product of several factors including the founding of the Hall Professorship at East Texas Baptist University in 1993 and, in the period after his death in 1994, the frequent comments of East Texans about the significance of Sam B. Hall Jr. By 1997 I developed the first notion of a book in his honor; the idea then was to invite and assemble the written testimonials of several dozen individuals—family members, congressmen, judges, and, simply, friends—who wanted Judge Hall properly remembered and honored. Therefore, the testimonials came, all of them revealing convincing insights into Hall's life, character, and deep influence on other persons. The testimonials, however, comprised an uneven collection that I recognized might fit better into a complete biography.

This biography is mostly the product of some 150 interviews and conversations between 1998 and 2003. Apart from a bale of wartime love letters to his beloved Madeleine, Sam Hall Jr. wrote letters that were brief and few. Consequently, his letters provide little to help fill out a biography; moreover, he kept no journals or diaries. Judge Hall's life record existed, and exists, chiefly in the lives and memories of those persons who survived him. The nature of the man, his relationships, and the biographical research process means that this book is certainly neither a critical exposé nor chiefly a political biography. It is primarily a biography that shows how Sam Hall Jr. majored in interpersonal relationships while engaged in his careers as a lawyer, congressional representative, and federal judge.

Therefore, I must thank so many persons, beginning with Madeleine Segal Hall and the Hall family, for agreeing to and cooperating with this project. Judge Hall's long-time secretary and administrative assistant, Sue Jordan, also provided encouragement and assistance. His law colleagues, his judicial law clerks, the congressional interns, fellow Members of the U. S. House of Representatives, and fellow members of the judiciary, all have helped me to identify and report the measure of the man. I also cannot neglect to mention his friends, fellow civic servants in Marshall, Texas, and beyond, who helped to prepare and promote him for leadership and shared their insights about him.

Ben Rogers of the Baylor Collections of Political Materials at Baylor University provided extensive and gracious early help with the Hall Papers. For the Hall family background and resources on Marshall and Harrison County, members of the volunteer staff of the Harrison County Historical Library and Museum (Hubert Bender, George Choate, Alice Barron, Ruth

Briggs, Edna Sorber, and DeLane Johnson Townsend) were very kind in directing me to the proper resources. Richard Fluker provided access to the Marshall Independent School District Board of Education minutes. Marguerite Glass Ratcliff's political scrapbooks—a treasure trove—and her boundless enthusiasm require my thanks. Throughout the project, the student workers in the Department of History and Political Science at East Texas Baptist University have helped with interview transcriptions and clerical work. I wish to thank Michael Porter, Katie Matthis, Brianne Hoffpauir, Carrie Joiner, Amanda McClaran, Derek Hatch, Jean Githinji, Tiffany Fitts, and Megan Hunter for their help.

My former and present colleagues have provided encouragement and advice: Charles Taylor and David Chrisman provided early encouragement; Jerry Hopkins and Linda Hudson have provided succinct and useful criticisms. Robert Ellison, Linda Hudson, and Archie MacDonald, Regent's Professor of History at Stephen F. Austin State University, reviewed and criticized the manuscript at various stages. Their recommendations have contributed to a much better book, though one with imperfections for which I alone take responsibility.

East Texas Baptist University helped with early research funding. Former Vice-President for Academic Affairs Donald W. Rominger Jr. gave support and useful comments on the manuscript. Vice-President J. Paul Sorrels gave an extra nudge to get the book done. The university institutional advancement staff is to be thanked: from 1998 until his departure to serve at another university, Vice-President for Institutional Advancement Jay Orr; more recently David Jones, Larry Wickham, and Catherine Crawford.

Finally, and most importantly, my wife Debra has never begrudged me the weekends, evenings and vacation times that have allowed me to complete this project while keeping a full schedule of teaching and departmental chairmanship duties. No one has supported me more; like her father, and like Sam B. Hall Jr., she makes good things happen. I dedicate this book to her.

A Foreword

By Charlie Stenholm

I had the privilege to serve with Sam B. Hall, Jr. in the U.S. House of Representatives for a little more than seven years, and for that reason it is a great honor to provide the foreword for Professor Summers' outstanding biography of the gentleman from East Texas.

In West Texas, we talk about "tractor seat common sense," and Sam possessed "East Texas tractor seat common sense" in great abundance.

Sam was a truly good, decent man, one of the finest I have ever known. My experience in Congress would not be the same if I had not had the opportunity to learn from Sam after I was elected in 1979. He was an excellent role model, and I benefited greatly from serving with him in the Texas Delegation.

I was a young cotton farmer from West Texas, and Sam had represented East Texas in Congress for several years. I quickly admired Sam's conservative common sense, his sound judgment and the strength of his character. He truly was a representative of the people.

He took seriously his service to his family, our country and God. It did not take long for me to understand just how central Sam's faith in God was to him. It may sound simple, but he always acted like the strong Christian he was. In particular, I recall his belief that Americans have freedom of religion, not freedom from religion. In this, he clearly showed he was a patriot.

Sam always voted his heart, even when his beliefs differed—sometimes sharply—with the Democratic Party line; in this, Sam and I were kindred spirits. I think it is safe to say that if only the Democratic Party had listened more carefully to Sam, our party would still be in the majority today. Indeed, if there were more Members like Sam in Congress I believe it would be a different, more civil institution.

Congress has changed a lot in the years since Sam B. Hall, Jr. walked these corridors. I admire Sam even more as the years pass because he exemplified the best traditions of the House of Representatives with his convictions and personal integrity. He was able to work with people he may have disagreed with a good portion of the time, but he could still differ with them in a respectful, honest manner.

The enduring lesson I learned from Sam was the power of one Congressman to represent more than one vote, particularly since he stood for conservative values and played an instrumental role in the Boll Weevils, an organization of conservative Democrats, now called the Blue Dogs. More junior Members regularly looked to Sam for direction on various issues and voted in accordance. I know because I was one of them.

This biography is just as much about Madeleine Segal Hall—Sam's partner, helpmate and fellow campaigner of 48 years—as it is about Sam. The spouse of a Member of Congress lives the Congressional experience just as much as the Member does, and I know Madeleine lived it all, the good and the bad, at Sam's side.

Professor Summers should be commended for writing a compelling biography of Sam. This book clearly is the product of years of meticulous research. I am particularly impressed with the many letters and other correspondence he exchanged with Sam's family and friends over the years in order to glean tremendous insight into the life and times of this remarkable legislator.

In addition, I want to commend the leaders of East Texas Baptist University for their vision in supporting and facilitating this project as a worthy tribute to their former student.

January 11, 1924—April 10, 1994

A time in the history of the United States of America when one man made a difference.

Introduction

People who knew Sam B. Hall Jr. learned to recognize and anticipate "the look," an expression he probably inherited from his mother and developed over a lifetime. With close family members, especially his daughters, "the look" could convey a range of emotions or warnings—that he was surprised, upset, or, it could mean a witty comment or prank was forming within, soon to erupt. "The look" was just one expression in his repertoire, inseparable from his attractive personality and impressive size, and just one reason Sam Hall distinguished himself memorably in many situations, with many people.

Born in 1924, Sam Hall Jr. grew up in an East Texas town that had more in common with towns of the Deep South than it did with Texas cities to the west, yet it was a distinctive environment also infused with a frontier Texan identity less than a century old. Hall was the son and nephew of lawyers who had risen to local and regional prominence. Inheriting the high visibility belonging to a family high in the social and professional ranks, Sam Hall Jr. had opportunities to do something positive with his life and he made good use of them.

This book tells the story of an enthusiastic, dutiful young man fully accustomed to and comfortable with his family background and upbringing, a young man who emulated the best models he knew—his father Sam B. Hall Sr. and uncle Reuben Hall, both of them lawyers and judges. He developed a successful, recognized law career, from which he received many personal and financial benefits. As a maturing civic servant and leader, Hall used his distinctive gifts, contributing time, energy and effective leadership to improve his community. Yet, he dreamed of serving his country in a greater way and did so, distinguishing himself in two relatively brief careers, successively, as congressman and federal judge. In doing so, he moved beyond the narrow confines of his East Texas background, broadening his perspective on the nation and the world. At the same time, Hall never left his East Texas identity and values. No longer simply an East Texas conservative Democrat, Hall demonstrated that his positive qualities—a gregarious, optimistic personality and a well-developed personal integrity—served him and those whom he served in every context. The experience was reward enough for him, but his peers, friends and family were motivated to honor him late in life for his exceptional service.

There are many ways to evaluate public figures: longevity and distinction in service, significant, enduring contributions, and comparison with others are familiar criteria. One may also examine the intricacies of conduct and personality, noting the quality of relationships and others' perceptions about the person who is the focus of the examination. Though this biography is the work of one author, it also is genuinely the product of many others' memories about Sam B. Hall Jr., mostly recollections of a varied group of East Texans. It is important in Hall's case to know what his colleagues in the Bar, the federal judiciary and the Congress thought about him. One who reads this book will know why these persons respected and loved him. His closest friends and family loved him even more, not only because they were intimates, members of the innermost circles of his life. Sam Hall was the kind of man who made any relationship rise above the norm, regardless of the circle to which one belonged. His professional colleagues and friends from his hometown and elsewhere, and his family all recognized that in Sam Hall Jr. they had someone who brought enthusiasm and confidence into their lives. His influence remained after his death, if only in memory and in the legacy of love and service he left among those he touched.

This book is not the blind celebration of a beloved individual. Sam B. Hall Jr. had his faults. Some resulted from his parochial origins or relatively modest educational and travel background, some from his limitations as a human being. He was no cosmopolitan. His conservatism and initial, limited experience beyond the borders of Texas sometimes ill-suited the demands of a congressional career, though his suitability to represent the people of East Texas was self-evident and appreciated, and his effectiveness as a legislator and member of congressional committees earned him the plaudits of his colleagues, constituents, and outside organizations. His congressional experience also bolstered his preparation to serve as a federal judge.

These general factors receive greater attention in the following pages. In them I hope the reader will become acquainted with, and willingly appreciate, a man whose intriguing personality, consistent convictions, personal integrity, love for people, and contributions to his community and country make him worth remembering.

1

The Hall Family Background

On a certain day, or perhaps on several, the young Sam B. Hall Jr. pulled a knife from his pocket and scored his mark on the Harrison County, Texas, courthouse. Inside, at the landing on the worn marble stairway, halfway between the rotunda floor and the second floor, the great cast-iron newel post had "SAM HAL" scratched boldly onto its broad top surface—the last "L" in Hall missing for lack of space. In the year 2000, the name showed even through layers of paint. One wonders whether Sam B. Hall Sr. ever noticed his son's mischievous work, or, if the etchings were actually those of someone holding a grudge against one of the Halls.

During his career as a lawyer and a federal judge, Sam Jr. made his mark in the old and the new Harrison County courthouses, as well as the federal courthouse in Marshall, all of them within hailing distance on Peter Whetstone Square. With those things alone he anchored himself deeply in the history of his town and county. But he also compiled an exceptional record as a local civic servant and as a Representative for the Texas First Congressional District. Thus he distinguished himself beyond all but a few native sons of Marshall, Texas.

The Halls, father and son, left their marks on the old courthouse in other ways. The old Harrison County Courthouse centered on the square was the third built on the site, on one of the higher hills in the town. As he had done with a dozen other Texas courthouses, architect James Riely Gordon drew its dimensions. A golden-domed structure of golden brick, Texas limestone, red granite facing and columns, and built in the Renaissance Revival style of the period, the courthouse opened in 1900, and by the time Sam B. Hall Sr. had become county attorney in 1942, it had served a full generation. His elder brother, Reuben, had been a lawyer and state's attorney in its courtroom. The county opened a new, more spacious courthouse in the 1970s. After a career of prosecuting and trying cases in the old Harrison

County courthouse, the senior Hall never felt at home in the new one. Sam Jr. lawyered in the old and new, even representing clients before his father, who sat as judge of the 71st State District Court. By the mid-1980s Sam Jr. presided as judge in the federal courthouse on the south side of the square, less than an easy stone's throw from the old courthouse.

Sam B. Hall Jr. was born in Marshall, Texas, to Sam Blakeley and Valerie Hall on January 11, 1924. His birthplace preserved traditions from the days of the Republic of Texas when, like numerous other southern families, the Halls relocated from states east of the Mississippi to Texas. A frontier community whose founders brought their southern culture and traditions westward in the 1830s and early 1840s, by the 1850s Marshall was the fourth largest city in Texas. The Halls settled in Harrison County between Marshall and Hallsville. Like their neighbors they bound themselves to the cotton culture and to the labor of the slaves that produced it and other crops. They brought slaves with them and increased the number of bondsmen they held up to the time of the Civil War.

Sam Jr.'s grandfather, John Will Hall, was the second son of Charles Maclin and Ambrillus Price Hall. Charles had been born in Tennessee, Ambrillus in Alabama. They came from Alabama about 1843 after marrying and starting their family—the records show her as a fourteen-year-old bride. In 1850 she was twenty-four, with sons "CO" or Clem, who was ten years of age, and "JW" or John Will, aged seven. John Will as an infant would have been too young to remember the trek to Texas in 1843. His younger brothers were C. M. or "Mont" and Rufus. His one sister M. Catherine was four years younger than he.

The Halls migrated with a larger family group that included Charles Hall's father, William Wakefield Hall, his mother Pamelia (Emily) Shropshire Hall, and brothers, Montraville J., John B., William W., Rufus C., and sister Ann E. Josephine Hall. Most of them, including William and Emily Hall, had come from Franklin County, Tennessee, but other members of the party came from Jackson County, Alabama. Related mostly by marriage, the families included some Blalocks, Mitchells and Prices. According to one family recollection, they journeyed to Texas by flat-bottomed boat. If so, their route would have started in northern Alabama on the Tennessee River, continued to the Mississippi at Cairo, Illinois, then down the Mississippi to the Red River, and up the Red to Shreveport, Louisiana, a short distance from Harrison County. Until their deaths in 1849 and 1854, Sam Jr.'s great-great grandparents, William and Emily Hall, resided with Montraville J. Hall at the plantation house later known as Edgemont. Slaves made bricks for its construction in 1845; the house still stands on Hall's Hill west of Marshall. [1]

In the year 2000 the family of Sam B. Hall Jr. still owned a portion of the lands originally held by a Hall relative, Samuel P. Hall, before the family settled in Texas. Sam Jr.'s great-grandfather Charles M. Hall began buying land in 1845, acquiring the first parcel of property, which remains in the Hall family to the present. On October 6 he paid his brother, Montraville J. Hall, $150 for 100 acres of land "about three and a half miles west from the Town of Marshall, in said County, on the waters of Potters Creek." His land adjoined that of his father, William Hall. The property either came from or adjoined the collection of larger tracts for which one Samuel P. Hall had gotten the patents, or certificates, as early as 1838, only a year or so after the Republic of Texas claimed all lands and the right to disperse them on the basis of previous legal arrangements. The 1838 patent involved almost three "labors" of land, about 525 acres, and the 1844 certificate involved a section or 640 acres of land on Potters Creek. [2]

The Charles Hall family lived on land bordering the properties of William McKinney, G. W. Morgan, and Ephraim Tally. In 1847 Charles M. Hall bought 320-acres for thirty-two dollars, 310 acres on Potter's Creek in 1856, 330 acres for $2,000 in 1857, and 220 acres in 1859. These transactions established him with lands sufficient to run a moderately sized plantation, which, like those of his relatives, could be worked with the labor of family and slaves. [3]

The Hall families owned enough slaves to work the crops on their plantations. Brother Montraville had fourteen, seven females and seven males, and his brother John B. held six, as attested in the 1850 census. Ten years later they had expanded their property, with Montraville holding the largest number of bondservants in the family, thirty-three. Charles M. had thirteen slaves, with two adult females at age 30, and four males, and eight were children under ten years of age. He had acquired some 1,200 acres, and he and Ambrillus had five or six children. Among them was John Will, their second son. [4]

Charles M. Hall died probably from pneumonia, and without a will, on March 24, 1862. John Will was named administrator of his estate sometime after the war. [5]

Sam Jr.'s grandfather, John Will Hall, attended Marshall University—a secondary school at best. By 1862 the Civil War aroused large scale response from Texans who volunteered for service by the thousands. Most Texan support went to the defense of Confederate positions in southern Missouri, Arkansas, and northern Louisiana, with over twenty regiments of Texans—cavalry, dismounted cavalry, and infantry—serving the Confederacy in the Trans-Mississippi District. At age nineteen, John Will joined his older brother, Clem, and other relatives and friends in

Company K of the 17th Texas Cavalry, Clough Rangers, under Captain Gil Mackay. The 17th Texas Cavalry was among those units dismounted early on as the generals needed infantry rather than poorly trained warriors on horseback. Family lore placed John Will and Clement at the Battle of Pea Ridge in late 1862, and later they appear to have taken part in the defense of Arkansas Post. In January 1863 when both armies suffered from soaking dampness and intense cold, John Will and Clement were among the men captured in the overwhelming Union army onslaught against the Post of Arkansas and Fort Hindman. John Will was held as a prisoner of war at Camp Douglas, Illinois, just south of Chicago. At some point before his capture he had been promoted to sergeant. The frigid weather and dampness hastened death for many of the sick and wounded during transport. Clem fell ill with pneumonia, yet lived long enough to be listed in prison at the St. Louis and Jefferson Barracks in Missouri, where he died on March 4, 1863. One uncle, Rufus C. Hall, was listed as dead in September, 1862, and another, William W. Hall, was imprisoned in St. Louis. Captain Gil McKay never returned home. [6]

John Will Hall spoke later in life about his reassignment after release from prison camp and his service with the Army of Tennessee in the Chickamauga campaign. Whether he served beyond that is uncertain, but at some point, perhaps after a bout with pneumonia, he was told the war was over and he could go home. Whatever the conditions or time of his release, Sergeant John Will Hall and other soldiers took an amnesty oath after Appomattox, perhaps at the courthouse in Shreveport, Louisiana, and then walked home. The returning Texans parted company at road junctions to go to their own towns. John Will Hall entered Marshall and passed Marshall University in the rags of his former uniform. Before he got through town, the cobbler had measured him for a gift of new shoes. At his homecoming—and before he was allowed in the house—Ambrillus had the black servants shave him, cut his hair and scrub him to remove the grime of months of neglect and travel. The two-story frame house had a gallery—a porch—all around the lower level, and John Will slept there for some time. He had a hard time adjusting to the house after living so long in tents, in the open, and in prison. [7]

The war, the loss of immediate family, relatives, and friends from Harrison County, were troubles to contend with during and after the war. John Will Hall came of age as a soldier, a prisoner of war, and as one of the blessed veterans to return home. He was for a time the man of the family until his mother Ambrillus remarried. In November, 1868, she married Captain John Blakley, a planter and farmer from Rusk County. Blakley (also spelled Blakely even in official records) and his large family moved to the Hall plantation. A neighbor lady watched as seven or eight girls clambered out of the "conveyance" and over a rail fence. She exclaimed, "John Will, your wife just jumped the fence!" That prophecy came true in February, 1872, when he married his step-sister, Alice, the tenth of eleven children. He was twenty-nine; she was three months short of her seventeenth birthday. [8]

Charles M. Hall's personal property was dispersed in an estate sale on February 19, 1870. The Blakleys bought as much as anyone, especially the household items such as bedsteads and chests, plow equipment, five bee-stands, two smoothing irons for a dollar, and a thirty-dollar cook stove. Four mules named Jude, Molly, Kit, and Sal, and two cows with their calves went to various buyers. [9]

On April 1, 1871, Charles's real estate, valued at $5,300, was distributed between Ambrillus A. Blakely (160 acres), his married children, John Will Hall and M. Catherine Livingston (83.5 acres each), and his minor children, Rufus (100 acres) and Josephine (103 acres). [10]

Sam B. Hall Jr.'s grandparents John Will and Alice Blakley Hall had eleven children; two died as infants, and a daughter, Sue, died of typhoid fever as a child. Eight boys came in rapid succession and shared lives of work, play, church, and school at the one-room Noonday schoolhouse in western Harrison County. Sam B. Hall Sr. was born on September 12, 1888, about five miles northwest of Hallsville. Some natural pairings in interest and occupation occurred. The brothers Norman and Chesley were telegraphers, Went and Fred were farmers, Richard and Grady became rural mail carriers, and Reuben and Sam became lawyers in Harrison County. They grew up after the Civil War and Reconstruction period, and their world was markedly different than the one in which their parents had come of age, met, married and built a family in postbellum Texas, a few miles north of Hallsville. For many years the Hall household included Owaisa, the orphaned daughter of friends named McPherson who died, their children sent to live with various families. From the time that John Will brought Owaisa and her small trunk to the Hall home, she was considered a daughter. She later married Ernest Lott and moved to California.

At some point the family—but not all—moved from the farm into Hallsville where the schools were better. John Will Hall believed in education and wanted its advantages for his children. The Freemasons commonly operated schools in Texas, and the younger boys and girls attended school at the Masonic Institute in Hallsville. The Masons employed a Mr. Ballard, who must have been an oracle, for Reuben idolized him and spent as much time with him as he could. Ballard taught Physics along with all the other subjects to the upper grades. Apparently he taught well, leaving his students excellently prepared. Reuben went on to the North Texas State Normal College in Denton and found he could not extend his education there; after about two weeks, he declared he would be better off farming. Mr. Ballard had covered their curriculum years before at Hallsville.

Reuben returned to Harrison County and after a few years passed the county examinations for teaching. He taught in various places including Gum Springs, near Hallsville, saving money to pay for tuition at the University of Texas when he was about twenty. Bartering for his room and board in Austin, he dealt with the proprietress of a boarding house, saying he would keep her table full of boarders in exchange for his meals, and exchanged daily chores for his bed. He worked odd jobs, sold suits and shoes, taught at a teachers' institute during the summer months, and did farm work. Later in law school, Reuben Hall worked for the state's attorney in Marshall during the summertime. By the time he entered private law practice, he had married Julia Anderson and started a family. With his law degree in hand, he served in Marshall as assistant district or state's attorney for three or four years. After John Scott decided not to seek another term as state's attorney in 1912, Reuben ran for the position, won and served three two-year terms in Harrison County. [11]

As youths, Reuben and Sam B. Hall Sr. chose to pursue careers in law. They found farm work ground on their souls, the cotton rows a sweaty bondage. The prickly, smothering oppression of sun and humidity in the cotton field convinced Reuben and Sam there must be a better vocation. One summer day when Reuben was twelve and Sam ten, they hoed to the end of a row and rested under a tree. Reuben declared he was "not gonna do this after I get grown." Sam asked what he planned to do. Recently in Longview, Reuben had visited the law office of Young and Stinchcomb and been impressed with the books and lawyers. He admired his great-uncle, lawyer Montraville J. Hall. Reuben said, "I'm gonna be a lawyer." They talked, and Sam said he would too. Neither of them knew what lawyers actually did, but each boy set his mind on becoming one. [12]

Some years later Sam Hall left the home environs in Harrison County for college at the University of Texas at Austin. He returned to teach school for five years, all the time studying law on his own until he took the bar exam on October 15, 1913. He passed it and formed a law partnership in January, 1914, with Joe S. Brown, but did not begin work as a lawyer until the school year ended in May, 1914. Hall was to work in private practice twenty-eight years, be district attorney for six years, and district judge for the 71st State District Court for twenty years. [13]

Sam entered the U.S. Army during the First World War and went to Camp Travis in San Antonio. His brothers, Reuben and Norman, visited him there, bearing a cake and a gift of muscadines that young Nell Hall had gathered for him. "I sent him a little sack of muscadines and I think that just about tore things up when he got those muscadines." He cried over them. He returned to Reuben's home after discharge from the army, in poor health after a bout with influenza during the epidemic of 1918. He sat by the hour before the fireplace, warming himself and counting his good fortune to be alive, home, and out of the army. [14]

Only a few years after they married, the Reuben Halls took in Joe Brown and the younger brother Sam, who lived with them for eight years until he married. They had a new house in the country. It had a power plant for electric lights and a telephone—a rarity in rural Harrison County. Sam's good nature, humor, and love for his nephews and nieces made him welcome, and the Reuben Hall household with its younger male guests was a harmonious, happy place. From the time she was two years old until her mother told her it was improper, Reuben's daughter Nell referred to Sam and Joe Brown by their first names. So Nell called them both "Uncle." Early each day Reuben's children, still in their nightgowns, came out on the house porch when Sam left for work. "He'd turn and go down the walk around to the car," Nell reminisced. "We would turn and go up to the edge of the porch. It was a high porch. And we'd go up there and we'd be up there waiting for the time he walked around there. We always hugged him and kissed him goodbye. Not our father, now, that was Sam." Sam gave them a hug and a stick of Wrigley's Juicy Fruit gum, which they dearly loved and for ever after associated with him. For his own use he alternated Juicy Fruit with chewing tobacco, especially in his young adult to middle years, keeping the gum in his desk to mask the taste of chewing tobacco and cigars. He had chewed since boyhood and chewed on a cigar if he was not smoking it. [15]

An exceptionally bad case of the measles made one of the children, Reuben Hall Jr., a lifelong invalid. The child's condition was so dire that the church congregation pleaded with God to spare his life. He had been the subject of one of the family's more peculiar stories. During the early fall when he was two, he saw the cattle being put through the dipping tank on the Vawter place next to the Hall family farm. Not knowing what he was not supposed to be able to do, he decided to dip the Hall cattle himself. He opened the corral gate and drove some ten head of cattle to the Vawter farm on Hinson Springs Road. The cattle did not know what he could not do, either. He prodded them through the dipping vat and drove them back to the home farm before anyone else knew it, except for the maid at the Lassiter place across the road. She declared, "Marie, ain't that the least boy you ever saw running those cows to the dipping vat?" [16]

Sam and Joe bought the family's first car. The 1913 Model T Ford tested their patience, so much so that Mrs. Reuben Hall was forced to prepare her girls before the young men left in the morning, plugging their ears with cotton. Invariably the process of starting the car produced utterances little girls should not hear. Said Nell, "The air would be filled with various and sundry oaths, the cranking and the driving." [17]

In January, 1919, Reuben Hall became the third member of the Hall, Brown, and Hall law firm in Marshall. Reuben and Sam were law partners for a time, and both eventually sought and gained political office as county attorneys. Like his elder brother, Sam Hall was well respected throughout Harrison County, and chiefly by the country people, from the time when he first ran for the office of county attorney. He concentrated his campaigning in the countryside, attended cemetery work days, church dinners-on-the-grounds, and country singings. Whatever events there were, he attended them. He remembered the people he met, if not always their names. Over the years he probably knew most people in rural Harrison County. His legal work had already shown people that a person was in legal trouble had hardly anyone better to help than Sam B. Hall. By then his brother had become judge of the 71st Judicial District of Texas, which included Harrison and Gregg counties, the same position Sam later held. Reuben was later the presiding judge from the 1st Administrative Judicial District of Texas. Reuben won election as an associate justice of the Court of Civil Appeals at Texarkana in November 1934, assigned to the position by Governor Miriam A. "Ma" Ferguson. [18]

Sam Sr. found his wife in the outer office of his law practice. Sam Jr.'s mother was Valerie Sidney Curtis, the daughter of Albert Sidney and Fannie Berger Curtis. Albert was a long-time sheriff and district clerk of Harrison County. Fannie, a housewife of Jewish parentage, also worked at the family's "Model Bakery" in Longview, and later served as county clerk after Albert's death. Sam Sr. and the family always joked that he married Valerie Curtis in order to get her out of the law office so that he could hire someone better. Sam's new secretary was Kathleen Casey, after whom the Halls named their daughter. Sam and Valerie went to Dallas for their wedding on March 22, 1923, where Gus Dunn, the renowned Church of Christ minister, could perform the wedding. Valerie joined the North Franklin Street Church of Christ in Marshall and remained a faithful member. She devoted a prominent part of her budget to buying flowers for the worship hall on Sundays, and seemed to consider it one of the best things she could do. It brought her joy, and the flowers brightened the building for everyone. [19]

Sam and Valerie made a complementary pair, presenting a blend of personalities that left a strong impression. Valerie's gruffness surprised people, while her humor delighted them. She had a generous spirit. Sam knew how to put people at ease, to present himself as their friend. He let people know they could open up, telling him what was important to them.

Sam Blakeley Hall Jr. was the eldest of Sam and Valerie's three children. A robust eleven pounds at his birth on January 11, 1924, for a time he wasn't shown around in the community. There was an epidemic of red measles, and parents were keeping their children isolated. Marshall then claimed 18,000 inhabitants as the largest city in East Texas. Around and beyond its town square were businesses such as the Russell-Graham Company department store, Matthewson Drug Company, Athos's Marshall Candy Kitchen on West Austin street, the F. W. Woolworth and Company on East Houston, M. L. Weisman's and J. C. Penney on North Washington, Smith Motor Company a block east of the courthouse, the haberdasher A. S. Zachary, Logan and Whaley hardware, and the Hub Shoe Store on Austin street.

The Marshall telephone directory identified the residences as occupied by white or "colored" families, and listed four cotton buyers, two cotton gins, and the Marshall Cotton Oil Company. There were eight blacksmiths, one chiropractor, and the ice company. There were at least twenty-two law firms. Listings of the Lodges and Halls of the Colored Knights of Pythias, the Elks, the Freemasons, and the Odd Fellows suggested the typical prominence of the fraternal organizations in the city.

During the week when Sam Jr. was born, William G. McAdoo was chasing the Democratic nomination for the presidency, speaking against "privilege," and appealing for lower income tax rates on small incomes. Pat M. Neff was governor of Texas. The local newspaper listed advertisements for the Smith-Phillips Motor Company and the inexpensive, new model Durant "Star Car." Joe Weisman and Company in Marshall advertised corduroy suits that included two pair of knickers for boys for just $5.95. During the following week, the United States government was calling China to account for bandits killing American missionaries and looting a mission compound. The local theater showed Hal Roach's new Pathecomedy, *Why Worry*, starring Harold Lloyd. And William J. Simmons, the founder of the revived Ku Klux Klan, was still claiming to be emperor of the Klan despite an order of banishment by H. W. Evans, the Imperial Wizard, and E. Y. Clarke, the Imperial Giant, of the KKK. On January 18, there was breaking news about the Teapot Dome scandal, a holdover from the Harding administration, brought to light only five months after Warren G. Harding died in office and Calvin Coolidge became President of the United States. [20]

Perhaps in the fall of his first year the proud parents took their son to the East Texas Fair in Marshall and entered him in the baby contest. He did not win, and, on the one hand, perhaps Sam and Valerie Hall were not too concerned about it; but, on the other hand, perhaps they were very upset at the outcome of the contest. As a grown man Sam Jr. gleefully dedicated his creative energies to a richly embroidered and tragic tale only remotely resembling the basic event. According to Sam the judges, horrified at the child with the big head and ears—possibly the ugliest child in East Texas—ordered the responsible parties to remove the little monster. Valerie and Sam retreated homeward, defeated, ashamed, heartbroken, blubbering, and inconsolable. The bigger the story got, the more Sam Jr. hoped it would annoy his mother. He loved the story as much for its creative possibilities as for the chance it gave him to tease her. He never tired of telling it. [21]

The Hall family lived in one or another of the Curtis and Hall homes that sat on a city block they largely owned; they were at 209 S. Wellington in 1924. Across the street was the Harrison County jail, where the inmates upstairs spent much of their days observing through barred windows all that occurred on South Wellington Street. As a toddler in his undressing stage, Sam Jr. gave the inmates some innocent entertainment on afternoons after Valerie had carefully bathed and dressed him. Left to sit on the porch of the house, he stripped off his clothes on a short trip from the front steps to the sidewalk. He even took the laces out of his shoes. Free of all restraints, naked as a jaybird, he ran up and down the sidewalk. Valerie knew the jail inmates would hoot at her if she chased Sam, so she sent Miss Ethel, the maid, to do it, even though Miss Ethel hated the embarrassment of the hooting and hollering from the jail crowd every bit as much as Valerie did. [22]

Valerie had another habit that Sam Jr. could have done without. Each afternoon at naptime she took a tree switch and whipped him until he cried. He did not want a nap, but after the whipping he cried himself to sleep. Until Sam caught on the whipping was a regular event. [23]

Born in 1927, Sam and Valerie's second son, William Sidney, died in April 1931 after an undiagnosed illness. Kathleen Hall recalled that her mother Valerie could never explain why William Sidney died, except to say that the illness started with seizures. They attacked suddenly, and when they came during the day it was Sam Jr.'s job to run to the neighbors' homes for help in case Valerie needed it. He returned breathless to help his mother as much as he could. [24]

The younger boy loved to sit in his Uncle Reuben's lap to hear stories about bears and other wild creatures. Normally a wonderfully sweet boy, William Sidney had a hair-trigger temper that often swelled to a rage. Valerie

The sons of John Will and Alice Blakely Hall, from left to right: Richard, Went, Chesley, Reuben, Sam, Norman, Fred, and Grady.

Sam and Valerie Hall were devoted parents to Sam Jr. and William Sidney. Valerie Hall never fully recovered from William Sidney's death.

Sam B. Hall Jr. with younger brother William Sidney - a "wonderfully sweet boy."

Sam Jr. at about 18 months of age.

Sam Jr. and Kathleen called each other "Bubba" and "Nan." The Halls lived in a new brick home on West Houston Street during the thirties and forties.

dressed the child in shoes with hard leather extension soles, terrible weapons when in anger he went for the shins of the closest person around. "Hot temper! Good Lord! He was just like a buzz saw," Nell Hall recalled. "If he got mad at you, he walked up and hauled off and kicked the fire out of you with those. He always hit you on the shin with that extension sole—I mean it would bring tears to your eyes!" He kicked the family housekeeper Miss Ethel so much that Nell was amazed she could walk. Ethel attended the boy's funeral, her shins still covered with bruises. [25]

The child's death knit the bond of protection ever more tightly between Valerie and her remaining son and later her daughter Kathleen. Valerie Hall never fully recovered from William Sidney's death. For the rest of her life at family Christmas gatherings, she carefully placed a toy on or under the tree—a toy that would have been an appropriate gift for her second son. His death affected her in practical ways. She somehow associated ground beef patties with his death; on the night that William Sidney became ill before he died, perhaps he had choked on some meat, or perhaps something else could have been wrong with it. Whenever she served her family ground beef it was loosely, thoroughly cooked. Her grandchildren never encountered a normal hamburger at her table. [26]

Sam's sister, Kathleen, came into the family on June 7, 1932. Her big brother Sam had the measles and so was not allowed to see her for a few days, and even then only through a window when she was five days old. The two had pet names for each other from early on; he called her "Nan" at least until she finished high school, and she called him "Bubba" for the rest of his life.

While the children were growing up, the Halls had a longstanding weekly ritual revealing the parents' great attachment for their children. For years, every Sunday, or very nearly so, rain or shine, Valerie Hall summoned a photographer from town to the house on West Houston Street. Everyone was ready for Sunday school, and thus dressed for pictures. The photographs from those sessions filled many boxes in the family collection. Valerie loved to dress her children well and could afford it. She especially favored Sam and got along more easily with him, or so it seemed to Kathleen, though if she were to be accused of partiality, Valerie would deny it. Perhaps her continuing grief over William Sidney's death reinforced the impression. Beyond that, however, it would be easy to speculate, perhaps simply to recognize, how the absolute devotion that Valerie and Sam Sr. had for their children enhanced Sam Jr.'s sense of security and confidence—characteristics he showed throughout his life. Sam Jr. began school at the age of five, probably too young to be in school, and his parents were anxious about him. Valerie parked her car at the school on the first day to watch him at recess time—to see whether he had friends and how he got along with the other children. William Sidney was in the car, too, and he cried out, "Daddy!" Valerie asked why he had called for his daddy, and turned to see her husband watching from his car. [27]

As he matured, Sam Jr. garnered respect out of a combination of his qualities, and being regarded a handsome boy did not hurt. The first time Charlene Carrington ever saw Sam Jr. was in the study hall at C. J. Collier Junior High School. She exclaimed that he was the best looking boy she had ever laid eyes on and asked who he was. Linda Thompson said, "Oh, that's Sam Hall." [28]

The young Sam Jr. enjoyed the advantages of a stable family and the certainty of his place in Marshall. His home life, church life, and schooling developed within a secure circle of family and friends. He never had to look far for others to confirm who he was, to know that he was loved and that he was naturally expected to fulfill certain roles in family and community—the roles of devoted son, brother and grandson, accepted friend, and representative of a leading Harrison County family.

2

Young Sam Hall to 1948

The family into which Sam B. Hall Jr. was born observed rituals typical of a time before television, air conditioning, and automobiles changed how people relate to their neighbors and to each other in their own homes. Sundays began with a horse ride before breakfast. After breakfast everyone dressed for Sunday school and worship. On Sunday afternoons there were long walks, often westward on West Houston Street, across the railroad tracks beyond the meadow and the county fairgrounds.

Meals were ritual. For many decades the Halls employed a black housekeeper and cook, Maggie Hiner, at the West Houston Street house. After the Halls built the new brick house on the north side of U.S. Highway 80 West, Maggie occupied a small house on the property about twenty yards away. A marvelous cook, Mrs. Hiner typically fixed two or three meals and retired to her own house in the evening. Close to Valerie's age and widowed many years, she lived into her nineties and died in 1997. Maggie was not "the help," but a friend, and virtually a family member even after retirement. Late in life she often visited the Hall home in town to demonstrate her recipes and cooking techniques to a family who knew how much her secrets and skills would be missed after she was gone. [1]

From the Hall home on West Houston Street one often heard the steam whistles or air horns of trains approaching from Hallsville and points west. When the wind calmed, one might hear rail yard sounds from the north side of town. There, the Texas and Pacific railroad employed more than a thousand men. Marshall's residents knew the train sounds, the echoing, metallic boom of a line of cars being coupled. Those who lived nearby could discern the progression of pops as couplers gripped each other in succession when the locomotives pulled on the line of cars. Townspeople checked their clocks by the steam whistle that announced the changing of shifts and the noon break in the railroad shops. The common wisdom told to children, akin to the wisdom of elders everywhere was about the dread and mortal danger of the railroad tracks: "Don't get too close when the train comes by, or it will suck you under!" One Sunday while crossing a set of railroad tracks Kathleen wedged a foot in the tracks and was forced to abandon her shoe while a train passed. She got the shoe back, but with added respect for the railroad presence that helped to define Marshall. [2]

As a teenager Sam Jr. was not allowed to travel to out-of-town football games if the school bus was to cross any railroad tracks. People needed no reminders about the hazards of collisions between automobiles and trains. Too, there had been a tragic accident that parents held in mind. In 1927, seven members of the Baylor University basketball team and three other students died when their bus crossed the path of a Missouri Pacific passenger train. Across Texas people remembered that tragedy and others like it. [3]

During the 1930s the Halls took long car trips, usually in Sam Sr.'s favorite Nash, and later in a blue 1937 Plymouth coupe. The most memorable trips were to Tulsa, where Valerie's sister lived. The family left Marshall around four in the cool darkness of a summer morning, on a drive that seemed endless in the days before major highways and interstates. A twelve-pound block of ice in the front floorboard cooled the air passing over it—at least for folks in the front seat. The Halls began long trips with a picnic basket stocked with Maggie's fried chicken, the tasty product of a frying session begun about three in the morning. But Sam Jr. and Kathleen usually had their pieces eaten before they passed the city limits. Sam Jr. favored the legs, Kathleen the breast. Years afterward, Sam Sr. joked that there would not have been so many dogs chasing the car if they hadn't been throwing out so many chicken bones. [4]

Valerie usually drove. On one trip Sam Sr. drove the family beyond Mt. Pleasant in Titus County as far as Talco. Valerie had been complaining about Sam's driving. They stopped. Sam Sr. got out, handed billfold and keys to Valerie and declared they could go on to Tulsa without him while he caught the bus home—but he did not, instead, he took the passenger seat, silent while Valerie drove. [5]

Opposed on principle to marital conflict, Sam Sr. generally took the closest way out, if necessary "taking a cold winter walk" out of the house. Asked how he and Valerie got along so well, he declared he never argued with her, but, "I want to tell you—I've taken a lot of those cold winter walks!" It was for him a winning way. Sam Jr. learned in his parents' home not to argue, and he would not in his own home. [6]

As brother and sister, Sam Jr. and Kathleen were close confidants throughout life. Hall had a strong protective urge for his sister. As an adult she frequently sounded out decisions and discussed problems with him; it was their habit to confer on the little things. After Sam Jr. died, Kathleen observed that many times when she faced a decision that reminded her of her wise older brother, she asked herself what Bubba would say about it. She called him "Bubba," the way she had said "brother" as a child; it was never anything but an endearing term to Hall. Even after he went to Congress, she called him Bubba: "I would call his congressional office and if Sue Jordan answered the phone, I would ask for Bubba. If she didn't answer, then I would ask for Congressman Hall." He called her "Nan" until she graduated from high school, "then it became Kathleen or sometimes 'Nuts.' I'd answer to anything he called me!" Kathleen always felt her brother's genuine affection for her. [7]

His love had its flaws. Once when he was sixteen or so and driving, Valerie had him take his sister to the cinema to a midnight showing of *The San Antonio Rose*. Embarrassed to have the little sister tagging along, Sam Jr. drove Kathleen "all over Harrison County," she later explained. He hoped that she would fall asleep and he could take her home before going to the movie himself. It did not work. As they rode he asked repeatedly, "Wanna go home?" No, she did not! Before the show time, Sam tried "to hustle me in there so all his friends wouldn't see him taking his little sister. We hadn't been there fifteen minutes and I was sound asleep!" [8]

Teenaged Sam Jr. bought a necklace for a girlfriend, Carolyn Hamil. They broke up, leaving him with the necklace engraved with an "H", so he gave it to his sister at Christmas. Deeply impressed to receive such a gift from her brother, in the 1970s Kathleen learned from Valerie why he had first bought the necklace. Madeleine Hall later told Kathleen that Valerie thought it too personal a gift for Carolyn, but he could give it to Kathleen. Apparently he did so with little or no complaint. [9]

As in former generations, the Hall family kept horses and rode frequently. Sam Jr. entered his horse into the show at the Central East Texas Fair. Lady got an energetic scrubbing, washing and grooming. At the fair, the horses and riders entered the arena. With Sam Jr. astride, Lady entered looking her best, but balked, going no further while other equestrians and their mounts passed by. His best efforts failed to get her moving. Sometime later Lady lay across an electrical wire and died—yet another frustration. Kathleen abandoned horses after an early, negative experience with one. She mounted a horse with a loose saddle—the horse had inhaled during cinching—so that saddle and rider ended up under the horse. She did not ride after that and considered it no loss. [10]

Sam Jr.'s identity as a son of the Halls of Marshall and Harrison County was secure by the time he enrolled at the College of Marshall (COM). No other educational institution had a stronger shaping influence on his life. At COM he prepared for law school, developed enduring friendships, and found his wife, Madeleine. That he did these things while living at home showed how the strong bonds with family and hometown shaped him first and always. Sam B. Hall Jr. never yearned to escape in order to find himself. He knew who he was, sensed where he belonged, and found adventure enough in familiar environs.

During the economic depression of the 1930s under President Franklin S. Groner, the College of Marshall struggled to keep students and survive financially. By the time Hall entered as a student, the college had added acreage and buildings from the former St. Joseph's Boy's Industrial Orphanage, which students called "The Vatican," adjacent to the original campus. There was a new girls' dormitory, Laura Groner Hall. The main classroom and administration building on campus remained Marshall Hall, which was completed and occupied in 1917. The college had been in operation only twenty-three years. It included a secondary-level academy as well.

There were new and old friends at the College of Marshall when Hall began as a freshman in the fall of 1940. Life at COM had many "family"characteristics because of the small number of students and the compact campus. The college offered personal attention, starting with the faculty and staff who enforced strict standards of etiquette and conduct that applied equally to "boys" and "girls." The social conventions of the 1940s imagined no reference to the students as "men" and "women." Unquestionably, the College of Marshall took the concept of *in loco parentis* (in the place of the parent) seriously and competently.

The college drew students chiefly from the villages and towns of East Texas, with a sprinkling of students from elsewhere in Texas, a few other states, and countries. Too, the college introduced young East Texans to the wider world, but also reflected the surrounding culture, including its Jim Crow segregation. In the 1940s there were public schools for blacks and whites, and the pattern played out in Marshall with COM and the private, historically black institutions Wiley College and Bishop College, one United Methodist, the other Baptist. Such was accepted as the proper social order.

Though at the time it may not have been so clear to him, Hall later confessed he had always been set to attend COM, mostly because of the influence of his friend Frank Groner. But he remained in Marshall for college due to strong family influence, which was perhaps not openly expressed, but nonetheless strong. The Halls tended to hold their children tightly, perhaps too tightly. As a high school senior, Sam Jr. received Representative Wright Patman's recommendation and consequently an offer to attend the United States Military Academy at West Point. Sam Sr. and Valerie wanted that experience for him, but they did not want him to be apart from them, either. It bothered them, too, that their son as a USMA graduate and commissioned officer could be called up first in time of war. The prospects for another global war looked too strong when Sam approached high school graduation in 1940. An alternative was to study at Abilene Christian College in West Texas, and a girlfriend, Evelyn Metcalf, would be there too. But on the eve of his departure for Abilene, with his bags fully packed, Hall decided not to go. He could finish his first two years of college while living at home, and so he did. That decision established him in a wider East Texas circle of friends and with his life's mate, Madeleine. [11]

One day in summer 1941 Hall and his cousin Fred Hall visited the city swimming pool, where they met Madeleine Segal and Jean Solman, Madeleine's cousin from Houston. Nothing came of Sam and Madeleine's immediate mutual interest until later in the year. [12]

At the College of Marshall in fall 1941, Sam Hall and Madeleine quickly developed an understanding that theirs was a special relationship, and they happily nurtured it amid a growing campus perception that they were an "item." They dated other people, especially after Hall left to study in Austin and was drafted into the Army Air Force, but their relationship was clearly different. It began when Hall made a special effort to welcome Madeleine to campus, surprising her by coming by the dormitory when she first arrived. He invited her to go for a drive a few times, but they did not do that. In September 1941, the Central East Texas Fair was held at the fairgrounds adjacent the Hall home on West Houston Street. Hall and James McClellan were parking cars for fair visitors. Seeing Madeleine and her cousin Sue Brayn, Hall asked if Madeleine would like to do some rides. They rode the Ferris Wheel, the bumper cars and the Loop 'O Plane. With that and their unmistakable mutual attraction, they began dating. Within weeks the pair dreamed and talked about the life they wanted to have together. "I knew that year other dates were meaningless, and that my life would not be complete without Sam," Madeleine later recalled. He brought up marriage early on; she assured him they needed to wait a few years, and they did. She was seventeen, he eighteen. Madeleine always remembered what she wore that day at the fair: a pleated skirt with a pink Angora wool sweater, and probably saddle Oxfords. Hall remembered those days as the "beginning of a life of happiness that I hope to God never ends." [13]

Soon after the first date, Sam showed Madeleine his sense of humor. Madeleine recounted what he did as they entered the Paramount Theater in Marshall: "I was waiting for him to buy the tickets, and he turned to me and said, 'Did you bring your money?' I was shocked, but managed to look at him and say, 'No, I did not.' With that, he laughed and showed the tickets to the doorman. I knew he was a fellow with a sense of humor." [14]

College life for Sam and Madeleine involved plenty of time doing "just little nothing things" such as going to the lake, taking walks or canoeing. Hall visited campus frequently, actually every day, spending considerable time with the other boys in the dorms. Though he lived at home with his parents and younger sister, he was able to drive a car to school. He was especially popular because in those late-Depression years "he was the only one with a car" and was willing to take people places in it. [15]

Popular and involved, Sam and Madeleine fit well in campus society. In his second year, Hall was a cheerleader and tennis player, and served on the staff of the school newspaper, *The Compass*, and the yearbook, *The Martian*. He belonged to the student council, choral club, men's quartet, and was president of the Pre-Law Club.

The intriguing listings from the campus newspaper, *The Compass*, of November 11, 1941, revealed how Sam and Madeleine fit in and how well the students knew each other:

> "Ideal Boy—The person whom I would like to be marooned on an [island] with, if he had the: Personality of Sam B. Hall, Jr.; Profile of George Cobb; Habits and qualities of Bunt Lovelace; Hair of Bill Henderson; Nose of Quinton Carlile; Eyes of Jelly Blankenship; Teeth of Harold Taylor; Smile of Jack Ritchie; Lips of Jack Abel; Leadership of Bill Crayton; Cooperation of Billy Posey; Sportsmanship of Herbert Smith; Physique of Laurence Minton; Neatness of J. C. Norris; Intellect of George Earl Bennett; Poise of Melville Womack. Well, if a man had all these traits, who would not mind being marooned with him??????? Ideal Girl—The girl that all boys would go to the extreme to be on an island with, if she possessed the: Personality of Mattie Don Glover; Profile of Mary Lee Anderson; Habits and qualities of Sarah Gayden; Hair of Jean Waldrop; Nose of Martha Lee Willis; Teeth of Inez Head; Lips of Jessie Gwynne Cooke; Smile of Doris White; Dimples of Dorothy Wyatt; Hands of Louise Johnson; Leadership of Clestine Pinson; Sportsmanship of June Gottholt; Intellect of Marcelle Ramsay; Figure of Madeleine Segal; Neatness of Alieen [sic] Tardy; Cooperation of Jean Shepherd; Poise of Cara Pat Aikin."

The College of Marshall also felt like "family" because the faculty and staff knew and watched well over the students. Madeleine Hall remembered how Professor Sallie Margaret Duncan, a tough teacher, intimidated students, but her bluff persona failed to hide her caring personality. After Hall was drafted into the Army in 1943, Miss Duncan heard that he was coming home on a weekend furlough. She offered

Madeleine a room at her home so that she could visit with Sam and his family and would not have to return to the dormitory by the 7:00 P.M. curfew time. Of course, Madeleine took the offer. [16]

There were wonderful teachers: Miss Sallie Duncan, who had studied at Texas University, Baylor, and the University of Colorado, was head of the English department and also Dean of Women. J. Wesley Smith, the Academic Dean, was an unfailingly sweet, kind, gentle man, truly interested in his students' welfare. J. Hubert Boyd, a M.A. graduate of Baylor University and Professor of Education, was Dean of Men and a favorite, beloved teacher. Sam's favorite was Director of Athletics Norman Earl Barnes, an Austin College graduate who had also studied in Arkansas and California, was young and single, and "one of the guys" but so much more because of the many hours he spent with the young men on campus. His death during the war grieved his students deeply. A University of Texas graduate and member of the Texas Academy of Science, Kenneth McCutchan taught science. Other teachers were John H. Hill, head of the History department; Irene Howard, head of the Romance Languages department, David Hansard, head of the Music department, Monroe Tolar, head of Mathematics, and Evelyn Malone, who directed women's Physical Education. Lois Pinson, Gene Clift, and Virginia Bell respectively taught Piano, Art, and Speech. Mary Kay (Mrs. Franklin) Armstrong served as librarian and publicity director. The teaching staff was very well prepared for their time and their positions at an institution such as COM. Dr. Franklin S. Groner and Dr. J. M. Garner were President and Vice-President, but on such a small campus where everyone was well known, all were important, and all had multiple duties, though perhaps none were more important than Bessie Carter, who directed the dining hall. [17]

Sam Hall Jr. brought his good looks and pleasant personality with him as a freshman. Not finished growing physically, he was just less than six feet in height. During his Army years, he reached his adult height of six feet, two inches. In 1940-1941 Sam participated in the Debate Club, Pre-Law Club as Secretary-Treasurer, Rifle Club, and Little Theatre. He sang well and took part in the Choral Club of 1941-1942, which Berniece (Mrs. Rex) Brown directed. He came to Mrs. Brown, announcing that he was there to sign up for voice lessons and that it was the same as with his taking piano lessons: his mother's idea, not his. Nevertheless, he did enjoy singing. In a quartet, he sang baritone, Gareth Joiner sang lead, Lon Bates sang tenor, and Franklin Deering, bass. There were songs such as "When I Survey the Wondrous Cross," "Lo, How A Rose 'Ere Blooming," and "De Ole Ark's a-moverin'." The quartet's other members alleged that Sam routinely was late to practices because he was involved in so much. Hall sometimes sang in more informal settings, as when students would gather on Sunday afternoons. One number Helen Williamson remembered as well as Hall's beautiful voice was "Amapolla, my pretty little poppy." The College of Marshall recital on May 12, 1942, included Frances Hennessee on the program. Hall presented solos such as Giordani's "Caro Mio Ben," Franz's "Dedication," and Brahe's "Bless This House." He and Mrs. Rex Brown also sang the duet, "A Perfect Day," by Carrie Jacobs Bond. [18]

Early in life, Sam Hall made lifelong friends. His COM classmate Harold Taylor was such a friend, six years old when he met Sam Jr. in Mrs. Maloney's Sunday school class. Harold was the only son of a man who named his chickens after the women in their neighborhood around Gordon Street in Marshall—a fact likely not well-known then or since. Harold and Sam were infrequent companions until sometime in high school, and then people expected to see one if they saw the other. They were not into heavy mischief, and Sam should not have been if he always honored his parents as much as others have claimed for him. They probably never did worse when together than on the day they were riding in the Hall family's 1927 Essex and one of them laid the broad side of a tennis racquet out the window to the back of a black girl's head as she walked on the roadside, knocking her down. The bad deed was hilarious for only a moment, then shameful. Reality set in with a harsh lecture from Harold's father. Sam Sr. probably never knew about it, or Sam Jr. would have earned a whipping. [19]

Taylor and Hall stayed close at the College of Marshall and later became roommates at the University of Texas. At graduation Hall inscribed Harold's COM yearbook, The Martian, with the sentiments of a six or seven-year friendship. He wrote:

> Taylor I want you to always remember that ole' Hall is behind you 100% in everything you do, providing it's legal—and of course I know you wouldn't do anything that isn't honest and uplifting (50¢ for that please) Well P. G. just never forget that you are about the closest pal I have, and one that I'll always remember.

It was signed "Your Pal Hall." [20]

Student pranks and what today many would barely define as misconduct did occur on the COM campus. In one instance some students had a dance complete with a portable record player in the Marshall Hall fourth floor chapel. Apparently they assumed the teachers were gone for the night, but the science professor, Kenneth McCutchan, was at work in his office and ascended the stairs to learn the source of the music and noise. His observations yielded a list of names as the dancers fled the scene; one who fled unnoticed and unlisted was Madeleine Segal. [21]

Sam Hall Jr. and some other young men stole outhouses from all over Harrison County, many of them constructed by the Works Progress

Administration, to put atop the homecoming bonfire. District Attorney Sam B. Hall Sr. learned about it and called Sam Jr. at Matthewson Hall on campus, "Son, where were you last night?" Hall knew what his father meant and said that he had been at the college. Asked whether he had been at the college all the time, he said no, that the boys had been riding around some. That was true enough, as one of the young men, Joe Berry Pyle, had borrowed from his family's lumber milling business a flatbed truck ideal for hauling privies. Sam Sr. told his son, "I tell you what I want you to do. I want you and those boys who were with you to go out and get those outhouses and set every one of them back up where you took them from." It was one of life's most humiliating moments for Sam Hall Jr. Recalling the embarrassment he reminisced, "We set every one of them up and had to start over with a bonfire from scratch—but we had a bonfire." [22]

In fall 1941 the College of Marshall entered its Silver Jubilee year, and the Sixteenth Annual Harvest Festival program of November 13 included the coronation of the Court of Silver Jubilee. Sam B. Hall Jr. was master of ceremonies. Mrs. Rex Brown arranged and directed a fantasy production called "The Enchanted Forest," in which Hall played the Prince. Students pitched in a "penny a vote" to choose the queen and her court for the Silver Jubilee. Madeleine Segal was crowned Queen of the Silver Jubilee Court; Miss Jean Shepherd of Marshall was runner-up for Queen, and among the ladies in waiting was Miss Jeanne Waldrop of Springhill. [23]

Madeleine roomed in the Laura Atman dormitory (now Merle Bruce Hall) with Mildred Cornelius, who married Quinton Carlile. Another girls' dorm and the dining hall also sat about where the Rogers Spiritual Life Center was built in the 1990s. Among the students who worked in the dining hall were Joe Lovelace and Helen Chapman (née Williamson). Helen's brother, Theodore K. "Ted" Chapman, was among the COM students who died in military service during the war. Madeleine worked in the office of Dean Wesley Smith and in the post office; all but a few of the students worked to help pay their way. The college was always strapped for cash but found some way to keep its students. Dean J. Wesley Smith routinely brought carloads of fresh produce and other food items that he personally collected from farmers. Madeleine majored in business and remembered how Quinton Carlile lent her some good help with lessons in an accounting course. [24]

Hall found other lasting friends in Marion Holt and Rex Narramore. The Holt family paralleled the Halls in that Marion's father, like Sam's, was a county attorney. Holt and Hall were to become classmates at Baylor Law School, along with Joe Lovelace. Narramore, one of the quartet members and the class president for 1940-1941, called his associations with COM, Hall and Lovelace, and his memories of Norman Barnes and Dean Wesley Smith, the best two years of his life. Among Hall's closest lifelong friends was Joe "Bunt" Lovelace of Linden, Texas, whom he met in 1940. Lovelace lived in Frank Davis Hall. He later reminisced that when he was captain of the basketball team and Sam was a cheerleader, Coach Norman Barnes suggested they switch positions to see if the team could build a better record. Another lifelong friend, Jack Ritchie, came to COM in the fall of 1941, a pre-law student who made Sam Hall one of his first friends in Marshall. [25]

During their first year at the College of Marshall, the young men recognized the possibility of their roles and involvement in the war that seemed increasingly sure to come. On December 7, 1941, after morning church services, Sam Jr. and his Uncle Reuben went fishing at a lake near Texarkana. They returned in the late afternoon to a somber atmosphere as families gathered around their radios to hear the news from Pearl Harbor. On the COM campus everyone considered what would come next for America and themselves.

As he looked to the end of his COM career, Hall contemplated plans to finish the bachelor's degree at the University of Texas before entering law school. What he had begun at COM he planned to develop carefully and was eager to reach his cherished goal of entering law school to become a lawyer like his father and uncle. He could do that at Texas but not at Baylor because their law department was closed due to the war. His experience with the law club at COM only confirmed what he already knew he wanted. He also knew absolutely that he wanted Madeleine Segal as his wife. Deeply in love, he knew they complemented each other well—he could see them together always. After graduation with his Associate of Arts degree, and before leaving for Austin in late summer, Hall worked at the Ford, Bacon, and Davis Company, which was later the site of the Thiokol plant in northeast Harrison County, in Karnack, near Caddo Lake. His work activities varied there, and in his break periods he wrote Madeleine, sometimes on the company stationery, adding his name to the letterhead after "Davis." He and Madeleine were a year along as a serious dating couple, and he did not like being apart from her "at all," though he was scarcely out of town, and then only during the day. [26]

Hall wrote almost daily from Austin. He wrote about a hundred words a page in a large, confident hand, to "Miss Madeleine Segal" at the College of Marshall, once writing about another young couple, newlyweds who were doing so well together he wished "we were in their shoes." Madeleine's portrait graced his desk in the dormitory. "Everybody that comes in wants to know who that beautiful creature is, and I tell them all that she is my future wife, and honey I mean it too, with all my heart." [27]

The early days at the University of Texas were exciting, filled with opportunities to meet new people. Hall and Harold Taylor became

Sam Jr. and Madeleine Segal. The reflecting pond was behind Laura Atman Residence Hall, College of Marshall.

Sam and Madeleine, the College of Marshall Harvest Festival, November 1941. Sam was Master of Ceremonies; Madeleine was crowned Queen of the Silver Jubilee Court.

Sam at Sheppard Field, Wichita Falls.

Mr. and Mrs. Sam B. Hall Jr. on honeymoon in Shreveport, Louisiana, February 1946.

roommates at Austin. They went to lunch with the "Phi Kapps" and to a reception with the Lambda Chi. "The A.T.O.'s (that Jack Baldwin fraternity) have already tried to get me but I gave them no definite answer," but he planned to go to supper and spend the evening with them. Both he and Taylor decided to delay joining fraternities. Hall had a southwest corner room in his dormitory, Brackenridge Hall 143-B. He wrote his parents to send his radio and the Marshall newspaper. A cold spell prompted a request for extra blankets. He was filled with questions about news from home and friends. "All of you see Madeleine when you can, and have her out to dinner some time. Please don't ignore her." In the same month the family was to come for a visit, and Hall pleaded, "Mother, if you do come down, please bring Madeleine. Mother, I want to see her bad, awful bad, so bring her with you if you come. Listen make dad come down, as I haven't seen you all in a darn long time." [28]

Sam and Valerie Hall had accepted Madeleine during the College of Marshall period; Valerie was delighted to see what happiness she brought her son. Valerie was "crazy about Sam—she knew how crazy he was about me and that's all it took," recalled Madeleine. The relationship between a mother and son could not be better than that between Valerie and Sam Jr. It was no trouble for her to support the two young people in their dreams and courtship. [29]

The almost daily letters to and from home and family could not be ignored. In one instance Hall declared he had better "answer pronto" to some recent letters in order to "keep another World War down." He asked how everything was at home, and, being unable to resist, wrote "How are the horses, hogs and Kathleen (ha, ha sis, how do you like where I put you. I didn't mean it really)." Hall was keeping up in his schoolwork, "not in the least getting behind in any of my studies, in fact I am ahead in most of them." [30]

On one occasion Madeleine took the train to Austin for the Baylor-Texas football game. She happened to board the train with an acquaintance, Todie Ray (later Mrs. Charlie Flowers), a student at Kilgore College. The two enjoyed each other's company but were far from alone. Unknowingly, Madeleine and Todie had boarded a troop train at Marshall, and none of the railway officials had forewarned them. Once underway they made the best of a novel situation; no earthly power could keep them from being the center of attention anyway. The soldiers loved riding across East Texas in the company of two attractive young women, and they presented Madeleine and Todie dining car napkins signed with all their names. The women left the train in Austin, finding Charlie Flowers and Sam Hall Jr. standing together, speechless because the soldiers were hooting and yelling out the windows, calling out their girlfriends' names. [31]

At the University of Texas, Hall met Ralph Watson, who came from Bonham and lived in Brackenridge Hall. Their schedules put them at various intersections and lanes around campus so that they became familiar to each other. The U.S. Navy took over the dormitories for its officer cadets, and the dorm students found lodgings off campus. Watson and Hall ended up next door to each other in the White Arms Apartments near campus. They found a "greasy spoon" diner nearby that fit their tastes and went there often for supper. As was the case with other young men, Watson joined the V-7 Naval Reserve and Hall was called up to the Army Air Corps. Watson and Hall later encountered each other in Longview during Sam Sr.'s 1948 district judge election campaign. Watson moved to Marshall as a distributor for Sinclair Refining Company, so he and the Halls remained friends, and he gave political and financial support when Hall ran for Congress. [32]

In Austin less than a year, Hall was drafted shortly after Harold Taylor. Taylor went on to serve as an Army Air Force pilot in Europe, where he was captured and spent time as a prisoner of war. Hall's service began with basic training at Camp Wolters, near Mineral Wells, Texas, in early April, 1943. Arriving on a Monday about mid-afternoon, he got a physical and moved into a tent—so he explained in a letter to Madeleine, "yes honey your ole guy is sleeping in a tent." Norman Bass from Marshall was three tents down the row, and Hall wanted to be assigned somewhere with him. On Tuesday, the recruits began learning to march, took tests, and got their uniforms. On Thursday Hall wrote, "I haven't the slightest idea what I will be in, or where I will be sent, but I am going to try to stay as close to you as I possibly can." His letters came in envelopes often embellished with miniature stick figures called "Agamemnons," a fad Johnny Lee Ward had started among students at the College of Marshall. Sam wished Madeleine could see him in his new uniform: "I got a darn good fit in everything, and must admit with a degree of pride that I look fairly well. I am going to apply for OCS [Officer Candidate School] just as soon as I can, and then when I have those bars on my shoulders, I want you to be kinda proud of me—will you honey?" [33]

Any draftee could reasonably expect to be transferred out to serve, if not in Europe or the Pacific, at least elsewhere in the United States. But Hall was assigned to administrative service at Sheppard Field in Wichita Falls where he remained throughout the war, working in an office under Master Sergeant Don Luna. The headquarters squadron handled basic training of recruits, and Luna had some 600 enlistees in his unit. Hall telegraphed Madeleine and his family every time his name appeared on the list for transfer overseas or to another base. The family all expressed relief each time they heard that he had been taken off the list. On the one hand, he doubted he would be lucky enough to be as close as Sheppard Field for the duration of the war, but wished he could. On the other hand, he dreamed of becoming a second lieutenant in the Army Air Corps, but his repeated applications were turned down. Otherwise robust, he had frequent migraine headaches that kept him out of Officer Candidate School and the possibility of flight training. [34]

In late 1943 Hall heard about plans for the College of Marshall's being renamed East Texas Baptist College and offering bachelor's degrees. He wrote Madeleine, "I hate to see that, as it will in my estimation kill the effect of the school, I don't know exactly how to say it, but I just feel it. I mean by that that place has some kind of way of getting into a person's blood . . . which never leaves." Others probably felt the same way because the new name would take the emphasis off of Marshall, which had given birth to the college in the community fund-raising campaigns before World War I. The Baptist General Convention of Texas took over the college's operations in the 1920s and kept it alive. So, by the 1940s the decision to rename the school East Texas Baptist College meant that the trustees wanted a wider, regional identity reflecting its Baptist connections. [35]

Hall's letters home revealed nothing unusual or earthshaking, though it is interesting to follow his accounting of checks he cashed. In one instance he recorded twenty dollars lent to "Henry," a friend so broke he could not turn him down, but who would repay the loan at the next month's pay day. He bought a new pair of shoes because he had a certificate to do so. Fifteen dollars went to his hometown friend Phillip Baldwin who had not been paid in three months because of confused paperwork, and Hall was to get the money back the next week. He was paying off the balance on $56.50 for a nice watch for Madeleine. He went into detail in his letters to his dad and mom about expenditures, attending church, and visiting the Wichita Falls home of a Mrs. Prince, the aunt of a fellow student in Austin. Mrs. Prince introduced Sam and Phillip "to some Wichita Falls girls—they were very attractive and we had a gay time yester [sic] afternoon." In the same letter Hall noted Mrs. Prince wanted him and Madeleine to accompany her, the nephew and Phillip, with their dates to Dallas, and, of course, he could use a bit more money, which he would pay back. Keeping accounts square, he added, "in fact, the money that I have already sent home in the past can count on this debt." [36]

Kathleen turned eleven in 1943 and got a letter from Sam Jr., who wrote, "I remember very well eleven years ago when I first saw you. You were as red as I was, remember I had the measles when you were born. Course I know you don't remember it." He missed attending his sister's party and eating some of her cake. He promised to send a gift when he got it in the mail. He hoped to get home soon. "When I get there I want you to have Maggie to fix me some fried chicken. I haven't had anything but pork since I got in the army." He called Kathleen by her pet name: "Nan I'll close and in closing I'd like to wish to the sweetest little girl in the world a very happy birthday. Always yours, Bubba." Because it was so important to be home for special events in the family if he could, Sam Jr. surprised them by coming home for Kathleen's baptism on her twelfth birthday in June of 1944. [37]

Hall wrote stronger, more frequent letters to Madeleine from his post in Wichita Falls, beginning with the first week there. "This army would not be half as bad if you and I were married dear, and we could live off the post." The young man confessed his first six days at Sheppard Field apart from Madeleine were like six years. [38]

On occasion Madeleine got letters typed on Army Air Corps stationery with an elite typewriter. Hall was a fast and accurate typist. In one letter, he apologized for writing so much but said it was "one of my most important jobs." He complained about the cat, "Junior," who had made a home in the barracks and who just then was on his lap, his paws on the typewriter keys, interfering with business. Hall lived to send and get letters, and complained that Madeleine's letters seemed to reach him quicker than his letters did her, even when he mailed them special delivery. He could send mail by free, military post, but it took too long. He sent her a special delivery letter, writing, "If you don't get that letter, I will start turning handsprings and having cats with rubber tails." The days dragged by as he waited for the war to end, for their reunion and marriage. "I want to see you so bad that it's getting where that is all I think about." But he was encouraging and absolutely open with Madeleine. "You know honey, it's really great to be in love with a person like you. I just think lots about how lucky I am to have a girl like you. Did you ever just stop and think and realize who wonderful it all is?" And, "You sure have a heck of a hold on me—but I love it." The next day's letter declared his efforts to get a pass to come to Marshall or to have Madeleine come to Wichita Falls in order to have as much time with her as possible. [39]

In late August 1945 Hall still sat at Sheppard Field in Wichita Falls, his military service having been starkly different from that of those who served in the battle theaters of the war, but still far from unusual. Years later, during one of his campaigns for Congress, someone asked whether he had served overseas in the military. No, but he had been told that "two years at Sheppard Field in Wichita Falls was like five years overseas!" [40]

Hall wrote how he thought of the day when he and Madeleine would "sit around and talk about these letters honey and how crazy it will seem then." He had great hopes for them.

> Yes, I have big things in store for the both of us Madeleine and I do believe that if anything ever happened

> to you that something within me would automatically go out. This in some measure might sound unusual to you but many times I have wondered just what I might do—who I might turn to if anything ever happened to you. It's truly wonderful that I know you and intend to marry you. No one, including yourself, knows exactly how much I love you. [41]

Like so many others in wartime, Sam and Madeleine were separated, but at least they had the advantage of keeping their courtship within the borders of Texas. Madeleine finished at the College of Marshall and completed a business degree at the University of Houston. Sam Jr. kept her informed about his possible leaves of absence coming up, typically through breathless, urgent telegrams, such as "Can get away the second possibility of a later date not certain can you leave Houston for a few days am vitally interested wire immediately love you. Sam." On many occasions Madeleine took the train to Wichita Falls. Those trips usually were hard and long, especially during the summer, and she quickly found out how easy it was to lose her seat if a military officer needed it. She learned to carry luggage that a soldier could lift from the overhead racks and place on the floor so that she could sit in relative comfort. "I rode more trains and buses during the war!" Usually, however, she met with Sam in Marshall so that when he got a weekend leave he could see both her and his family. [42]

Late in the war one of Hall's trips home involved a sad occasion. His COM teacher and friend, Norman Barnes, had been killed in action in the China-Burma-India theater of the war, while flying over the "Hump" of the Himalayas. His aircraft, one of dozens lost in the high mountains where weather conditions were among the worst anywhere for aviation, was supplying the Chinese Nationalists against both the Japanese and the Chinese Communists. Cloyd Taylor remembered how in 1945 he had just returned from the service after two years in the European theater of the war and was told that on that very day, the memorial service for Norman Barnes was to be held. Sam B. Hall Jr. was there to serve as a member of the military honor guard. He was also present as a pallbearer at the funeral of another classmate, Marine Lieutenant John Milton Cornelius, who was killed in action at Okinawa. Barnes and Cornelius are memorialized with the other College of Marshall war dead, their names engraved on a pink granite marker at the northwest corner of Marshall Hall on the East Texas Baptist University campus. Congressman Hall was on hand to help dedicate the marker on October 1, 1993. [43]

Hall had an appendectomy while he was home in Marshall on a weekend pass, either in late 1944 or early 1945. Back at Sheppard Field, the military doctors examined him, found a hernia, and performed surgery to repair it, thus his hospital stay was longer than expected. Valerie and Kathleen Hall visited him, bringing a quart of chocolate ice cream they had begged to buy from a Wichita Falls merchant, a Mr. Hall at Allison's Drug Store. He found a lifelong friend in the base hospital at Sheppard Field. Robert Wainscott was on sick leave and in the same room. During Wainscott's two stays at Sheppard as a cadet-in-training, probably no more than six months at a time, he and Hall spent many hours together. Wainscott remembered that "We weren't out chasing after women or barking at the moon; we just had a good time together." Besides, Hall was not interested in other women anyway, he was so wrapped up in Madeleine Segal. He talked about her all the time. It was "Madeleine this, Madeleine that," so Wainscott knew he was thoroughly in love with her.

Hall was the only guy Wainscott knew who had his own car, and they drove off base whenever they could. He went to Marshall with him at least once and stayed with the Halls. When the war ended, Wainscott was still in pilot training, but he was sent to the South Pacific to do radio communications work. Over the years, he and Hall stayed in touch. In 1976 Bob and Florence Wainscott visited the Halls in Marshall, not knowing when they came that Hall was running for Congress. They came to Washington for his swearing-in as a Congressman, and made several other visits. As a new Congressman, Hall went to Durham to see Wainscott and ended up helping him sweep out some new office space. Wainscott called Hall's office so much that Hall's administrative assistant Sue Jordan learned to recognize his voice. [44]

Hall's situation changed considerably after discharge from the Army Air Corps. Instead of returning to the University of Texas, he enrolled in the School of Arts and Sciences at Baylor University for a term, waiting for the law school to reopen. He found it tough to focus on his studies. He and Madeleine were supposed to marry at the end of term and would have to schedule the wedding around final exams. In a December 7, 1945, letter he professed "It will take a long time for me to give you all the loving that we both want," and eagerly looked forward to a long line of Christmases with Madeleine. A week later he confessed how hard it was getting after four years to write the daily letters—letters he wouldn't think of not writing, of course. "I know my letters must sound like a phonograph that has been played a thousand times." Neither he nor she minded, but in comparison to the letter writing from the years of war and courtship, for the rest of his life Hall only occasionally wrote personal letters, and those he wrote, aside from his characteristically brief business letters, were concise and to the point, though usually sprinkled with humor. He always preferred the telephone. [45]

Responding to a letter from Madeleine less than two weeks before their wedding, Hall pumped some teasing into his response:

> So you occasionally get goose pimples—well I don't see why you should—this business of getting married is a pretty old thing you know. Incidentally I saw a beautiful bedroom suite today with the cutest little set of double beds that you ever saw. I just love to sleep on those things. Honey are you throwing things yet? [46]

The college and wartime years had allowed Sam and Madeleine to complete some educational goals and to mature, so that they were ready to take on the responsibilities of family life by the end of the war. Hall's parents heartily supported the marriage, but the wedding and the transition in their own family life were inordinately difficult for them. Sam Sr. and Valerie had poured great attention and energy into their own marriage and their children. The father-son relationship was remarkable. Soon after meeting Sam Jr. in college, Madeleine was amazed at how Sam Sr. and Sam Jr. communicated when they were together. Sam Jr. was the first young man she had ever seen who hugged and kissed his father each time he said goodbye. He continued to do so as long as his father lived. [47]

On the day Sam and Madeleine married, Sam Sr. was so upset that he took to bed and would not get up until his brother Reuben came and scolded him: "You've acted the fool long enough!" Sam Sr. was going to leave the bed and go to the wedding. And he did. [48]

Sam and Madeleine were married at the First Baptist Church in Marshall on February 9, 1946, repeating their vows before Dean J. Wesley Smith. They chose him to officiate as a trusted, much respected and admired teacher and friend. First Baptist was appropriate for the wedding; Madeleine as a Baptist also wanted organ music, something not to be had in the Church of Christ where the Halls worshiped. It was a large wedding party for the time. Harold Taylor was best man, as Sam also was for Harold later on when he and one of the bridesmaids, Mary Nell Durie, were married. The army friends from Sheppard field, Don Luna and Bob Wainscott, were there. Sam's cousin Catherine Curtis was maid of honor, and Minnie Frances Grantham was the other bridesmaid. Sam's sister Kathleen and Madeleine's cousin Dorothy Ann Leiser were junior bridesmaids, and the four groomsmen were Don Luna, Hulon Huffman, Sam's cousin, Fred Hall, and Steve Warren, who married Sam's cousin, Carolyn Curtis, Catherine's twin sister. [49]

The evening of the wedding was wet and cold, the weather anything but ideal. As the church had no place for dressing, Madeleine arrived completely dressed for the ceremony. People held umbrellas over her on the way into the building. It was so cold that after the reception, when the couple got into the car to drive away, the tin cans the groomsmen had tied to the car were frozen to the ground and had to be pried loose—the clatter must be had regardless of the weather.

After a two-day honeymoon in Shreveport, Louisiana, the couple went to Waco where Hall was to enter the Baylor Law School. Despite the scarcity of housing right after the war, they found a small apartment, originally the maid's quarters, over a garage behind a home on Austin Street. The apartment had a large bedroom and closet, a bath, and a sitting area that doubled as a kitchen. The modest "kitchen" had a two-burner hotplate and an icebox big enough for a 25-pound block of ice. On ice delivery days, Sam rushed home from classes to make sure they got a new block of ice. They washed dishes in the lavatory. After discovering a colony of bats in their stairwell, the couple abandoned that apartment and rented another from a chiropractor who had three efficiency apartments, each replete with a small bath and kitchen, and a living and sleeping room with a closet that contained a fold-down, Murphy bed. It was typical postwar housing for newlyweds. [50]

Madeleine at first worked as a secretary with the Joe D. Ward drafting firm. The work was good and the men were gracious, but she was young and, the only female in an all-male firm, missed not having other women around on the job. Soon afterward she interviewed with Truitt Grant at Baylor University for a secretarial position in Pat Neff Hall, the administration building. A much better position, the job also put Madeleine in contact with Baylor University President Pat Neff. One day Grant came to Madeleine, saying that his wife, Neff's secretary Margaret, was ill, and that the president needed someone to take a letter. She and Sam stood in awe of Neff, a former Texas legislator and governor, but his welcoming warmth calmed her fear of taking a letter for the great man. Sam quipped to Madeleine, "If we have a son, I'm going to name him 'Pat Neff Hall.' That ought to be good for a scholarship!" [51]

The Baylor law department occupied the third floor of the Carroll Library building. Margaret Harris (Gordon) Amsler was interim dean when Sam entered as a member of the first postwar law school class. Leslie Jackson succeeded Amsler in 1946, and Abner McCall became dean in 1948. Angus S. McSwain Jr., who graduated with Sam Hall in 1948, returned the following year to teach. As the first female law professor at Baylor in 1941, Amsler, who graduated at the top of her class in 1937, continued her teaching career that would last almost a full thirty-two years. The practice court was an important part of law school training. Frank M. Wilson, who served as Judge of the Tenth Circuit Court of Texas, began teaching the practice court along with Judge Joseph W. Hale in 1947. [52]

In the Baylor law school Hall enjoyed taking several courses under Abner McCall, who taught evidence, and developed a strong student-mentor relationship. Hall admired McCall, who was ten years his senior, had made the highest score on the Texas bar exam after graduating in 1938, and who had served with the Federal Bureau of Investigation before returning to teach at the law school in 1946. There was the tendency after the war for veterans, who were virtually the entire postwar class, older and more mature than most other students, to be treated more as peers and colleagues. That was the case with Hall and McCall. McCall later supported Hall during his congressional campaigns and was present at his funeral in 1994. When McCall was president of Baylor University, Sam and Madeleine's daughter Becky worked as a student secretary in his office. [53]

Every member of the small, first post-war law department class at Baylor except for one was a wartime veteran. Hall joined Vernon Smith, Marion G. Holt, John Luther Smith (later a state district judge), W. A. "Bill" Hughes (later a state district judge and member of the court of appeals at Fort Worth), Byron McCullen (later a state district judge in Gatesville), Enos Jones, W. C. Davis (later a state district judge in Bryan, and until retirement a member of the Texas Court of Criminal Appeals), among others. H. Hart Nance and his wife, J. B., were fast friends from the law school group. John Luther Smith said of those years, "That old, poor bunch that came from World War II. Some of us lived in the Baylor Homettes that they provided for veterans. A good many of us were married. I was and had a little young daughter. As I think back, and we have often kidded about it, you couldn't have gotten a poorer bunch together." [54]

Rex Houston, an attorney specializing in liability law in Henderson, Texas, and a 1992 Baylor Lawyer of the Year, also graduated with Hall, who was honored as Baylor Lawyer of the Year in 1991. Hall's cousin, Fred C. Hall Jr., also attended for a time.

Bill Cornelius of Jefferson was enrolled during Sam's second year. Ever after, he and Sam cultivated a lifelong, collegial relationship, and were sometimes on opposing sides of a legal case. Cornelius entered practice with his father, James R. Cornelius Sr., and his brother, James R. Cornelius Jr., in Jefferson. [55]

Joe W. "Bunt" Lovelace and his wife, Margaret, were at Baylor to share experiences with the Halls. Margaret went into labor with her first child; she and Joe had no car, so Hall took them to Hillcrest Baptist Hospital where he "walked the floor" with Lovelace until the baby came. The maternity nurse brought baby Joe B. to the nursery window. Sam exclaimed, "My Lord! He looks just like Guy Hardin!" It was a joke at Joe's expense—Guy and Helen Hardin shared a bathroom with the Lovelaces at the trailer park where they lived. The "G.I. housing" at Baylor featured tiny trailers, the "Homettes," placed in pairs with a small connecting bath. To share the bath, Lovelace recalled, "You would knock on the door, and if it were not hooked, you went in and hooked the door on their side, then unhooked it and returned to your quarters." [56]

Lovelace went on to build his law practice in Linden, but Grover Sellers, a former Texas attorney general, offered him a job with AT&T. Lovelace called Hall for advice:

> I told him I would go to Dallas and the good salary and benefits. What did he think? He answered without hesitation, "Don't take it. They may send you to Dallas now, but to get ahead the next step will be New York City, and that will not work." He said he could see Margaret now—walking down Fifth Avenue with her shoes in her hand—looking for the bus home to Mississippi. Margaret agreed. [57]

As a law student Hall demonstrated analytical abilities essential to being a decisive lawyer. In particular, he could to distill evidently complex problems into rather simple points. His classmate, Vernon L. Smith, recalled that Hall kept a "big, big notebook," the largest in the class, and was regarded as much an authority as a student could be, one whose notes were often useful to others after class. Hall preferred to do much of his writing and all of his examinations on the typewriter. His penmanship was poor; besides, the typewriting was faster and more legible. [58]

Finished with his law studies in May 1948, Hall took the bar exam, failing to pass by one point. Soon afterwards he retook the exam, and while waiting on the results, returned home to help Sam Sr. in his election campaign for the district judgeship. Soon Marshall, Texas, was to have a new lawyer. The prospect of becoming an attorney in any other place never occurred to him or anyone who knew him. Sam B. Hall Jr. was going home to start a family and a career.

Sam and Madeleine moved into the garage apartment adjoining the new Hall family home at the farm on U. S. Highway 80 West near Marshall. The living arrangements on the farm lasted only briefly, and the couple occupied a rent house on Nathan Street in Marshall. But soon they returned to the Hall property, this time living in the old family house, Sam Jr.'s birthplace that had been moved there, just fifty yards west of the Hall Seniors' house, from South Wellington Street. There they remained from May, 1949, when their first daughter, Linda Rebecca, "Becky," was three months old, until in 1962 they moved into a newly renovated house in town. With that, Sam and Madeleine strengthened their already deep roots in the Marshall community. [59]

3

Judge Sam's Son, 1945-1976

When I started practicing law, we had a law firm that wasn't open on Saturdays. The hardest guy to sell on closing the office on Saturday was Sam Hall, Jr., just because he liked to work. . . . I am not sure if he wouldn't go to that office even if he didn't need to. It was just kind of a tonic for him. But he loved to work, and you know, that followed him into Congress. Those people work hard. — Franklin Jones, Jr. [1]

Under normal circumstances, Sam Hall Jr. would have entered into a law partnership with his father, but as Sam Sr. became District Judge in 1948, Hall joined the father and son firm of William and Walter Lane. That partnership lasted approximately two years until Hall joined Ernest F. Smith's firm that by 1959 included William M. Huffman, and much later, a son-in-law, W. F. "Pinkie" Palmer.

Bill Huffman's family went back three or four generations with the Halls, and his father, Perry, had run a general mercantile store near Hallsville. After graduating from Texas A&M, he planned to work as a researcher for Ralston Purina Company. Hall told him he should think about law, which Huffman could not see himself doing. Nevertheless, during his U.S. Army service at Fort Hood, Huffman, an officer, represented enlisted men in special courts martial for misdemeanor charges. Army regulations did not require representation by a lawyer. His familiarity with the *Uniform Code of Military Justice* and his resolve to do his best with the task earned a commendation from his commanding officer who encouraged him to study law. During his last two years in the army, Huffman enrolled in the Lasalle School of Law correspondence course, became a student member of the American Bar Association, and, after returning from a European tour of duty, at the urging of Smith and Hall enrolled in the University of Texas Law School. With books Hall gave him, Huffman left with the promise of a position with the firm when he returned. With another Marshall native, his friend and roommate Don Rives, he drove his new Mercury to Austin. Huffman became a partner with Sam Hall Jr. and Ernest Smith on the first day of 1962, and Rives commenced his own practice in Marshall. [2]

Don Rives had taken time off from school to tend the family farm after his father's heart attack in 1955. Already interested in law, he took spare time to visit the courthouse where he observed Judge Hall and Sam Jr. in their respective roles. He was impressed with Sam Jr.'s quick thinking, effectiveness with argument, and apparent good preparation. [3]

Hall enjoyed being a lawyer much as his father did. He enjoyed criminal defense work, the courtroom atmosphere and proceedings, and the anticipation of taking a case to court. He prepared his cases well and built a reputation as a capable courtroom lawyer. In what may have been simply common practice in the profession and a feature of the times, he never brought his legal work home, never discussed his cases with Madeleine or the family, and did not want his wife in court. Madeleine never heard him argue a case. The same was true of his mother, Valerie, who never heard Sam Sr. argue a case in court. [4]

Small-town lawyers like Smith, Hall, and Huffman were used to putting in long hours, arriving early to the office and staying as late as necessary to get the work done. They never considered "punching the clock" but worked six full days a week, and sometimes early on Sundays before church on unfinished business. Hall and his ilk were not nearly as clock-hour conscious as the profession later became; he was likely unable to account for the number of hours involved in a case. Bill Huffman remembered that Hall worked intensely in the office. He prepared cases thoroughly, trying to avoid surprises and costly mistakes. Sometimes he worked far harder than was justified, but his diligence inspired confidence and trust. Reminiscing on the investment of time and attention in legal work with Sam Hall Jr., Huffman wrote, "Our best times were when we were working on a lawsuit together, many times sixteen hours a day. His commitment was to provide the best representation for a client, regardless of whether the client could pay for all the time that was spent." [5]

As well as Hall and Huffman worked together, their respective strengths invited comparisons. As he was later as a judge, Hall favored the terse decision based on careful consideration of the facts; these decisions were often more intuitive, however, than based on the detailed review that Huffman favored. Bill Huffman in fact relished detail and was meticulous in his legal work. Both men produced good work; they simply approached it using differing strengths.

Ernest Smith and Hall also were great partners, as Rodney Gilstrap described them, more like brothers because they spent so much time together—more than they did with their wives—and got along so well. Nonetheless, Hall reserved time for family and a great deal of activity in civic clubs and church. Somehow, though, he was able to confirm the impression that family came first. [6]

Smith, Hall and Huffman once accepted a lawsuit everyone considered impossible to win. It involved a waitress in a "honky-tonk" café between Longview and Kilgore in East Texas. Homebound one Saturday night, she was left injured and comatose after large truck struck her car. Despite a remarkable recovery, and with no memory of the accident itself, she needed compensation for injuries and medical bills. The truck driver claimed to have had a green light; she had pulled her car directly in front of him, and the crash was unavoidable. The police reports provided no help. The Longview city engineer said the light then was not cycling red or green but was a flashing caution light. If that were so, then the woman had a red light, and the truck driver had a yellow caution light. The attorneys' personal knowledge of that traffic light conflicted with the engineer's report.

In their situation as a low-budget law firm, they would rarely, if ever, hire private investigators, so Hall and Huffman went to Longview on a number of Saturday nights when the light was due to switch to flashing yellow. It never switched. A closer look showed that if a truck driver, higher off the ground, were approaching the intersection he would see not one light—at that intersection—but the one beyond it as well. Actually, it would be easy to see only the second light, which at the time of the accident displayed green. Indeed, the truck driver had seen a green light, albeit the wrong one, but the woman also had told the truth.

After a month of Saturday nights, Hall and Huffman had evidence and hired a television cameraman from a Shreveport television station to video the sequence of the lights at those intersections. He mounted his camera on a stepladder at the height of the truck driver's eyes. Hall's theory about the lights proved true, and they won the case. They proved a point with Joe Lovelace, too. After the client's accident, he had teased Hall and Huffman that they went to Longview not to sit for hours watching the traffic lights. That was too boring; he suggested there must have been something else they were up to. The evidence proved Lovelace wrong. [7]

Another side of Hall's office activities reveals much about his personality. His office was a social center and a workplace. He took time to visit with friends and clients. There were lengthy conversations. Family members frequently dropped by. Hall liked to talk on the telephone and accomplished a great deal of work on behalf of civic organizations and boards. A law student and family friend, Jerry Beane sat with Sam one day. The telephone rang. Sam answered, listened and said, "Lady, you have the wrong number—you need to call a service station." Hanging up the phone, he explained, "That was Madeleine; she is picking up one of the girls and has run out of gas." Immediately he phoned and a local service station brought gasoline for his stranded wife's car. [8]

Attorneys' offices normally see a steady turnover in clerical and secretarial help. This contrasted greatly with the record for Ernest F. Smith, who bragged that in fifty years of practicing law he had only two secretaries, and each had served about twenty-five years. Consequently, the secretaries in such a stable situation were not only essential to the workings of the practice but were true professional partners. [9]

The law office placed heavy demands on the secretaries. Even succinct briefs took hours to type, and the firm's business load often meant long weekdays and extra hours on Saturdays, sometimes even on Sundays, and usually not for extra pay. After Hall served in the Congress and saw the secretarial pay scale in Washington, he admitted to Beverly Hines Harris that she and the other secretaries had worked many years for inferior pay. Though she would never trade the experience of working in the law office for anything, Hall's admission pleased her. His secretaries so respected him that in 1965 he won the "Boss of the Year" award from the Harrison County Legal Secretaries Association. [10]

Hall had little patience for verbosity and detailed written reasoning, which he claimed he found in his detail-oriented partner, Bill Huffman. Beverly Hines Harris worked many years typing legal briefs and records. She remembered how it irritated Hall that Bill Huffman put so many words into a brief or pleading. Many times Hall asked what Hines (later Harris) was typing, read it and exclaimed, "He's had you type fifteen legal pages when he could have said every bit of that in one paragraph." True, that was not his style, and one could not find a more conscientious lawyer with a detailed knowledge of the law than Bill Huffman, but Hall also enjoyed needling Beverly Hines about the differences. For her it was all the same, as Hall produced equivalent work for her in other ways. [11]

Beverly Hines (Harris), Gladys Kornrumpf, Dolly Moore, Laura Muckleroy, Blanche Turlington, and Sue Jordan worked with the firm, but not all at the same time. Beverly and the other secretaries submitted a memorandum to the firm of Smith, Hall, and Huffman, pleading for relief from Saturday duties, recommending that only one secretary be in the office on Saturday mornings, and arguing that not much got started or done on Saturdays anyway. The bosses responded in an "Original Answer," denying the "outlandish allegations of cruel treatment" made in the memorandum. It was a lawyerly, litigious, but entirely good-humored response: "Wherefore everything being considered, and after having read the indictment which produced exhilarating effects and much inward laughter we have convulsively and amorously acceded, yielded, consented and concurred in your ultimatum." Smith, Hall, and Huffman affixed their signatures, and the secretaries got their relief. [12]

Client peculiarities posed a humorous challenges, as with an elderly lady who always telephoned the law office asking for Sam Hall Jr., assuming the secretary to be Mrs. Hall. Beverly Hines finally stopped trying to convince her otherwise. When asked, "Mrs. Hall, could I speak to your husband?" she simply took a message or forwarded the call. [13]

Hall's reputation as a competent trial lawyer grew during the 1950s and 1960s. Franklin Jones Jr. who represented the Woodlawn, Texas, school district, recalled how Hall had handled the consolidation of the Marshall and Woodlawn districts, a controversial case. "We were trying to defeat that consolidation and wound up in the courthouse with it," Jones recalled. Hall and Jones represented the respective sides. "I thought we had all of the improbables going in our favor. We had a big, hungry school district and a city that had reached out and gobbled up a little one-room schoolhouse, but Sam tied them up. It was not easy to do, because we had the emotional appeal on our side of that case." [14]

Sam Hall, Ernest Smith and Bill Huffman did oil and gas work. Hall also tried personal injury cases and otherwise was engaged in general practice. During the sixties and seventies, he sometimes defended insurance companies, mostly with automobile accident cases, and was known for it, as few others did similar work at the time. [15]

Hall and Smith were imposing lawyers and men by virtue of their abilities, height and girth. They liked to eat. Hall kept candy in an office drawer and did not like to find it missing. The two tried a liquid diet on which, indeed, they grew heavier. The legal secretaries observed that Hall and Smith downed their "diet shakes" enthusiastically, supplementing them with great dollops of ice cream. Great shakes, great weight gain. Sam Hall topped the scales at around 275 pounds, another reason that he, like Ernest Smith, had an Austin tailor, Mr. Dalton, visit to measure them for custom fitted suits. [16]

Sam B. Hall Jr. had the natural gift of a booming voice to match his size—an asset in an argument or, as it happened, in court. Attorney Ned Dennis recalled the sound of Hall's forceful voice as it penetrated the closed double doors to a courtroom; he was cross-examining a witness. Knowing the power of his voice, Hall spoke in order to inspire, to encourage, to strengthen, and probably to intimidate. Used to his or another's advantage or as the voice of authority, it was a distinctive strength. [17]

Scotty Baldwin always was impressed at Hall's ability to speak *ex tempore*, with few or no notes, with continuity and color, so that he was easily understood and persuasive. Hall once shared with the younger Baldwin the key to success in law, to bypassing failure and mediocrity: "There's a whole lot of room on top and a whole lot of room on the bottom, but there is very little room in the middle." With hard work, one could be on top. [18]

Hall believed his purpose was to help people with legal problems. He often seemed almost too good to be true, but his earnest desire to do good wore well, and people remembered him for that. He enjoyed providing legal services for people who could pay little or nothing, sometimes simply helping a friend, or thinking ahead to when he or she might need benefit of a will. Hall anticipated and met needs as he saw them. Ann Hall, a Wiley College alumna retired many years from teaching in the Marshall schools, recalled Hall's honesty and availability in helping to settle a tricky will. Ann's husband, Robert, appreciated Hall's pointed, productive inquiry into a matter of veteran's benefits due him. [19]

Hall did not fit the popular stereotypes of lawyers because he followed his heart and relational tendencies. His compulsion to serve dominated, and as long as he met the financial needs for his family, financial arrangements were secondary and negotiable. He lent money to clients and friends who had none well before payday. He never received repayment for some loans, but he did not dwell on that; he could not abide doing nothing. He wrote wills, insisting that a person must have a will before anything else. Some went for five or ten dollars, some more, others nothing. Jewell (Mrs. U. S.) Gray remembered the day she and her late husband Principal Price T. Young were walking on the square in Marshall. Hall met them and directly asked, "Do you two children have a will?" They did not. He took them immediately to his office, and they had a will when they left. [20]

Some clients who could have paid for legal services chose simply not to do so, or paid their bills out over time; some accounts simply were zeroed out. As a plaintiff's lawyer, Hall sometimes decreased his fees to give the client more money from a settlement. As a matter of course, attorneys do *pro bono* work to benefit the public; he did the same. His law practice prospered, which let him serve beyond the financial needs of his family. [21]

Mrs. Charles Wilson, a member of the school board (one of only two African Americans at a time on the board), and an advocate for integration through her work on the board and the NAACP, had occasion to employ Hall as a lawyer. After getting his assurances that he could divide business matters from school board business, Mrs. Wilson asserted that she would know when a lawyer was representing her well. Hall asked how, and she responded, "When I win!" [22]

Hall got some of his service ethic from experiences with people on the other side of the color line. His upbringing, many of his enduring relationships, and his career cannot be understood completely without remembering how he lived in a mixed black and white society. Society and community were officially and publicly segregated before the 1960s in East Texas, but on a more personal level, there could be, and was, a richness of relationship and interaction one cannot comprehend without having experienced it. The Halls had always known, employed, befriended, trusted, respected, and relied on individuals—the descendants of slaves—whose lives intertwined with their own. There was always a black housekeeper or cook in the Hall home. At the Hall property west of town lived the black hired hands and their families, who tended the land and its crops for Sam Sr. and Valerie well into the 1960s.

There were several dwellings on the Hall land west of Marshall. Junior Ruffin lived in the cabin that Sam Jr. later made his special retreat. Squire Ruffin and his family lived in another cabin. Sam and Madeleine's eldest daughter Becky Hall used to run to Junior's house to show him her report card before anyone else saw it. James McClellan was the general handyman and taught Sam Jr. to drive. James had worked with the Halls since his teenage years, and the Hall children included him in some of their earliest memories. Hall once gave McClellan a Chrysler everyone called "the Box," and McClellan's death came in an accident when his wife ran over him with that car, backing it over him in the driveway. [23]

The Sam and Valerie Hall children and grandchildren grew up going to funerals of black and white friends, and frequently went to funerals within their extended families. At many funerals, Sam Sr. and Sam Jr. were asked to offer a eulogy. Shortly after Amanda Hall married Tom Wynn, she commented one morning about the afternoon's funeral for a black friend of the family. Wynn had no plans to go; he did not know the man. Amanda replied, "You're in the family. You must go." She appealed to her grandmother, Valerie, who laughed when she saw how upset Amanda was. She said, "Honey, don't ever make him go to a funeral. He'll have time to do that." Nevertheless, attending funerals was a part of marrying into the Hall family, and Tom Wynn adjusted to it. [24]

Another black family close to the Halls lived a few miles south of the Hall home place, near the Perky power plant, on Finklea Road. The family of Adell Dixon Sr. included six children. Mr. Dixon farmed, raised horses and worked in real estate. His daughter, Verta Williams, recalled the kind of relationship they had with the Halls: "We all, you know, there wasn't no way in the world we could be separated from them!" The third child in her family, Verta remembered much time spent in the fields behind the mule and plow on her family's land. Adell Dixon Sr. sometimes took his six children in the horse-drawn wagon to watch proceedings in Sam Sr.'s courtroom. "We had a chance to hear all the trials and everything. I think that made us some good children." [25]

Sam Sr.'s brother Richard was the rural mail carrier on the route where the Dixons lived. In season, they left watermelons at the mailbox, and Richard gave the children dimes or quarters. When Mr. Dixon took jobs out of town or out of state, the family knew they could rely on the Halls for help if they needed it. Otherwise, "Mr. Sam" was often at the house, or Adell was off to "see Mr. Sam." Recollecting the relationship between the families, Williams said, "A lot of people maybe had things against them, but we never—we wouldn't talk that way. They were just good, you know. If we didn't know things, we'd go to them and ask them; they'd give us advice. And my daddy was always close to them, and it made us close to them, too. Always close to them, very, very close." Williams remembered they did not fear white people despite the social segregation. The family had trusted friends they could count on. Sam Sr. and Sam Jr. were such friends, admired because "they always looked out for the welfare of their fellow man." [26]

Sam B. Hall Jr. felt at home in the courtroom. Comfortable with himself and the demands of courtroom legal practice, confidence, competence and humor entered the courtroom with him, even when matters went against him. Court cases could have moments with an entertaining bent. Hall once defended a client in an unusual case, as Judge Bill Steger recalled when, as a U. S. Attorney for the Eastern District of Texas, he prosecuted a case and Sam represented the defendant at the Jefferson federal court: "I was prosecuting a pet shop dealer who developed a clandestine business on the side of selling smuggled baby parrots from Mexico," Steger wrote. "After a spirited week of trial, the matter was disposed of by Sam's client receiving a probated sentence." [27]

The issue of conflict of interest always was an issue in court, and in small-town courtrooms, there are always many opportunities to test the problem. Bill Palmer appeared for jury duty one day when Hall and F. Scott Baldwin Sr. were on opposite sides of a case involving some local citizens. Both lawyers were relatives by blood or marriage to the families, as was Palmer's wife. Scotty Baldwin asked how Palmer was related. Before he could respond, Hall stood and said to the judge that if Mr. Baldwin would agree to it, they would both stipulate that Bill Palmer's wife was related to everyone in Harrison County. The stipulation was good for a laugh. [28]

In the years immediately after Hall began his law practice, his father was building his reputation as a judge. Well known and well regarded in the county, Sam Sr. became noted for his fairness, his strong sense of justice, an impressive courtroom demeanor, and a knack for getting to the heart of the issues in a court case and reaching a judgment that would stand—few of his decisions were overturned. Sam Jr. later shared those qualities as a federal judge. Sam Sr.'s courtroom became the focus of changes that anticipated desegregation and perhaps a subtle move toward better justice. F. Scott "Scotty" Baldwin Sr. recalled how he and Franklin Jones Jr., both out of law school less than a year, agreed to defend a black man charged with murder. The case had come to Marshall from another venue where the district attorney wanted the death penalty. Still, in the fifties the courthouse was segregated—the drinking fountains, the restrooms, and the courtroom. The defendant, one Mr. Burdine, was alleged to have cut the throat of an elderly, white farmer, and an all-white grand jury returned an indictment of murder. Reluctant to deal with such an issue so early in their careers, but wanting to give the defendant every opportunity, Baldwin and Jones raised the issue of the all-white, all-male jury as a detriment to the defense. Judge Hall diplomatically heard them out, but the racial composition of the jury was already set, and the trial was to proceed. The defendant received a life sentence from the jury. There was no federal impediment to Negro participation on juries, but the states allowed jury selection policies consistent with segregation practices. Soon after in cases involving blacks, however, and for the first time in Harrison County since Reconstruction, blacks sat on the petit juries; the first mixed venire in Harrison County was on September 12, 1955, which happened to be Judge Sam Sr.'s birthday. It was also in Judge Hall's court that a woman sat on a jury in Harrison County for the first time since Reconstruction, or perhaps, ever, but only after 1954 when Texas State law permitted it. [29]

The roles of the Halls senior and junior in the county courthouse suggested great changes since the 1950s, because in many instances Hall represented clients in his own father's court. That practice would not only raise eyebrows today, the law would not tolerate it. Father and son respectively recognized the need to avoid partiality to the point that it was more difficult for both. Surprisingly, no lawyer ever tried to get a case moved if Sam Jr. was on the other side in a suit coming to Sam Sr.'s courtroom. Many lawyers knew and respected the judge for his impartiality and fairness, but some wondered whether Sam Sr. was truly fair with his son, and whether he might rule too heavily in cases his son represented.

Lawyers from out of town were leery of trying cases against Sam Jr. in his father's court. There was no indication that clients ever suffered an unjust decision. The courtroom relationship between Sam Sr. and Sam Jr. drew from the father's desire to hold his son to the highest standards, to dispel fears that the son would take advantage of his father in his own court. Judge Robert Parker recalled going to trial as an attorney with Sam Jr. on the other side. Sam Jr. objected to something Parker had said. Judge Sam Sr. responded, "Sit down Sam." Moreover, lawyers sidestepped the risk of partiality by requesting, and getting, jury trials instead of allowing cases to be decided on the judge's opinion alone. Nonetheless, there remains a legendary tradition regarding the tendency of Judge Sam Sr. to favor the side of clients whom Sam Jr. represented. It is, however, likely just that, a tradition counter to the facts and the integrity of Sam Sr. Some would argue, moreover, that Sam Jr's. positive reputation as an effective litigator enhanced his desirability as counsel regardless of the fact his father was the presiding judge. [30]

Whenever Hall represented a client in his father's court, father and son took pains to guarantee that the judge's decision would not influence the lawyer's fee, as in contingency cases where the fee depended on the judgment and any fines levied in the case. Bill Huffman heard more than one lawyer tell Judge Hall that he was unfair to Sam Jr., sometimes ruling against him even when he knew he was right. The concern was that such a ruling might harm the client's case. In later years the courts, the state bar and state law prohibited close relatives being involved in the same trial, so that neither lawyers nor judges nor clients suffered undue personal pressures or bias. [31]

Frank Finn once tried to take advantage of Hall's practicing before his father to get the edge in a case. As he recalled,

> Sam B. Hall, Jr., was commencing his trial experience. When I discovered this significant fact, and thinking and hoping that it would curry great favor with Hall, Sr., I hired Hall, Jr., as "local counsel." Sam, Jr., was to handle all the objections, plead the case with the Judge, and interface totally with Judge Hall, Sr. To my amazement and delight, none of the local Marshall lawyers objected. It was perfectly all right with them for Sam, Jr., to sit with me and to represent my client and me before his dad. I soon learned why. It made absolutely no difference. Judge Sam Hall, Sr., used the same even hand and judicial approach as before. He would lean forward, resting his arms on his great bench, and say, "Now, Sam, you know we can't do that." Today there would be an immediate Motion to Recuse. [32]

Ernest Smith and Sam Hall Jr. often tried cases together, as Smith did with the other partners. Smith and Hall were a regular team, though Sam tended to do more courtroom work. Even so, Ernest Smith also mentored Hall in the profession of law and courtroom procedures. Other attorneys regarded Hall as fearless, ideally suited to the courtroom. To try a case before one's own father might be comforting, but there were other courtrooms, and Hall performed just as well in them. Attorney Franklin Jones Jr. commented that for a courthouse lawyer "to lose his guts" was the "worst thing that could happen." Hall never did. [33]

There was another advantage to trying cases before one's own father, knowing that the mutual esteem and unqualified love of father and son imparted confidence. So Hall's transition from observer to active participant in the court of Judge Sam Sr. was all the easier. Hall Sr. kept a tight rein on his own son in court, but also gave him the benefit of constant, close association outside the court. One wonders how many days Hall accompanied his father and other members of the court across the courthouse square for a butcher's block lunch or to a hot meal in the diner at the drug store. The butcher in the general store, seeing Judge Sam, Don Rives, and others heading his way, laid sardines, crackers, cheese and cold cuts on butcher paper and offered Cokes to drink.

Sam Jr. strode in the company of his father, "Mr. Sam," a local legend and the brother of another well-regarded East Texas lawyer and judge, Reuben Hall. Judge Sam Hall Sr.'s life, habits, personal tics, and forthrightness contributed to an image of comfortable Texas Southern gentility. People got out of the way when he approached the courthouse square in his 1960 Chrysler Imperial Sedan, intent on finding his parking place by the courthouse. He drove with white-gloved hands, as much aiming as driving the car some said. His Juicy Fruit or Beeman's gum, chewing tobacco and cigars were legendary. A southern gentleman unfailingly gracious to women, paradoxically, like some men of his era, he habitually referred to his wife as the "Battle-ax," a term only somewhat endearing at best. Like other state district court judges, he never wore a robe on the bench. In court he kept a spittoon, his cigars, gum, and a nail file close at hand. [34]

Sam B. Hall Sr. had friends and acquaintances galore and loved their society, but he, and Sam Jr. after him, had trouble remembering names. Glenn Link, a former Harrison County clerk, recalled the judge's difficulty remembering names. Link remembered a typical exchange: "Hall Sr. said, 'Glenn, what's that fellow's name over yonder?' I said, 'That's Rex Pickens; but Judge, you won't remember that.' He said, 'Yes, I will.' He'd get down there and say, 'Hi, fella.'" [35]

Marshall Attorneys Franklin Jones Jr. and F. Scott "Scotty" Baldwin once savored a few spare moments at the new county courthouse. Judge Hall Sr. recounted an "apparent cross-examination," that is, when a lawyer gets an opposing witness whose story ranks with gospel. Such a witness has an "affidavit face," and, as Jones put it, "honesty drips from him everywhere; everything he says has a ring of truth to it." It is hard to cross-examine someone like that. A handwriting expert, an exceptional witness under cross-examination, swore under oath that the a contested will was a forgery. A young lawyer was to do the cross-examination. Judge Hall advised him, "Listen, you're going to cross-examine him and you're going to ask him three questions. You ask him where he was the night that will was signed,

Sam B. Hall Jr. administers the oath of office to his father who had been elected to another term as State District Judge.

Judge Sam B. Hall Sr. and Sam Jr. in Houston at the Annual Convention of the State Bar of Texas, July 1956.

you ask him whether he knew so and so [the person contesting the will], and you ask him how much he was being paid. You don't ask him anything else!" The lawyer retorted that he was going to take the witness apart. Jones said he would never forget how Judge Hall crossed his hands, sat on his desk, and said, "Boys, he was like a young tender bird in the hands of a big hungry tomcat!" The judge had given the young lawyer a way to avoid cross-examining such a witness—looking as if he had cross-examined and been the better for it—an opportunity he foolishly ignored. [36]

Sam B. Hall Sr. received appropriate honors in later years. On Wednesday, November 6, 1968, his portrait was unveiled in the new Harrison County Courthouse; a luncheon followed at the Panola-Harrison Electric Cooperative Community Room. Planning to retire on December 31, he noted that except for the Texas Constitutional Amendment on mandatory retirement age, "I believe I could have served four more years." He told how he and T. Whitfield Davidson were on opposing sides of a lawsuit over land on Hynson Springs Road in Harrison County. The jury was deadlocked, and the foreman sent word asking whether it might be legal to deny both parties the land and instead give the 50 acres in question to the Red Cross. Reluctantly, the judge denied the jury's request. In a later interview, Hall Sr. recalled how he and Davidson frequently argued cases lasting three or four days. The courtroom audiences packed sack lunches for murder cases so they would not miss any of the proceedings. Fred Erisman, former district judge of the 124th Judicial District of Texas, said his relationship with Judge Hall was "the finest post-graduate experience any lawyer could have." Various speakers praised his integrity, humanity, balance, and one imputed his success and character to his parents. Thomas Fletcher, a Houston attorney, said of John Will and Alice Hall, "Those parents endowed their sons with the birthright of undaunted character." Judge T. Whitfield Davidson commented that he had met Sam's father, John Will Hall, a former Confederate soldier, at Hallsville. [37]

His superb training by the example of his father did not keep Sam B. Hall Jr. from mistakes. He once represented a man accused of cattle rustling, a crime akin to timber theft in East Texas, and filed a motion for a continuance before a full courtroom, claiming that his client was ill and unable to attend trial. Judge Hall asked whether District Attorney Phillip Baldwin had a response; Baldwin suggested the motion might be valid, but to pass over it and call another case. He asked the sheriff to have the county health officer visit the missing defendant. The sheriff returned later with the health officer and whispered something to Baldwin. At the proper time, Baldwin asked to present evidence on Hall's motion for a continuance. "So I call Dr. Norman Holcomb who was the county health officer, and I said,

'Have you seen the defendant today?'" He said he had. Baldwin asked, "Was he sick?" Holcomb replied, "Well, I don't know; he was out in the field plowing when I saw him!" To Sam Jr.'s embarrassment, Judge Hall said to the sheriff, "Go get that man and bring him in here!" [38]

Sam Jr. did not get along with everyone. He showed his temper in a disagreement by stacking a client's files outside his office and telephoning the client to pick them up. [39]

In another instance, Sam Jr. defended a client in a seven or eight-month long felony case. He filed a motion for continuance, explaining that he had hired a state legislator, Reagan Huffman, as counsel, which meant an automatic continuance since the legislature was in session. Baldwin allowed that the continuance was probably valid and legal, but first called just one witness, as Judge Hall directed. Said Baldwin, "I said 'Swear Mr. Sam Hall Jr.' I put Sam on the witness stand and I asked him how long he had been in the case. He responded, 'Six to eight months, a year—something like that.' I said, 'Now, when did Mr. Reagan Huffman join the case?' 'Well, we hired him yesterday.' And I said, 'So, in your motion what you are saying is that the law firm of Smith and Hall is not capable without Mr. Huffman being at the counsel table—Is that right?' Well, he couldn't say yes!" [40]

Sam B. Hall Jr. was well established as an attorney when Sue Jordan came to work at his office. A high school graduate from Ore City, she may as well have been in midtown Manhattan or Dallas, at least. In 1964 as a high school student she observed a trial in Gilmer. "The trial that we were observing was a divorce matter involving a well-known attorney from Gilmer. He was represented by Ernest Smith and Sam B. Hall Jr. Little did I know what an impact these two lawyers would later have on my life, especially the one named Hall." [41]

Jordan came to Hall's office at the age of 28 after working five or six years with Don Rives, another Marshall attorney. Rives had been invited to become the executive assistant to William P. Hobby Jr., the lieutenant-governor of Texas, and Sue wanted another position in Marshall. She came to Hall's office on a Saturday morning, found the front door unlocked, entered, heard some rustling in the back, walked to the library where Hall was, and began the interview. Sam was a great listener, but he did most of the talking because the big man with the big voice intimidated Jordan. "The interview lasted about an hour," she remembered, "most of the time being spent with him telling me stories." He showed her the office and asked her to come to work. Thus ended the interview, and thus began a long and happy working relationship. The nature of her work changed as she moved from the position with Don Rives to Hall's employ. Attorney Don Rives' work in law had been mostly title work, and he did not enter the courtroom nearly as often as Hall, who was, though a general lawyer, very much a trial lawyer, thus she had new things to learn. Jordan was to serve with Hall from 1974 until 1994 when he died while serving as a federal judge. [42]

When Sue first met Hall's mother, Valerie, the white-gloved, genteel appearance and conduct of that southern lady overwhelmed her. She felt herself to be an underdressed, unsophisticated girl from small-town East Texas. Madeleine Hall declared she thought the new secretary never would see the light of day, seeming not to come out for several weeks after taking the job with Hall and Huffman. [43]

From the first, Jordan was treated as a lady and much more. The Hall family soon regarded her as virtually part of the family. She worried about what to wear to work. One day Judge Sam Sr. declared, "You look very nice today, lady!" She wore a light green, polyester dress and put so much stock in his opinion that for some time afterwards her working wardrobe tended toward pastels and polyester. Jordan thought of herself as an Eliza Doolittle, the heroine of "My Fair Lady" or *Pygmalion*, one who in Hall's employ rose from humble origins to become an administrative assistant to a man of influence. Hall simply encouraged her to do her best work and expected no less. She trusted him implicitly and gave him full loyalty. He and Madeleine treated her like a daughter, giving advice with major decisions just as they did their own three daughters. Especially when Hall was in Washington, and Jordan's family was far away in Ore City, Texas, Sam and Madeleine watched over her much as they did their own three daughters. [44]

Thus, Sam B. Hall Jr. developed his skills and built his legal practice during the fifties and sixties, benefiting from the guidance, collegiality, and friendship of his legal associates, secretaries, and his experienced father. He found in the profession of law not only a productive and profitable vocation, but also a means of affirming his relationships and roles in his East Texas community.

4

Family, Friends, and Church Life in Marshall

As a young married man and attorney, Sam B. Hall Jr. found numerous ties between the lives of his family of origin and the one he was to build. Among his roles was that of intercessor in a few matters concerning his sister and parents. In 1950 Kathleen enrolled at Baylor University in Waco to major in music. Grief-stricken, her parents Sam Sr. and Valerie went to bed in tears, and Sam Jr. and Madeleine conducted Kathleen to Waco. Later, at the "Lions Loonies," an annual program of the Lions Club in Marshall, Kathleen played piano accompaniment for John McLendon, who was a salesman for Armour and Company. Eventually, Kathleen wanted to marry John but knew how her father would be about "Daddy's girl." Valerie told Kathleen, "that drummer will leave you high and dry," so she had doubts about Kathleen's prospects with John. Thus, John and Kathleen went to Sam Jr. and Madeleine as intermediaries. Sam Jr. actually spoke first with his father. Once the ground had been prepared and John's way eased to broach the subject in person, he visited Judge Hall in his office and got permission to marry Kathleen. [1]

Neither John nor Kathleen knew that Sam Jr. was long since satisfied that John would make an acceptable husband for his sister. He had met McLendon at James Neely's Brown Pig Barbeque café. Hall was a regular customer, and Neely introduced him to McLendon. Later, Hall completed a personal background check on McLendon, interviewing John's former employers around town, asking detailed questions about his character and behavior. The family knew nothing about it until Hall and the family underwent investigation at the time of his nomination as a federal judge. Hall told McLendon that he had investigated him many years before. Beyond being merely satisfied, the Halls drew McLendon into their loving family, so that he, an only child, came to regard Hall "the only brother I would have," a real bonus to his wedding Kathleen in 1955. [2]

There are men who make ideal fathers for daughters. Sam Jr. was such a man. Frequently asked whether he missed having any sons, he usually responded, "What would I do with one?" He was happy with daughters and enjoyed them as much as possible. His fathering impulse went beyond meeting needs; it pleased him to please his daughters if he could, just as he did life's other leading women, his mother Valerie and wife Madeleine. Madeleine gave birth to Linda Rebecca in May 1949, and Sam was ready to fulfill his duties as a husband and father. Present at the hospital on the night of Becky's birth, but excluded from the delivery room, as was the norm, he stayed the night with his wife, left for breakfast at the Ginocchio Hotel and returned. Madeleine required more time to recover from a Caesarian section, so he made sure she stayed as long as necessary, providing a private nurse for a time. In the meantime, he liked being the first parent to change diapers, and to bathe and dress his infant daughter, at first spending more time with the baby than Madeleine. [3]

In 1951 the birth of their second daughter, Amanda Jane, allowed Sam to reprise his attentive role as father of a newborn. He lavished attention on her, helped as much as possible, and held Amanda a lot, as he had Becky since she was first born. Caring for his girls brought out his affectionate nature; his unabashed affection for his daughters was consistent and obvious to everyone.

Sandra Blake was a later arrival in 1959, unexpected at first, but welcomed just like the first two girls, who were thrilled to learn they had a sister. On the first Sunday after Sandra's birth, Sam brought the two elder girls to the first floor, and asked the hospital staff to bring Madeleine in a wheelchair to fix their hair. They were dressed for church, and properly, but their hair was too much for him. During the week he took the newborn Sandra from the hospital, drove her to Becky and Amanda's school, and allowed them to see her through the chain-link fence. The other girls were old enough to help raise her. Becky proudly carried her infant sister on her hip, acting almost as a mother to her. With Becky and Amanda ten and eight years older, Sandra had more of an only child's experiences once her sisters became teenagers. As a true only child, Madeleine's world changed greatly with three daughters—her mother's model of child rearing did not suit the situation—so she adjusted. Fortunately, Sam's family experiences and nurturing personality assured a comfortable transition for him.

Sam and Madeleine had inherited consistent beliefs about disciplining children and applied them as necessary. Amanda remembered well the time when she got a "beating." On the first day of the first grade year, she ran all the way from the old Stephen F. Austin grade school to the Hall house near the fairgrounds on West Houston street. She did not want to go to school: "I didn't enjoy buying school supplies, so I knew I would never enjoy using them." Becky had "run away" from school earlier, going across the street to the meat market and calling home to Madeleine, who ordered her back to school. Knowing that, Amanda decided there was no use asking, so she simply left. "I asked to be excused by my first grade teacher, Mrs. Sternberg. I remember vividly going to the little girls' room. I looked down the long hallway, saw no teachers, no students, no nothing, and thought 'This will be a good time to go,' so I exited." A lady member of their church, Vivian Ann Ford, lived in the house on the hill by the fairgrounds, the house the Halls Sr. had built in the thirties. The maid let Amanda in to wait for Mrs. Ford who was just then showering and dressing. "I asked her to take me home because I had carnival tickets to sell to my mother," Amanda reminisced. "She knew that was probably a lie, but she said I was crying and so hysterical that she knew she had to do something. So here we go in her car: we cross the railroad tracks, and here comes Grandmother in her car. I dropped my handkerchief on the floor of the car until Grandmother passed. I thought, we've made one more." Valerie did not see her in the car. [5]

At the house on west Highway 80 they found a concerned welcoming party. The parents, grandparents, and the county sheriff waited in the driveway. They feared the worst, such as a kidnapping connected with the outcome of a recent murder case in Sam Sr.'s court. Terrified, Madeleine and Valerie had been crying, and Sam Sr. urged his son not to spank Amanda with the tree switch he went quickly to get. Amanda recollected that "To me, of course, he was the biggest man I had ever seen; it was the longest switch I believe I had ever seen. Daddy never said a word; he just kept holding my hand. He told me why he was spanking me—of course I knew. Lord, he was crying, I was crying—it was horrible. I'm not upset because of the spanking, just the memories. I committed a cardinal sin of disappearing, which I never did again." [6]

Amanda thought she had achieved her objective when the family sat down to lunch, but afterwards her father told her to brush her teeth, comb her hair, and they would go back to school. "I couldn't believe it. It never crossed my mind he would make me go back to school that day." She protested, but her father ordered her to apologize to every person who had searched for her, especially her teacher Mrs. Sternberg, and apologize for disrupting his or her day. Sam Sr. had dismissed court, but she was not taken to court for an apology. Hall dropped her at the school with a kiss and a reminder that he loved her. [7]

Sam and Madeleine insisted their daughters do what was right without question. That is the impression they caught as young children and others noted as a reliable pattern in the couple, just as it had been with Sam Sr. and Valerie. The Halls had high expectations, and the girls knew those expectations would be consistently applied. Even so, there was always a light-hearted love of fun and an appreciation of the unique characteristics of each daughter. The youngest Hall daughter, Sandra, recalled, "Daddy was a real stickler when it came to manners and respect. When I started school, he told me that even if I could not always make good grades I could sit in class and keep my mouth shut. Well, I was a very friendly little girl. I made a very low mark in conduct and hid under the dining room table when he came home from the office. I understood from that day on what would happen to me if I ever made that mark again. I always wanted to quit school. I believe I started wanting to in the third or fourth grade." [8]

Sam wanted his daughters to share his love of horseback riding. Amanda and Sandra enjoyed riding, but Becky hated both the thought and the experience. It took only one instance of terrified screaming for Sam to know Becky was not going to be a rider. At age three she got her first bicycle. Madeleine considered it a bad idea, but the child enjoyed the bicycle and had no problems with it. A horse threw Amanda when she first learned to ride. Sam ordered her back on the horse, and Madeleine objected. Amanda, unhurt though slightly shaken, remounted the horse while her dad reasoned that if she did not then she never would. [9]

Hall played with his daughters and the rest of the family. From the time in the fifties when the family lived in the country on the road to Hallsville, he had a 1949 Jeep that he took out on the property or into the woods with his daughters. He had an adventurous streak that he showed in a worse way with farm equipment, but he liked to make a trail rather than follow the road. "Anything that was over an inch tall, Daddy went over in that Jeep. He didn't care if it was a big tree. He figured the Jeep could go over it and try to scare you to death. He was having fun with us!" [11]

The Halls were an intimate family. As it was with Sam Jr. and his father, so it was with Sam Jr. and his daughters. The granddaughters revered Sam Sr. and Valerie, who adored their grandchildren. Amanda's personality most resembled that of her father. Judge Sam Sr. regularly used an office in the law firm. Beverly Hines marveled that Amanda came to her granddad's office sometimes to sit quietly for a considerable while with him, typically without conversation. Beverly sometimes thought Amanda had left, but she had not. "They—I guess it was comforting to have the presence of each other. She's just always coming to see that granddad." [12]

Amanda was twelve years old one day when she asked her father what she could be when she grew up. On their way to the grocery store, Hall pulled the car into a parking lot and gave her an answer. He declared that she could be anything she wanted to be, do anything she wanted to do. The way he said it impressed her thinking and assured her of how much he cared for her future. [13]

During her high school years, Amanda sometimes walked from the school eastward on Houston Street to the courthouse in order to observe her dad in trial proceedings. Her grandmother Valerie, who had never observed her husband in court, claimed Amanda had no business being there, but Sam was pleased, and insisted that if she enjoyed sitting in court, then she should be allowed to do so. Aside from whatever interest the trial itself presented, Amanda was proud of her dad and took deep pleasure in seeing him, hearing him, in the courtroom. [14]

Hall took the time to attend whatever programs his girls were involved in as he knew his presence and encouragement was important. Hastening home from Dallas the afternoon of a Marshall High School choral performance, Sam and Madeleine reached the auditorium just in time to learn that the choir director, Mr. James Matheny, had selected Becky at the last minute to present a solo. As she sang, Hall, overcome with tears, left the auditorium, but soon returned once he had composed himself. He was proud to watch Amanda as a junior high cheerleader and to see his daughters chosen to the Marshall High School Homecoming Court. [15]

Hall's daughters regarded him as a hero. It is an edifying thing to be the daughter of a man with a reputation for honesty, integrity, and loyalty in his business and legal affairs, civic activities and duties, and in his role as public servant in both the Congress and the Judiciary. Amanda reported that people regularly mentioned the ways her father had helped them and how they thought of him as a friend. [16]

Hall enjoyed shopping with his daughters, sometimes going out at the change of the season to watch them model the clothing items they were trying on. His opinion counted a great deal, and his good fashion sense learned from his mother delighted them, so that his recommendations often were their choices. He went each time Madeleine and one of the daughters chose a wedding dress. [17]

Hall enjoyed shopping with and for Madeleine who was not an enthusiastic shopper. But he encouraged her. He enjoyed the occasional extravagance for his wife, the unusual and extraordinary, especially jewelry. He always wanted Madeleine to have the gift he thought suited her best. Having come from a family that parted with money harder, the conservative Madeleine learned to accept the extravagance of the gift and of an attentive husband who anticipated needs and sometimes discerned her desires. Hall often gave what she wished for but had not let herself want. "It was there before I ever thought to ask for it." [18]

Dorothy Runnels, the wife of the late congressman Harold Runnels of New Mexico, marveled at Sam's shopping habits with Madeleine. "I remember Madeleine telling how he would take her shopping and help her select clothes. *Now, that's a really special man!* One of the most endearing things I remember is how his daughters talked about "M'daddy." They never referred to him as their father, or their dad; it was always "M'daddy said . . ." or "M'daddy did . . . ." Sam grinned broadly whenever he heard himself called 'M'daddy.'" [19]

The Halls belonged to the Marshall Symphony Association and League, which revived the Southern debutante tradition at the annual ball. Her proud father presented Sandra as a debutante at the inaugural Symphony League Ball in 1977, when the ball was held at the new Marshall Civic Center. [20]

Hall's enduring practice at Valentine's Day and on other occasions was to select candies and gifts for his daughters at Matthewson's Drug store in Marshall. As long as he lived, he had them sent to his daughters, both before and after they were married. [21]

The civic servant and politician can easily fall into a pattern that includes family less and less. Hall was away from the home a great deal. It is difficult to survey his active professional and civic life without assuming his family came second or third in priority, or that his family felt neglected. While he did not neglect them, there were times when the daughters longed for more time with their father. In a sense, each daughter had a different father, as each one related to him differently out of her own personality, and he responded to different personalities while being so powerfully the devoted father. By the time he went to Congress the daughters were fully grown, two were out of the home and married, yet his presence in Washington rather than Marshall made a greater difference for the family. Nonetheless, whatever the circumstances or the time in the life of the family, Hall consciously sought to be fully present when at home. He left his work and other commitments behind, keeping work and home separated as much as possible. It worked the other way, in addition, as Madeleine Hall asserted she never once came to court to observe him during a trial. For Madeleine to have done so was something that occurred neither to her nor to Sam Jr., and it probably helps to explain how Hall could move so easily from work to home to work. Paradoxically; the family members frequently visited his office. [22]

Hall's civic service and numerous memberships entailed long hours in the office and courtroom and with various organizations and boards, so he remained fully occupied away from home. Becky Palmer observed, "He was very family oriented, and he was very emotional, but he also had that side of him that had the need to serve, and that was his way of doing it. Now as a kid it was kind of hard to realize that, but as an adult you can look back on it and see that he was fulfilling two sides." [23]

Hall believed in taking life seriously, but not too seriously. He was an optimist. Difficulties did come, and when the girls complained or whined his favorite question was whether they did not have enough to worry about: "Are you gonna let a little thing like that bother you?" Minor problems did not need magnifying. [24]

The father of three daughters should have a firm view about dating and curfews. Becky had a 10:30 P.M. curfew when she started dating. Her first boyfriend "wanted to know what time I had to be in as we were driving out the driveway." It was 10:30, and he thought that was too early. She said, "Well, you can go back and tell him." They were back at 10:30.[25]

There were always other young people around the Hall home while the daughters were growing up, particularly during the teen years. Sam Hall Jr. attracted young people because of the positive acceptance they could sense. Tempered with gentleness and love, his gregarious personality, size and confidence left them feeling secure and valued. Dennis Watson was like a brother to the Hall daughters, particularly Becky, with whom he graduated high school, and he spent a great deal of time at the Hall home. Madeleine kept ice cream, especially the ice cream bonbons that Dennis liked. "Ice cream time" rallied everyone at the house. Playing football for the Marshall Mavericks on Friday nights, Watson often heard Sam Hall bellowing, "Ice cream time!" Watson played for Baylor University. "There could be 50,000 screaming fans in the stands, and I could recognize Sam's voice yelling 'ice cream time,'" he recalled. "I would look around, and there he would be with a big grin on his face." During Watson's high school years, his father died, and Sam Hall consciously did things to help, becoming a father figure for him. Later, as best man at Watson's wedding, he slipped $200 to him when he and his bride set off for their honeymoon. [26]

The boys, Dennis Watson and Mike Chapman, for example, did not come to the Hall home just because three girls were there. "It was Daddy," said Amanda Wynn. "They absolutely adored him. He was Dennis Watson's best man in his wedding. They loved him, loved to be around him, and loved anything to rub off of him to them." Having lost his father also, Chapman confessed that after his father died, everything he did with Union Pacific Railroad or otherwise in his career he did as a direct result of what Sam Hall said or expected, and he looked to Hall for approval. Chapman once asked Amanda what she thought was the most important thing her parents had done to raise their daughters to love them as they did. Amanda knew it was respect, utmost respect. [27]

During their Baylor University years, Amanda and Becky were members of the Atheneans sorority, which had an annual party for the parents at Homecoming. In a meeting at Waco's Cameron Park, when the time came for people to say a few words, Sam stood and said, "I'm trying to solicit help for my daughter Amanda. Becky came to Baylor and found herself a husband, but Amanda has been through the football team, the basketball team, and the baseball team and she hasn't found one yet." Amanda was mortified, as was the basketball player she was dating at the time, but Sam's exaggeration delighted everyone else. His humor endeared him to his daughters' friends. [28]

Hall was proud to have his three daughters graduated from college. Sandra recalled the electrifying moment during her graduation when her dad made a scene: "As I was graduating from Baylor University in 1981, all of the family came to Waco for the ceremonies. As I walked across the stage and received my diploma, I heard a booming voice from the back of the auditorium saying, 'Aren't you glad you didn't quit in the fourth grade like you wanted to?'" [29]

Years after his daughters were mature adults he took delight in their families and work. In Beaumont, Texas, during a trial, Judge Hall stopped at a child's clothing store to check on the selection. A court reporter, Erin Rienstra, was with him. There was more to his visit than the purpose of checking on clothing for the grandchildren. Second daughter Amanda operated a similar business in Marshall, designing and producing a line of

There are men who make ideal fathers for daughters. Sam Jr. was such a man. With Becky and Amanda, aged three years and one year.

dresses for little girls. Asking whether the Beaumont shop had any "Manda Jane" brand clothing, he was told that "Manda Jane" was one of the best lines of clothing made for children. Quietly, but obviously, he was proud to hear that. [30]

The Sam and Madeleine Hall family took an annual summer vacation, and Sam's love of the water usually guaranteed they would go to the Gulf Coast, just west of Destin, Florida, to a small hotel that had good access to the beach. It was a relaxing place, nice, with good food. In some years the family went to Pensacola or Miami. Hall loved to travel, and, like his uncle Reuben, loved the Gulf Coast; his parents did not enjoy it. Aside from the water itself he loved long walks on the beach. [31]

The Hall family's long tradition of taking fried chicken on the road continued with the Sam Hall Jr. family. Maggie Hiner, the long-time cook and housekeeper for the Halls Sr., prepared a fried chicken feast for the journey. U.S. Highway 80 was the major east-west thoroughfare to Louisiana, and the trip took the family from Marshall through Waskom, Texas, and Greenwood, Louisiana, then to Shreveport and beyond. Maggie's irrestibile fried chicken lasted no farther than Greenwood or Shreveport, less than forty miles into the trip. And, in homage to the family tradition, the cook and the eaters, the family joked that dogs chased the car for miles, following a trail of discarded chicken bones. It was normally an exaggeration, but not in one instance. Madeleine and the girls once accompanied a basket of Maggie's chicken, without Sam, on a trip to Houston. Pausing at a rest stop, they screamed when a large dog, no doubt overpowered by the aroma of southern-fried yard bird, tried to enter through the windows and jumped to the car's hood.

On another trip, Becky remarked she thought she had just seen one of the girls' hair dryers—the kind with the separate blower unit and elastic cap in a flat, square box—fly from the luggage rack of their well-laden station wagon as they approached a bridge. Indeed, it had, landing near a black woman's house. She and Hall chuckled as they collected the appliance and he lashed it more securely to the luggage rack. He thanked the elderly lady for her help and shook her hand, leaving a folded bill. [32]

Hall had abiding love for history and a nose for historical relevance. In 1957 during the Little Rock Central High School confrontation between Governor Orval Faubus and the federal government over school integration, the Halls went to Little Rock to pick up a niece, John and Kathleen's daughter, Melanie, for a visit with the family. Hall saw what was happening in Little Rock and was determined that the family had to see history in the making. They went to see for themselves. Arkansas Governor Faubus had called on the National Guard to keep nine black students out of the school. When

Hall saw the National Guard troops with their rifles surrounding the school the anger rose in him; using the military to enforce a policy bothered him greatly. The addition of federal troops later only deepened his anger. [33]

In 1969, the Apollo 11 astronauts were nearing the first moon landing while the family was on the road in Texas. Hall insisted that they stop, so they rented a motel room with a television in order to see the event. Such an unprecedented, once-in-a-lifetime historical event was not to be missed. Whenever possible, Hall made sure their vacation route passed by Civil War or other battlefields and other historical sites. He liked to quiz his daughters about them before they reached their destination. Beyond that, whatever the circumstances and the purpose of a gathering, or a family trip, Hall was in it to enjoy other people. He loved to make regular, daily life and new experiences opportunities to celebrate, which surely they were. [34]

The son of a Church of Christ elder, as a church deacon Hall kept himself and his family active in the Burleson Street Church of Christ in Marshall, later renamed the Eastern Hills Church of Christ. When Sam and Madeleine married in 1946, it was clear that they would attend the Church of Christ. Madeleine was the only child of Maurice Joseph and Margaret Segal of Jefferson, Texas. Her Jewish father was a merchant and the son of a merchant. Her mother "Maggie," the daughter of lumberman Meredith Manning and a member of the Christian Church in Jefferson, was "a woman of great strength and independence" who taught Madeleine self-reliance and confidence in the goodness of life, "that life was good and I should strive for the best it had to offer." Madeleine grew up in Jefferson, going to Temple Moses Montefiore in Marshall only occasionally for such things as her cousins' Bar Mitzvahs, and attended the First Baptist Church in Jefferson. She decided she could very well make the transition to Sam's church. Hall demanded nothing of her, but was so positive and consistent in his Christian commitment that she had no problem belonging to his church family as well as the Hall family. [35]

For Hall, church was a non-negotiable part of life. He led congregational hymn singing for many years and in later years became active with other things, staying as involved as anyone in his congregation. With Deacon Emmett Baker supervising, Hall helped a large team landscape the church property one Saturday. He arrived at church Sunday morning joking, "I wouldn't work for that Emmett Baker. He works you too hard, but we got everything done yesterday." For Hall, religious devotion, intense effort and liberal giving defined his churchmanship. Bob Wagner, the church's minister during Hall's later years, was impressed that he helped people and the church, so quietly that even he as minister did not know of his service. [36]

Attorney Richard Anderson described the image people developed of Hall as a Christian, saying that Sam was what people observed him to be. "Some people will wear religion on their cuff; with some it's held closely in the left pocket of the coat, right over their heart," Anderson said. "It doesn't just come trippingly out; but you have a sense that you know it's there by the way that they invoke the name of the Lord—there's a great profundity to it—that was him." [37]

The Hall family was so regular at church that, as a teenager who grew up close to the Halls, Mike Chapman wondered aloud whether Hall was the only church member with a key and so always had to be there. Whatever else the Hall family did on Sundays, they had to be back for evening church at six o'clock. [38]

The Christianity of Sam B. Hall Jr. and of the family in which he grew up involved a lifestyle of commitment to God and church, matters not to be taken lightly. The family held to a strong moral and ethical structure, professed an uncompromising sense of right and wrong as well as a thorough understanding of personal responsibility. Those essential values had endured in the home of Sam and Valerie Hall and continued in the home of Sam and Madeleine Hall.

Hall was highly respected in his church. His daughters Becky and Amanda belonged to his Sunday school class for a time during high school; for many years, he taught teenagers and young married adults. He enjoyed teaching, and, where knowledge of the Roman law was useful, as in the trial of Jesus, he was memorably effective. His ability to teach through stories made him a great teacher in his students' eyes.

Hall helped serve the Lord's Supper, the typical term for communion in his congregation, every Sunday morning. In leading prayer, his thoughts and phrases revealed his focus on God and worship. He tended not to repeat patent phrases or habitual sentiments that often intrude into extemporaneous public prayers. Without writing them, he planned his prayers beforehand. As a congressman his awareness and sympathies broadened considerably and his prayers reflected specific concerns for the nation and the world, thus he communicated a broader vision that many of his fellow church members appreciated. Above all else, Hall was regarded an exemplary Christian man purely by virtue of his character and conduct. Importantly in East Texas society, he was a staunch non-drinker, avoiding alcohol and recommending that others do the same. His friends noted his dogged consistency as a teetotaler. Regardless of the situation, he simply would not take a drink. There were no platitudes; he did not produce scripture verses or religious aphorisms; he simply professed to live as he understood he should. [39]

A survey of Hall's personal library revealed his love for history, military history and biography, humor, and political and judicial biography. Sam Hall as an attorney should have gotten more than enough reading during the workday, but he read in bed and elsewhere at home, and while traveling. A favorite was Douglas Southall Freeman's *Lee's Lieutenants.* He had collections on World War II, general military, naval and air history. His shelves held biographies such as James Reston's *The Lone Star* on Governor John Connally of Texas, and various titles on Sam Rayburn of Texas and Thomas P. "Tip" O'Neill of Massachusetts, both of them admired Speakers of the House of Representatives. There were a Masonic edition of the Bible, books on public speaking, and collected sayings and jokes. An Authorized "King James" Version given as a gift from his parents at Christmas in 1953, his personal Bible was marked with his favorite verse, Philippians 4:8. It read, *"Finally brethren, whatsoever things are true, whatsoever things are honest, whatsoever things are just, whatsoever things are pure, whatsoever things are lovely, whatsoever things are of good report; if there be any virtue, and if there be any praise, think on these things."* The verse likely best encapsulated Hall's ideals, beliefs and attitudes governing life. Other considerations aside, his life took its foundation from earliest childhood in a family and circle of relations who on their best and worst days professed New Testament Christianity.

The Halls belonged to a supper club that met monthly from the 1950s. Its original members included Ralph and Verlin Watson, at whose home the first supper meeting was held; Joe and Phyllis Hirsch; Tom and Mary Dinwiddie; Bill and Amelia Palmer; Don and Glenda Knutsen; Ray and Mona Lawson; and later Frank and Joanne Fuller, among others. The Watson daughters, Cecelia and Suzanne, and Hall daughters, Amanda, Becky and Sandra were almost as close as sisters, taking part in each others' weddings and maintaining strong friendships into adulthood.

Sam and Madeleine's circle of friends included Frank "Bodie" and Joanne Fuller. Frank came from Dallas in 1945 to teach band and choir at the high school. Working at first with a "scratch" band composed of untrained students, he got help from the Lions Club and Ernest Smith to buy new band instruments. Sam's sister, Kathleen, played piano for the choir at school and was dear to Fuller. After Hall completed law school and returned to Marshall in 1948, he and Bodie became friends. Despite the success of the band program with its two consecutive First Division titles, Fuller found after six years that he could make a better living in the insurance business, and moved to Paris, then Waco, and returned to Marshall in 1986, just after Hall resigned from Congress to become a federal judge. Hall was Fuller's only friend to call and say that he wanted to buy some insurance from him!

Bodie Fuller called the supper club "just a gab session," and Hall always contributed his humor, love of storytelling and rich knowledge of East Texans. Fuller remembered Hall as a "true man's man" and a wonderfully entertaining person. Joanne Fuller had a running battle of humor and teasing with Hall for many years. His friends knew to watch out for practical jokes. Hospitalized because of a respiratory infection, Hall got out just in time to meet the supper club at the home of Ed and Martha Key. Joanne had visited him in the hospital, so he planned a trick, hoping to play on her sympathy. Though still weak, he could not pass up the chance to pull a joke on Joanne as she entered the house and passed through the crowded room. Hall pretended to fall into a dead faint on the floor. Obviously the wrong victim, Joanne simply asked what he thought he was doing, turned and left the room, having ruined his act. [41]

The supper club members often played bridge, and people early on thought that as smart as Hall was he should make a great bridge player, but no. Phyllis Hirsch wrote, "Sam held the best cards of any of us—his mind never relaxed enough to get into the game. He was so happy when the phone would ring and one of his many clients would need his advice or time immediately—that ended his Bridge career."[42]

The Halls had dear neighbors, none more so than Ruby Yates and her daughter Patty. George Yates was killed in action in Italy in December, 1942, and Ruby never remarried. Hall was godfather for Michael, Ruby's grandson, a father figure for Patty, and helped with legal matters for Ruby over the years. He knew the deep devotion Ruby had for her late husband remained years after his death. Twenty years to the day after George's death Hall presented Ruby with a duplicate Marshall High School graduation photograph of George. She had forgotten the anniversary, and that Hall remembered it moved her deeply. [43]

Ray and Mona Lawson were good friends to the Halls. Ray Lawson met Hall in 1952 when he came to the law office to repair a door. Lawson had a new business, Martex Glass, and he was still learning how to do the work. He repaired the door and got acquainted with Hall. The new friends became neighbors for eighteen years. Lawson and Hall worked more closely after Lawson was appointed to the Board of Education in 1962 and Hall was attorney for the school district. The Lawsons' son, David, attended Baylor University, as did the Hall daughters, so the Halls and Lawsons traveled to Waco many times for university events just as they had at Marshall High School.[44]

Hall would do almost anything to stir up encouraging relationships. He supported the Marshall Mavericks football team in all the ways a father of high school students and a fan could do. W. G. "Buck" Buchanan typically coached defense for the Marshall Mavericks football team in the 1970s. Several years in a row, Hall brought him a box of chewing tobacco at the beginning of the football season, wishing the coach a great year. [45]

Close friends got help, too. Ernest Marshall was a long time friend and fellow member on the board of education. Hall's friends knew who they were, and Ernest Marshall's son Mark was no different. On a particularly hot summer day, he and a friend dismounted bicycles at the law office, entered the door, swept past the secretary, and went directly to Hall's office. He asked what he could do for the boys, and Mark replied, "Sir, we were really thirsty and needing a Coke, but had no money, so we wondered where we could borrow a quarter from. So we passed your office; it hit me, maybe Mr. Sam might help us out." He provided the quarters for the Coke machine in the outer office, and as they left he called after them, "If you ever have any more trouble, be sure to stop by!" In 1971, Mark experienced a severe injury in a sports accident and required extensive convalescence and therapy. The Halls were among those who pitched in to help. They made numerous visits to the hospital in Shreveport while Mark was comatose. In recovery, quadriplegic and in a wheelchair, Mark still wanted to finish high school, and Madeleine helped gather volunteers to attend him at school and take notes so that he could pass his classes.[46]

Don and Marguerite Ratcliff were fast friends for several decades. An engineer for the state highway department, Don trusted Sam Hall Jr. perhaps as he trusted no other man. He and Marguerite later helped with congressional campaigns when they lived in Cass County, and after they returned to Marshall. Marguerite liked to reciprocate Hall's impish pranks. A strategically-intrusive banana tree placed in his office as a "gift," or a worn, rusted sweep cultivator blade gift-wrapped to make Hall think he was receiving a fine Stetson hat, were ways to keep the friendly pranks going. Don Ratcliff retired in 1978 while the Halls were in Washington and could not attend his retirement dinner. A "Regrets" telegram belied the fact the Halls actually planned to attend, which they did, arriving in Atlanta during a rare East Texas snowstorm. In later years Hall read from his favorite Bible verses when he eulogized Don Ratcliff. [47]

People remain amazed that Hall served effectively on so many committees and boards. His community and civic service best explain why he was so well known and appreciated. Early in his career, while in his twenties, Hall pursued an ascending career in civic service, rising through community organizations such as the Jaycees, becoming their Outstanding Marshall Jaycee in 1953, having served as president of the Marshall chapter, as Vice-President of the Texas Jaycees, and as a national director from Texas in 1953. Friends considered him reliable and typically involved in more than his fair share of the work, whether as a Kiwanian or a member of the Junior Chamber of Commerce, or other organizations and boards. As a Jaycee he attended state conventions with Joe and Phyllis Hirsch, and Louis and Audrey Kariel, both of whom held several community offices. Their work together continued with the Greater Marshall Chamber of Commerce. Hall served as Chamber president and supported Louis Kariel later as president when he served. [48]

Through the years his and his family's interests involved him in such organizations as the Community Concert and Symphony Associations and the Harrison County Farm Bureau. As a member of the Kiwanis Clubs International, he was president and a lieutenant governor for the thirteenth district of Kiwanis. He was on the boards of the Boy Scouts' East Texas Council and Marshall Camp Fire Girls. Hall belonged to the American Legion, was a Thirty-second Degree Mason as a member of the Masonic Lodge, Hella Temple, in Marshall, and was an honorary 33rd degree Scottish Rite Mason. A Thirty-Second Degree Mason since 1952, Hall was honored as a Knights Commander in the Scottish Rite Order in November, 1977. Named the Outstanding Citizen for 1970 in Marshall, on January 14, 1971, Hall was described by Carlos J. Caccioppo as "a man who had dedicated his life to working for the community, the church and to ensuring a better tomorrow for the young people of the city, county and state." [49]

Hall's experience as the chairman of the Executive Committee of the Harrison County Hospital Association gave him the opportunity for concentrated service. He chaired the Marshall Memorial Hospital Growth Fund's Initial Gifts Division and Official Family Gifts Division. As president of the hospital board, he showed the ability to lead to consensus, to smooth over difficulties, and to foster cooperation. In the early 1970s, the hospital board under his leadership responded the need for improved hospital facilities. Hall, Carlos Caccioppo, and A. G. Carter Jr. led in a $1 million local fund drive for a new hospital addition in 1975 costing $4 million, and in the 1990s, in respect of his contributions and leadership over the years, the new skilled nursing unit of the Marshall Regional Medical Center was named for him. He took great pride in the development of the hospital and loved serving on its board of directors. In 1983 he declared, "People have heard me say before that there are no more important agencies in the community than its schools and its hospital, and I am very proud to have been associated with both. Health care and education are the two factors whose quality determines the value of a community." Hall took a positive approach to having the black physicians in town finally admitted to staff privileges with the hospital. His other crucial board service was on the Marshall Board of Education, during a time of transition for the community. W. F. "Pinkie" Palmer judged that "he really enjoyed being on boards. And after having been on a few in my life, I don't know how he did so many and enjoyed it, but he did."[50]

Hall loved to serve; it was never a burden, but a constant source of pleasure that others recognized in him. Friends described Hall's priorities, and he himself was nowhere near the top of the list. Patsy Smith-Gasperson described him as a man dedicated to "family, fellow-man, and country." His Christian heritage and patriot heritage were crucial to him, and he passed it on enthusiastically. A teacher and school administrator, Smith-Gasperson wrote,

> I remember Sam B. Hall, Jr., and the heritage he left as a patriot. He was likely to appear unannounced in my classroom and enter into the singing of patriotic songs. He was the impetus for a school-wide patriotic program, "Take the Torch." He shared books and teaching materials about history and patriotism, giving freely of his time to let students benefit from his experiences. He had a keen interest in disadvantaged and troubled youth, giving freely of his time and money to encourage and assist them. [51]

Hall's public service pursuits had nothing directly to do with his law practice, either. Franklin Jones Jr. reflected on Hall's stellar leadership in Marshall, saying, "I recall a story I always told when I spoke to any of the civic clubs: I'd always heard that the Rotarians owned the town, the Kiwanians ran it, and the Lions enjoyed it. Well, Hall ran the town." [52]

Sam B. Hall Jr. may not have run the town, but he clearly worked hard and exercised strong leadership. As to where he got the energy and drive such work required, his father's example may be a source. During one of those times when lawyers and judges wait on a jury, Sam Hall Sr. related to Franklin Jones Jr. and Scotty Baldwin that as a kid he spent a lot of time during the summer hoeing cotton—the hardest work the Hall boys ever had to do. The July sun made a rising storm cloud welcome because a boy could go to the house and put the hoe down. After a thirty-minute rain, the sun came back out and it was back to the hoeing. Jones had not known that Hall Sr. had worked on the farm like that, but he knew that no lawyer or judge worked harder, and that helped to explain the work ethic of the Hall family and Sam Jr. [53]

5

A Young Man's Bid for Congress -- 1962

In 1928 a young man won election as congressman for the First Congressional District of Texas. That young man was Wright Patman. During the late 1920s the First Congressional District of Texas had been a district of farms and ranches, of new oil leases and the timber industry. Heavy industries such as lignite coal mining for power generation and steel were not yet developed, but when as in the case of Lone Star Steel they were developed with help from Congressman Wright Patman, they provided a stronger financial base, which also supported many medium to light industries in northeastern Texas. The largely rural, small-town identity of the region endured throughout the century. During the half-century Patman served in Congress, agriculture abandoned the traditional cotton culture almost completely by the 1970s, and the railroads declined while highways and automobiles grew in importance. Dairying, poultry farming for meat and eggs, and cattle ranching grew more important after World War II, as did plantation-style production of pine timber for lumber and pulpwood.

By mid-century the population of the county seats and larger towns and cities ranged from 10,000 to about 25,000. In the northeast corner of the district, Wright Patman's hometown, Texarkana (though he grew up in Hughes Springs, Cass County, Texas), straddled the state line with Arkansas and doubled Marshall's population, but the Texas side of Texarkana surpassed Marshall by about five or six thousand residents. Other nearby East Texas cities such as Lufkin, Nacogdoches, Tyler, and Longview lay outside the First District (except Longview for a time due to redistricting), as did the Shreveport-Bossier metropolitan area in Louisiana, but, nonetheless, they exerted an economic and social influence on the Texas First Congressional District. During Wright Patman's long tenure in Congress from 1928 to

1976, the First District grew from ten to twenty counties, and, as the district grew, so did his influence. [1]

The decision of Sam B. Hall Jr. to challenge Wright Patman for his congressional seat in 1962 provided one of his most important lessons in life and politics. No minor matter, it was an attempt to unseat a living institution. When East Texans heard the term "congressman" they thought "Wright Patman." He had a career reputation as a populist dedicated to guarding and promoting the interests of his largely rural district. His impoverished upbringing and convictions about the rights of citizens over against the government motivated his dogged stance as a congressional committee chairman overseeing the Federal Reserve and the commercial banking industry. During the economic depression in the early thirties he supported granting a cash bonus to veterans of the Great War, and in the New Deal congresses he supported President Franklin D. Roosevelt's economic and social initiatives. His reputation and influence only grew through the years that two or three generations of East Texans knew him as their congressman, and few people had not benefited in some way from his service. His political grip on the district was such that at election time Patman could say he first learned about his Republican opponent when he went to the polling place to vote and saw the name on the ballot. [2]

Patman's committee positions, seniority and accomplishments benefiting East Texas enhanced his influence in the Congress and with his constituents. During the Second World War, he worked to direct into his own district such beneficial projects as the Longhorn Army Ammunition plant at Karnack and the Red River Army Depot and Lone Star Army Ammunition Plant near Texarkana. Patman directly helped to assure the permanency and growth of Lone Star Steel after the Second World War. East Texans had wall calendars with his picture, they received copies of his portrait for display on their walls, and his office sent out recipe books, among other things, as friendly reminders of his concern for the voters. His recognition and proven effectiveness for his district meant that he was trusted, much as a doting uncle or grandfather would be. That is how it was for a constant majority of East Texas voters for over thirty-two years. Thus, a great reservoir of trust and loyalty had established him unshakably in the First District. Sam B. Hall Jr. was going to challenge that. [3]

Wright Patman could not lose in 1962. Another challenger to Patman asked B. B. Boon of Linden his opinion about the people and Patman. Boon declared he was uncertain about the townspeople, but out in the country it was different. "As soon as you get out of the city limits, you walk into one of these houses and there's a picture there, about eight by ten, and it says, "God bless our happy home"—a great big picture of Wright Patman on the wall." Boon got into trouble in Linden. He and a physician owned adjacent vacant lots, and Patman supporters got permission to post campaign signs on the doctor's lot. Boon caught them placing signs on his property and directed them to the other lot. "All over town, I had people calling me thinking that I had done something bad. I had them check the record. It was rough times in those days if you went against Wright Patman." [4]

Lyndon B. Johnson used to tell about the fellow with a limited education whose political opponent in a Texas election was a Harvard graduate. The Harvard candidate emphasized the difference in qualifications, so the other retorted, "Well, I may not be very smart, but I wasn't dumb enough to oppose Wright Patman in the last election!" [5]

The "why" of Sam Hall Jr.'s motivation to run for Congress must have something to do with his desire to serve and his conviction that he could provide important service for East Texas. He hoped he could do it in Congress. When asked about his motivations, many people responded that Hall simply had always wanted to be a congressman. He was ambitious. On the other hand, perhaps going to the Congress was a more recent aspiration. An insight into the prospect of congressional service comes from the time after he finished at Baylor Law School. Hall was a new lawyer in Marshall. The Texas Democratic state leaders visited Marshall on one occasion. Congressman Sam Rayburn and Senator Lyndon Johnson met with the local Democrats, the lawyers and political leadership, at the home of Colonel Myron Blalock, who had been a member of the National Democratic Committee. Blalock lived just outside of town and had a lake where Sam Rayburn liked to fish when he visited. [6]

Rayburn sat in a swivel chair in the middle of a large room so that he could turn quickly to converse with the individuals around him. Hall recalled that Rayburn and Johnson wanted to know something about the men in the room. Might there be suitable candidates for this or that position? The Texas Democrats operated on the principle that congressmen such as Sam Rayburn or Wright Patman or Jim Wright would best be selected by their late twenties to early thirties so that they could build tenure in the Congress and rise to leadership. Of this selection process Marshall attorney Michael Smith said, "You leave them there forever so that they are committee chairs. That's why Texas always did so well in Congress, why we had speakers and committee chairmen. So they were always looking for the younger people whom they could plug in." Wright Patman by then already had twenty years or so in the House, and no one knew how long his tenure would be, so the party leaders wanted to identify possible candidates for the Texas First Congressional District. Rayburn asked who among those present might be a possible candidate. The men surveyed the room and presently many pointed out Sam B. Hall Jr. In later years one of his law-school classmates, Marion G. Holt, explained Hall's rise to leadership: "He was what I term a born leader. That is, he had natural talents to lead; that which you cannot learn, but must be God given. Hall did not brag or push to get up front. We pushed him." [7]

Hall got his introduction to politics as a matter of course, having been born into a family where Sam Sr. and Uncle Reuben had been elected to their positions as district attorneys and state judges. His father's political campaigns and daily activities were constant lessons in political life and public service. Hall pulled with the rest of the family in the political campaigns. Uncle Reuben and Sam Hall Jr. were as close as uncle and nephew ever could be, and Sam remembered helping with his uncle's campaigns from the time he was eleven. Hall also got direct experience with administrative matters when he served on the Marshall Board of Education and the local hospital board. His experience with the school board began when he represented the district as a lawyer during the late 1950s and early 1960s. He served during the crucial years when the board laid plans to accomplish the orderly integration of the schools. In 1958 the Marshall board hired a new superintendent, Von Rhea Beane, who had been serving at Mineola, and assigned him the task of preparing the schools for integration, a process not completed until after he had left the position. Hall served during those developments.

Before entering the congressional primary race in 1962, Hall conferred with Joe Lovelace, his long-time college and law school friend from Linden. Lovelace thought Hall was foolish to challenge someone who was unbeatable, but he listened when his friend spoke about the need to change things. Hall believed voters would respond to him as a youthful candidate and "give a young man a chance." Lovelace wrote, "I inquired about his organization and who would be his campaign manager. He turned to me and said he was looking at him. I could not resist such a friend." Hall had not come to Lovelace to get help making up his mind; he wanted to know whether he would stand with him. [8]

The campaign began on March 15, 1962. Sam Hall's closest supporters included Lovelace, Don Rives, Charles Thompson, Frank Hall, and Tom Lanier Sr. They had their first meeting in Frank Hall's new bomb shelter. Their use of a bomb shelter as a meeting place and the outcome of the 1962 primary election suggest an irresistible symbolic association between the two events. The Cuban Missile Crisis was still months away, but the Bay of Pigs debacle in April the previous year, the bad blood between President Kennedy and the Soviet Premier Nikita Khrushchev, and the construction of the Berlin Wall had put Americans in a defensive mood. Frank Hall had built a sizable reinforced concrete bomb shelter.

Joe Lovelace recalled what it was like to enter a political campaign amid such circumstances. He wrote,

> A few conservatives agreed to support Sam although none of our group had money. Our kickoff was in Mt. Pleasant at a semi-formal dinner that was broadcast. Sam had attacked Mr. Patman about the Supreme Court and his failure to assure that the justices had taken the proper oath to defend the Constitution. This was good talk in the South in 1962, and he received a rousing reception from the overflow crowd. The next day Sam received a telegram from Mr. Patman charging libel and demanding a retraction or he would sue. It did not upset Sam, but the rest of us thought he meant it, and we were concerned.

Although the candidate himself took the threat of lawsuit in stride, his associates absorbed more of the dramatic tension it generated. Lovelace was so upset he lost his stomach over it. Equally upset at the time, Don Rives, the campaign manager for Harrison County, later claimed that his ulcer did not heal until the statute of limitations for libel had run out. [9]

The candidates pursued the escalating give-and-take of campaign and speeches, assuming postures best seen in the newspaper campaign advertisements and reports. By later standards, the campaign leading to the Democratic primary in 1962 was brief, lasting from mid-March until the May 5 election.

Early in the campaign, Sam Hall Jr. accused the Congress, and, by implication, Wright Patman, of being soft on communism; of course, he himself would not be if he were elected to serve. Patman's campaign responded to Hall's inferences, citing the Communist Control Act of 1954 that declared the Communist Party should be outlawed. [10]

At his April 5 rally in Mt. Pleasant, Patman argued that Hall's views on limited government would keep the government from providing for the "general welfare" of the nation. He equated Hall to the right-wing Republicans. At the same time Hall characterized Patman as a liberal, a crony of the Americans for Democratic Action whom he considered an ultra left-wing group. That would make Patman among the most liberal members of Congress, particularly among the committee chairmen. [11]

After officially starting the campaign on April 5, the Patman campaign committee bought large advertisements in the newspapers emphasizing the seniority, influence, and many accomplishments of their candidate as he had served East Texans. The ads emphasized his support and development of veterans' programs, especially the G. I. Bill of Rights, and one ad clearly aimed to characterize Hall as a negative person, simply against this or that, whatever it might be. The ad admonished Hall to "Light somewhere, Sam, and let the people know! You've been shuffling All

Over the District Saying You're 'Against This' and 'Against That.'" The clever hook at the bottom of the page read, "In Fact, Sam, Are You For the People? . . . Wright Patman Is!" [12]

Hall had stated his philosophies and platform two days before, emphasizing the dangers of excessive government, saying,

> Our founding fathers were suspicious of the shackles of government controls. They fashioned and established a government of limited powers. Now we find the people of this country saddled with more and more controls and regulations—all originating in Washington. All of this central control and centralization of power in Washington means heavier burdens on taxpayers at all levels of government and warns of ultimate nationalization of vital industries which are no longer able to withstand the many restrictions and regulations placed upon them.
>
> I am opposed to the runaway trend of centralization and power and authority in Washington. I favor the strict limitation of the powers of the Federal Government as provided for by the United States Constitution.
>
> I believe the 10th Amendment to the Constitution of the United States means exactly what it says when it declares "The power not delegated to the United States by the Constitution, nor prohibited by it to the states, are reserved to the States respectively, or to the people." [13]

Hall clearly represented a strong states' rights position opposed to the strong populist stance of Congressman Patman, a leader who had participated in the development of a stronger federal presence in the lives of the people from the time of President Franklin D. Roosevelt and the New Deal. On the one hand, Hall criticized Patman's style and pattern of voting in the House of Representatives; on the other, Wright Patman continually challenged Hall's identity as a true Democrat. Speaking in a meeting at the Excelsior House hotel in Jefferson, Patman declared himself "almost ready to welcome him into the Democratic Party, but strictly on probation." But that would be possible, said Patman, only if Hall became focused about his policy positions instead of wandering "all over the political map, campaigning against all my programs as being 'socialistic' and 'communistic.'" Patman charged that Hall was unstable in his politics, sometimes supporting the Republican ticket, sometimes the Democrats, and, worst of all, "in the last election he supported the radical Constitution Party." [14]

Hall tried to draw an unsavory association between Patman and Jimmy Hoffa, the president of the national Teamster's Union. It was both a geographical and an ideological stretch. At an open-air rally in Sulphur

Springs, Hall produced a newspaper report as evidence that Jimmy Hoffa considered Wright Patman to be one of the five congressmen who voted most favorably on the issues Hoffa, and, presumably, the unions thought important. Given the political cleavage of the time, it is no surprise to find Hall, a conservative Democrat, attacking the voting record of Wright Patman, a long-time populist Democrat. Clearly, the labor unions would appreciate Patman's populism and his legacy of support for New Deal initiatives. Hall suggested that Hoffa's associations with organized crime made Patman look bad. The Hall campaign ran a large newspaper spread the same day clarifying those allegations: "Patman Votes 'Right' with Hoffa!" and "If You Want a Congressman Who Will Never Vote to Please Hoffa—Vote for Sam B. Hall, Jr." [15]

The Hall campaign published the details of the Hall platform on April 22. The Patman campaign responded similarly, citing the numerous responsibilities and accomplishments of their long-tenured candidate. A week later, the Hall campaign followed up with a "Platform for Positive Progress." The Hall campaign at that point was operating with less than a $10,000 budget, with less than $4,000 either paid or owed. The Patman campaign countered on May 1, chiding Hall for the last minute publication of his new platform, and declaring it too late to make a difference. [16]

A Hall campaign brochure, "Let A Young Man Serve," expressed Hall's integrity, quality, training for leadership, described him as a "dedicated foe of the Communist conspiracy," emphasized his desire to provide a country suitable for his children, and proclaimed his "proper regard for Christian values." A brief statement of his political beliefs read: "The political philosophy of Sam B. Hall, Jr., can be summed up in a few words: he believes in the preservation of the private enterprise system, national solvency and the inalienable right of the individual and the local community to manage their own affairs." [17]

One of Hall's key campaign rallies was in Marshall on April 24, 1962. At that evening rally influential individuals turned out to voice their support, including the campaign chairmen of the various counties. The Stardusters, a group from Paris, provided music, as did the Kay Sisters, a trio of Leneda, Linda, and Leta Kay. [18]

Hall's friend from college days and Marshall businessman Charlie Flowers served as master of ceremonies, and J. R. Perkins, the minister of the East Burleson Street Church of Christ in Marshall, offered the invocation. Hall's law partner, Ernest Smith, introduced the first speaker, Judge T. Whitfield Davidson. A twenty-six-year veteran of the bench, Davidson had been a state senator and lieutenant governor of Texas. He set the tone of stability with his presence and his appeal to a time many decades past when he had a good friend in John Will Hall of Harrison County and J. W.

Hall's sons Sam and Reuben were his colleagues in the legal profession. In line with tradition, then, Davidson's friendship with the Halls continued with Sam Jr. Judge Davidson reminded his audience of the historical legacy of Presidents Washington and Jefferson and their desire to maintain the good faith and credit of the United States of America, a task Hall Jr. believed in and would uphold. Said Davidson, "Washington said, in time of war, in time of trouble, you may have to make a debt, but as soon as the trouble is over, get that debt paid. Get it paid, balance your budget, and create a sinking fund. I bear evidence of the spirit of patriotism, voiced by George Washington." [19]

Joe W. Lovelace of Linden spoke briefly, emphasizing that the campaign would urge the citizens to let a young man serve—an obvious criticism of the age and long tenure of Wright Patman. "We find throughout the district," Lovelace said, "that the elderly people are recalling those words made in July of 1928 when the incumbent asked that a man not be allowed to inherit the office of Congress. Let a young man serve, should the door of hope be closed to those who would serve their country." [20]

Lovelace introduced Hall's former law school professor, the president of Baylor University, Judge Abner McCall, whose friendship with Hall had begun in 1946 at the Baylor School of Law when the younger man was his student. McCall exclaimed that sometimes it took an outsider coming in to tell people what they had in a candidate. "Very often," said McCall, "the home folks don't really recognize the true value to one of their neighbors until some outsider comes in and more or less objectively tells you, you have a non-puerile among you, entirely worthy of serving in Congress, and you're lucky to have such a candidate who offers himself. [21]

Hall was "a patriotic citizen, an able lawyer, and a Christian gentleman in the best sense of the word." McCall lauded Hall as the kind of conservative who would support economic progress and the ideals of the nation, a "conservator of the free enterprise system, and in that respect, he is a conservator with compassion for his fellow man." He would not support any movement toward a "totalitarian type of state." McCall expressed it thus:

> I am for a conservative who wants to conserve individual liberty. Not only because it's economically beneficial, but because Americans have always held individual liberty sacred and dear to their hearts, close to their souls. I don't want to have to answer my children—God forbid I have to answer my children—what did you do in the hour of decision, in the hour of crisis, when this system that preserves individual liberty was threatened from abroad and threatened from within, what did you do? I voted for a man who wanted to

> increase the power of the Federal Government, who wanted to push us on towards the welfare state? I sold your liberty for a mess of pottage? I don't want to answer that way. That's the reason I'm here tonight; that's the reason I suggest to each of you, and urge each of you, that you vote in such a manner that you will not have to answer your children and your children's children this way. I'm proud to endorse and stand up Sam B. Hall Jr. on this occasion." [22]

Sam B. Hall Jr. rose to speak, thanked his hearers for coming out to support a young man, and appealed to a letter Wright Patman had written in 1928. Reading from the *Lamar County Echo*, Hall quoted Patman's plea, saying, "The door of hope should not be closed in the face of the young manhood of our country." The Hall campaign had a "Youth for Sam" division active, perhaps to underscore the need for younger representation in Washington. His newspaper ads urged the voters to "Let A Young Man Serve," while one Patman campaign ad read "Patman is young enough for us, Sam." [23]

Hall then referred to a statement in the *Congressional Record* in March 1944 in which Patman denied the possibility a government could go bankrupt. Questioned about the prewar German inflation, Patman said, "The Government had plenty of money to pay its debts. Of course, the money was worthless, but they paid their debts with worthless money." Characterizing the statement as "that silly, silly kind of talk," Hall asked whether Patman was suited to represent "reasonable men and women anywhere in the nation, much less the people of the First Congressional District," at a time when the national debt was increasing dramatically, and Patman consistently supported measures which deepened the debt. He denounced Patman's support of deficit spending and declared, "The national debt must be reduced in a systematic manner." It would take cutting out unnecessary expenses including foreign aid to communist countries, a $20 million aquarium for tropical fish, and $1.2 million for a study "to determine why baby monkeys loved their mothers." Hall declared that his audience was the only source for money to spend in such a fashion, and that Patman consistently had promised more, especially for the elderly, than he ever delivered:

> Every two years he's going to raise the pensions of the elderly people of this district. Every time he says that, he's also going to raise the dam on Caddo Lake five feet. A man said the other day that if he had raised the dam every two years five feet, there would be water from Caddo Lake backed up to Fort Worth, Texas! [24]

Alleging a conflict of interest, Hall proceeded to disclose an inconsistency between Patman's denials that he had private business interests with his membership on the board of a Red River barge company subject to government agency approval in its operations. He doubted Representative Patman's support of the Constitution, and referred to his opponent's facility for sidestepping issues on his record with constituents. The implication was that Patman lacked full integrity in his dealings with constituents and supported governmental fiscal policies that oppressed American taxpayers, especially the elderly. [25]

In a subsequent interview, Bill Bradford of KSST radio in Sulphur Springs questioned Congressman Patman about Hall's claims against his record. Responding to Hall's claims, Patman characterized his participation on the barge company's board, begun after the operator had received the permit, as a "labor of love" to benefit the constituents of the First District and the Gulf Southwest region. He would not profit personally from it. The development of barge traffic between the Red River to the Cooper Reservoir promised great economic benefits to the region. Also, Patman again also cast doubt about Hall's identity as a conservative Democrat, characterizing him as a "Constitution Party man" who, in 1960,

> scratched the Democratic ticket and voted Constitution Party. The Constitution Party is a party known as a party of haters in the nation. They are the ones that want to do away with even school buses and school lunches. That's the party that says that everything is unconstitutional except law and order, the courts, and the army and navy. National defense—everything else is unconstitutional—can't do it. They want to repeal everything: social security, veteran's benefits, all farm bills. They want to go back to the law of supply and demand on farms, and, of course, that would ruin the farmers. . . . Furthermore, soil and water conservation—all those laws would be repealed. . . . If he's ever voted the Democratic ticket, I don't know it, and I've been unable to find out. [26]

Citing his conversations with Bascom Perkins of Mt. Pleasant, Patman clearly implied that Hall was probably the "mystery voice" of 1952 and 1956 that came on the radio anonymously,

> kinda like an Axis Sally or Tokyo Rose, wanting the people not to vote that terrible Democratic Party—vote the Republican. Now, of course, Mr. Hall came back later and said he voted the Democratic ticket in 1956—voted for Stephenson. And I can't dispute it; he knows and I don't. And I guess it's possible for a man to talk one way and vote another, and possibly he did that—I can't say that he didn't.

> But so far as being a Democrat is concerned, he selected to be [sic] the Constitution Party in 1960. The last opportunity that he had to declare, he didn't vote Republican, didn't vote Democrat, voted Constitution Party. And that Constitution Party is terrible! Why, it'd ruin the country; it'd repeal all democratic laws. [27]

In the Bradford interview, Representative Patman recalled his 1928 theme, "Give a young man a chance, a young man who has a platform." Patman remembered how, either in 1928 or early in the depression, people who disagreed with his efforts to pay the veterans "in full, in cash," (the World War Veterans' Bonus Bill) and to install federal old-age pensions had called him a "Bolshevik" and "I.W.W." and "bomb-thrower." Nevertheless, he followed through on his programs. Taking Hall's measure, he said, "And now then he's a young man with no program at all; he's a Constitution Party man; he's a wrecker; he belongs to the wrecking crew. I belong to the construction gang. And he wants to come in just because of age and wreck what I've done." Patman reminded the radio audience about the advanced age of Judge Sam B. Hall Sr., twice re-elected at an older age than Patman was in 1962. But Patman's age would not influence the voters this time. He also was expected to and did become the chairman of the powerful Committee on Banking and Currency, a position sure to benefit the Texas First Congressional District; it was an unprecedented opportunity Patman hoped to gain in 1963. Obviously, a new representative from the First District, lacking experience and seniority, would not have earned that opportunity, and so the district would not benefit. [28]

Clearly, Hall had encountered a formidable challenge to his identity as a Democrat—a challenge sure to provoke doubt among voters, including the Patman faithful, though of course Patman's accusations could not diminish Hall's commitment as a Democrat. But just as a candidate's liberal populism might be construed socialistic or worse by many arch conservatives, a strong, constitutional conservatism, especially one differing from Patman's brand of New Deal ideology or the majority Democratic definition in Texas, resembled Constitution Party or Republican Party principles in some people's eyes. Beyond that, Wright Patman's words might be interpreted as showing he knew how to cast the aspersion of undemocratic fascism Hall's way. Clearly, both candidates were capable of political charge and counter-charge, and the ideological differences between them were stark, inviting comment. Thus in a number of exchanges both candidates—the seasoned veteran and the younger novice—gave and took familiar politicians' barbs.

In an interview given in early spring, 1962, Hall characterized himself as a Democrat "born and raised in the Democratic Party." His uncle, Reuben Hall, and father both were Democratic judges. Hall said, "I consider myself as a Democrat of the school that believes that the Constitution of the United States and its division of powers is the best method of government of the people of the United States. And I think that those divisions of powers have been abused. And if I'm called a conservative, that name fits me all right, but my belief is in constitutional government." Hall resisted a clear label for his conservatism and denounced governmental encroachments on the judicial system, against strong centralization, and against the development of a welfare state in which people become "dependent on the federal government for a handout" or "the payment of welfare checks to persons which have made the bearing of illegitimate children a profitable thing." [29]

With the primary election only two days away, about 2,000 persons attended the Hall campaign rally at Linden. On that Thursday evening, May 3, the Riley Crabtree band from Sulphur Springs played. [30]

The Halls attended another barbeque dinner and rally, during which he shook every hand in the room, greeting and thanking every supporter. He took the hand of one lady who said, "It's me, Madeleine." He replied, "Thank you for coming, and thanks for your support," as he stepped away to shake the next hand. [31]

The Patman campaign bought newspaper space, emphasizing in near divine or at least paternal terms, the "guiding hand" and "know-how" of the candidate, his reliability and accomplishments. In a comparison to the Prudential Insurance Company's advertising of the day, Wright Patman was "Solid as the Rock," that is, as the Rock of Gibraltar. [32]

The last minute campaign sparring centered on the issue of the Congress and oaths for federal and Supreme Court judges. In 1947 the Congress had enacted an oath for federal judges, and Wright Patman had supported the vote. More recently, Senator Strom Thurmond had introduced a bill (S. 735) to amend the United States Code, explicitly requiring justices, especially Supreme Court justices, to say a particular oath. Rep. John Bell Williams of Mississippi had a matching bill in the House. Thurmond alleged that Section 453 of the Code did not require judges "to support the Constitution in compliance with article VI" of the Constitution. Hall supported legislation similar to that which Thurmond proposed. [33]

Thurmond had written Hall about his doubts that the U.S. Justices were taking the proper oath of office. Apparently, Patman had denied Hall's support of this, and Hall asked why he had been dishonest by claiming it was not part of Hall's platform. The Hall campaign platform revealed that the 1947 oath did not explicitly require a Supreme Court justice to support the Constitution of the United States, and Patman had voted for that faulty oath. Hall believed the oath should be corrected; if elected, he would introduce legislation to accomplish that. [34]

A *Marshall News-Messenger* editorial on May 4 supported Wright Patman, citing his chairmanships, experience, and the various projects he had brought to East Texas. Patman had brought valuable water projects, the Longhorn Ordinance Works at Karnack, and the Small Business Administration office at Marshall. He had gotten a federal court placed in Marshall when the General Services Administration would not provide one in Jefferson, and other cities in the district were competing for it. The editor also addressed the issue of the oath, writing, "The campaign opened with a major charge that the congressman voted to eliminate an oath of allegiance to the Constitution by the Supreme Court judges, an allegation later proved without foundation as Congress has no authority to repeal any portion of the Constitution." [35]

On election eve, E. B. Germany, the president of Lone Star Steel, used newspaper advertising space to declare that in view of Patman's work to assure the development of Lone Star Steel many years previous, East Texans would be worse than ungrateful if they did not vote for Patman. After all, he had brought them a $35 million steel plant. [36]

On the same day the Hall campaign ran a pictorial ad with a charming photograph of the candidate, his wife, Madeleine, and their three young daughters. Otherwise, the ad simply read, "If you see fit to elect me to the Congress of the United States, I will never give you cause to be sorry you let me serve." [37]

The campaign ads ended with Hall's supporters responding in a huge advertisement to a perceived smear campaign against their candidate. Some details remain unclear, but it read:

> In the March 16, 1962, edition of "The Texas Observer" newspaper appeared an article entitled "Religious Tussle Enlivens Politics" which pretends to describe an alleged dispute between Sam B. Hall, Jr., and a certain preacher at the East Burleson Street Church of Christ in Marshall, Texas. We, the undersigned members of that church, were present at the meeting on that date and time at which such incident is claimed by the newspaper to have occurred and state without qualification that <u>the charges against Sam B. Hall, Jr., in that article are wholly false and untrue</u>.

Twenty-seven signatures followed the statement. The advertisement asserted this was a poor attempt of Wright Patman to regain lost votes; he was to be defeated, and he knew it. [38]

A hotel room in Mount Pleasant was a regular meeting place for strategy planning during the campaign. Hall had reduced but did not fully stop his legal work in order to campaign. Ernest Smith and Bill Huffman, Joe Lovelace and Charles Thompson, among others, invested countless hours with the campaign. Smith and Huffman were partners with Hall; Lovelace and Thompson were friends and law partners. One day late in the campaign, sitting in chairs on a flatbed semi-trailer, their speaking platform at a rally in Linden, they waited for the program to start. Someone noticed that Charles Thompson's shoes did not match—one was black, the other brown. Amused, Joe Lovelace teased his law partner, asking, "Charlie, if we can't get our shoes on right, how do you think we're going to win an election?" [39]

Candidates often have used antique automobiles as moving billboards. Gerald Smith of Smith Steel Company in Marshall provided the Hall campaign a vintage automobile touted as having been built the year that Wright Patman went to Congress; the Chevrolet coupe, two-toned dark green and black, had been brand new in '28. The Patman supporters bridled at the inference their candidate and beloved congressman was out of date in 1962 and questioned the use of a company car for the political campaign, but Ernest Smith advised that if the Hall campaign had rented the car its use would be legitimate. In any case, the car was rented, whether beforehand or after the Patman campaign organizers criticized its use. [40]

Madeleine Hall remembered only one instance of rudeness toward her during the campaign. At an automotive service shop in Gilmer, someone absolutely refused to welcome the campaigners. People had been so polite and welcoming to that point, and Mrs. Hall was greatly surprised but said, "Thank you," and left. Campaigning in Avinger, Madeleine Hall had her daughters Becky and Amanda with her. A man followed them to their car and introduced himself as a plant worker from Daingerfield. He wanted to know why he should vote for Sam Hall. Madeleine's response must have convinced him, because he showed up soon at the campaign headquarters in Marshall, got a supply of campaign placards and signs, and became the main campaigner for Hall in his workplace. That plant had been considered closed to the Hall campaign, but with the man's help, Hall gained supporters there. [41]

Except for Sandra who was just two, the Hall daughters campaigned for their father on weekends. Twelve-year-old Becky and ten-year-old Amanda sometimes said a few words to the campaign crowds from the deck of a flatbed trailer in towns throughout the district. Becky never forgot the rudeness she and her friend Karen Hayes encountered on a rainy Saturday when she offered a leaflet to a person who threw it down and ground it with his foot. Nonetheless, the Hall girls easily joined in the excitement, and of course, their dad's exuberance and confidence was infectious. This made it all the harder when on the day and night of the election defeat they saw his exuberance drain from him.

Hall's law partner, Ernest Smith, had counseled him to campaign unofficially as much as he could without announcing, waiting for the time when Wright Patman would no longer be able to run because of age or ill health. Hall would be prepared to move into Patman's place; he would be well known among the constituents of the Texas First District. The 1962 campaign revealed Hall's impatience to get on with campaigning and to replace Patman. Confident he had the qualities and support to win, Hall lost to an experienced campaigner whom an appreciative East Texas public had long since confirmed as their perennial choice to represent them. Hall's defeat led him to say on many occasions that he lost to Wright Patman "because nobody could beat Santa Claus." Consistent voting patterns in the First District were such that any one candidate or group of candidates who faced Patman would get no more than perhaps 28 per cent of the vote, election after election. Charles Thompson recalled what a revelation it was: "You could just move in here and sign up and get 28 per cent of the votes; 28 percent wouldn't vote for Patman, but everybody else did!" [42]

Hall and Bill Huffman rode around Harrison County on primary election day. Hall said, "Bill, I've lost, I know." Huffman told him he did not know, but Hall was certain of it. After midnight on Sunday, May 6, Hall conceded the race, having lost both the district and his home county. There were votes still to be counted, but the trend was clear, and Wright Patman would win. After confirmation of the results, Hall responded gracefully, at least in public. [43]

The family was heartbroken; his schoolgirl daughters, Becky and Amanda (Sandra was a toddler), knew that their dad had missed something big, what with the excitement, the anticipation, and then the bruising disappointment. Becky had never seen her father so devastated, and it was an unforgettable shock for her. The daughters, especially Becky as the oldest, felt the pain of their dad's defeat very deeply and never forgot it. As schoolgirls, it was tough, too, when their classmates teased them the next day at school. It was incomprehensible to them that their dad actually lost the election. On election day Hall had told Becky that he was going to lose. "He had written down and put in his desk by how many votes he was going to be beaten, and he was pretty close." Shocked at his vote predictions, Becky glared at the numbers. She and Amanda hated to leave their dad's office; they wanted to squeeze more votes for him, and they certainly did not want to go to school. It was hard for Madeleine and the daughters to be out in public after the defeat; for a short while Madeleine dreaded leaving the house. [44]

The 1962 primary campaign taught Sam B. Hall Jr. and his supporters a priceless lesson about inexperience and overconfidence; however, the campaign also familiarized the voters with his name until later he would have an opportunity to run again. Moreover, he had in fact gotten more than 28 per cent of the vote; his 39 per cent tally of the vote showed strong, respectable support. During the campaign, Hall made new friends, friends that he kept through the years. As he had done before the primary election defeat, he called his contacts and friends regularly from 1962 until the 1976 campaigns, every week in some cases. He sought their opinions and strengthened personal bonds with telephone calls at Christmas and other special occasions. He thought of his friends frequently and almost as frequently called them. He also kept in touch with Wright Patman and the Patman family, and that contact later paid off as it encouraged them to endorse Hall in 1976. Regardless of his expectations for the 1962 campaign, Hall never doubted that he had the capabilities of a winner. It is unlikely that he intended to use the 1962 campaign as preparation for the future; those who knew him best say that was not the case. His closest friends and associates, including Bill Huffman, doubted that he was looking beyond the 1962 election. Hall did not run a strong campaign in 1962 simply because it increased the chances of winning another time. Huffman and others knew both intuitively and rationally that the prospect of winning over Wright Patman was slim, but, then, "loyalty and wishful thinking," as Huffman put it, are powerful motivators. [45]

Texas First District Congressman Max Sandlin later spoke out of his own experience about Hall's situation, noting the reality of the challenge and the long odds of his winning in 1962. Said Sandlin, "Once you're in the middle of a race, you've convinced yourself that you can do it. You can't force yourself to get up and go each morning unless you believe you can win some way. Then, when you lose, you're devastated and disappointed, although any independent person would say that there wasn't any way for you to win from day one." [46]

The candidate himself had no trouble believing his numerous contacts all over East Texas represented political support. He had nurtured many allies in East Texas, adding many new friends and acquaintances while he served as the district governor for the Kiwanis Clubs International—it was convenient that the Kiwanis district roughly coincided with the congressional district. Perhaps some were political friends only, but Hall's personality and political beliefs attracted the support of many East Texans. It was no great logical leap for Hall to consider running for Congress in the same region. Although he had not been campaigning for political office in that and other types of service, his cordiality and love of people communicated easily during the 1962 political campaign, as they would later in 1976. Thus, Hall gained lifelong supporters and friends, including some who took a political risk by supporting him. [47]

Bill Huffman recalled having first met Sam B. Hall Jr. near Hallsville at a Gum Springs Cemetery workday sometime in 1948, before the fall elections. Aside from the purpose of raising a few dollars for cemetery upkeep and having a considerable labor force to clean up the cemetery, the workdays also gave politicians a chance to mix with dozens of people. It was a more time-efficient way to visit with people than going door-to-door, especially in the rural areas. Sam Jr. and Madeleine were there along with Judge Sam Sr., and Madeleine was expecting their first child. They were helping with the campaigning for the district judge's seat. Even then Sam Jr. made a positive impression with people, being at ease with them, just as he would later while campaigning for himself. Another example of his gregariousness occurred some years later in the 1960s when Hall, Bill Huffman and Louis Williams, a Marshall insurance agent, went to Longview. On the return trip they stopped for coffee at Hallsville. Williams and Huffman sat, but Hall was on his feet, pumping hands and exchanging greetings with everyone in the restaurant. Williams said he had never seen anyone enjoy campaigning as Hall did. Hall was not running for office, but it was in his nature to act as if he were. Often seated with family or friends in Johnny Cace's seafood and steak house restaurant in Longview, he habitually surveyed the other patrons to see anyone he knew or might like to know. He sometimes spent little time at his own table. One often wondered when Sam Hall ever actually sat down to a meal in public. [48]

Some among Hall's friends and acquaintances discerned a natural progression from his community service leadership and work as an attorney to his congressional service, as if it were the most natural thing for him to do, being where he found his niche in life. In retrospect, people believed that he would eventually win election to Congress. Hall might even become a senator. Representatives commonly served a few terms before election to the Senate, but Hall apparently had no interest in the Senate; the House of Representatives seemed the more natural and reasonable place for him. Moreover, he seems never to have entertained pursuing office in the Texas State Legislature. The question remains whether Hall, as a conservative Democrat from East Texas, would be able to get adequate support from across Texas for election to the U.S. Senate. Clearly, some parts of Texas would respond more favorably to Hall than others. First, did they have predominantly Democratic or Republican constituencies, and, second, did those constituencies tend more toward conservative or liberal politics. That is, liberal Democrats were less likely to support him, but he could get support from Republican voters who shared his basic social and political values and ideological convictions. In any case, Hall now had the time to gain experience and maturity and wait for another opportunity to campaign for Congress. [49]

6

Marshall and School Intergration

During the post-Civil War Reconstruction period and beyond, into the twentieth century, Marshall, Harrison County, and other East Texas counties with large African-American populations resembled the Deep South. The end of Reconstruction in 1877 meant that white Democratic party government would be restored there much as elsewhere in the South. The post-Reconstruction institution of Jim Crow segregation continued in towns such as Marshall well into the 1950s and 1960s, until the Civil Rights Movement took effect in federal legislation for civil and voting rights. The federal laws that ended segregation in public places, in particular the schools, began a transformation completed only in the 1970s in Marshall. Though legal desegregation had been implemented, integration leading to a truly united community remained incomplete.

Change was easiest to see in the desegregation of the public school system in Marshall. Civic leaders, white and black, negotiated the integration process too slow for some observers, too rapid for others. Sam B. Hall Jr. was only one of many community leaders and school board members who were forced to deal with the necessary, and inevitable, process of school desegregation. One interpretation held that East Texas whites, including Hall, began with their customary segregationist perspective. Over time, for personal and moral, professional, political, and legal reasons, they came to recognize that official, sanctioned segregation had to end. It simply could not be allowed to continue. From the 1950s into the 1970s, Hall had prominent associations with the Board of Education, as a lawyer for the board, and as a member or president.

There were complex processes and perceptions associated with school integration. Some outsiders, after all, might have had trouble identifying with either traditional white attitudes and practices or the thoughts and desires of the African-American population of the 1960s. Apart from experiences beyond their own home society, the members of segregated society understood only what they knew directly. There was no question which part of society dominated politics and the local economy, though blacks developed their own social networks and means of living as best they could in an uncomfortable accommodation to reality, and they had extensive, usually amicable, relations with whites. Nevertheless, like slavery before it, racial segregation still had the stigmas of social, political and economic inferiority. It was still a social institution in which, for example, a white man typically did not breach the social barrier by something as benign, or sociable, as a handshake with a black man, and vice versa.

The process toward desegregation in the Marshall schools began only some years after the 1954 Supreme Court decision in *Brown* v. *Board of Education.* In 1958 the school board selected Von Rhea Beane as superintendent of schools. He had served in a similar position in Mineola, Texas. In addition to his experience and qualifications as a teacher, coach and principal, his perceived character and ability to communicate commended him as one who could lead in the process of integration in a community highly resistant to it. With no previous plans and numerous hurdles and initiatives to accomplish, Beane integrated faculty and community meetings, and implemented a stair-step plan to accomplish integration gradually. Integration of the schools was voluntary at first; in the first year only one black child applied to attend what had been an all-white school—Sam Houston elementary. A voluntary program was sure to produce small results, but then, any result at all threatened the existing order of things to the point that school officials and members of the Board of Education acted cautiously. Beane and Sam B. Hall Jr. took part in getting the black child into the school on the first day before the usual opening hour, to avoid a public confrontation. By the time school started, while protesters waited outside for her arrival, the child was long since inside the school building. [1]

Yet, there was no "Negro" membership on the school board. During the 1950s and into the 1960s the Bi-Racial Committee, composed of five white and four black members, reported to the City Commission on matters related to city and schools. The school system was under city government authority, and the Marshall City Commission appointed the members of the Board of Education. In the early sixties, leaders considered forming an independent school district. [2]

Gradual integration was only partial at best, though other changes came after the first year of voluntary integration. During the academic year 1969-1970, the Marshall Independent School District responded to a warning from the U.S. Department of Health, Education and Welfare that the district must comply with Title VI provisions of the Civil Rights Act of

1964. The district was required to achieve complete integration. The Department of Health, Education, and Welfare (HEW) was involved; beyond that, the United States Department of Justice warned that failure to comply would provoke a lawsuit. The Marshall school board passed an integration plan and got tentative HEW approval for it in August, 1970. Designed to replace the "freedom of choice" plan, the new plan based school integration on geographic zones. Even then many white citizens wanted to resist integration, but the board reasoned that any further delays would only harm the education of all Marshall school children. The board met many late nights, deliberating and planning the changes. On August 3, 1970, Sam Hall announced, "Tonight culminates the efforts of many Marshallites who have served on the school board over the past nine years to come up with an acceptable plan. . . . The plan presented tonight is not just something we made up this week." [3]

The first day of full public school integration in Marshall's history was August 27, 1970. Over the next decade, further adjustments under HEW directives were to assure fully balanced integration to match the racial composition of the district, which had a population somewhat more than 50 per cent African-American. [4]

Generational differences accounted for some of the resistance to integration. Many of the most vocal opponents came from the older generation of white citizens who were segregationists since before the 1950s, while many younger people in their teens and twenties had no strong feelings either way. But everyone anticipated big changes.

Hall served on the school board when Ray Lawson was chairman, and the process of integration quickened because of the legal implications if it did not. As a leader during the period, Sam B. Hall Jr. adopted a cautious attitude toward the speed and the character of the integration process. His sensitivity to those who wanted to slow it down probably did influence him, so his actions frustrated people who wanted quicker integration. Otherwise, he and the school board clearly understood the direction of developments and they did what they could to assure a smooth transition. Nevertheless, with all his caution and care to balance perceptions of what was going on, and efforts to retain good will among whites and blacks, the process was too slow. Leaders from the African-American community believed there could be no reason for delay except the reluctance of many white leaders to see school integration accomplished. Precisely what Hall thought about the process remains uncertain. One can survey the developments in the process, however, and perhaps not fully understand the myriad dynamics involved. In any case, the school board bore responsibility for the progress made and what many people considered unnecessary delay. The board was committed to full integration to satisfy the law and the courts and wanted to avoid a federal lawsuit against the school district. During his tenure as board president, Hall led in assuring that compliance leading to integration occurred in an orderly, peaceful fashion. [5]

As things turned out, few people were fully happy; whites accustomed to segregation over the generations since slavery ended found that they were being forced to change. Blacks found that desegregation of the schools did not accomplish a softening of attitudes toward integration of most other features of East Texas society. Thus, the Marshall and East Texas experience of integration was an unfinished project, revealing the greater challenge of developing equality in attitudes, of banishing prejudice throughout the society in general. Yet there was a significant change from the days in which racial animosities were pronounced and Jim Crow dominated. [6]

Some people believed that, for all his influence, Hall could have spoken up more assertively for integration. He could have and should have acted sooner, asserting his influence for the good of all citizens. A strong leader must have a concern for all people, black, white or otherwise. Those who thought Hall too cautious with white segregationists wanted that kind of leadership in Marshall. A strong, influential leader could better afford to take chances, and even some who respected him personally were disappointed he did not do more, sooner. [7]

Ora Asa Johnson served with the school district for thirty-eight years during and after segregation as a teacher, coach and principal. He knew Hall personally and professionally. His daughter Lydia and one of the Hall daughters were in the same Homecoming Court at Marshall High School, and his grandmother, who owned land near Hallsville adjoining Hall property, had thought well of the Hall family. Expressing a conciliatory attitude, Johnson remembered Hall as a statesman of sorts amid the new process of integration. Apart from his early role as lawyer for the Board of Education, Hall showed he could keep his concern for people, especially the schoolchildren, uppermost in his mind and conduct. Johnson considered Hall to be caught in the middle in the school desegregation conflict, and as he got to know Hall he found they shared the common goal of treating each other humanely, openly, and putting the children of the district first. He believed Hall had done what was right during the controversy and negotiations leading to school integration. He considered Hall faithful in dealing with the light God gave to him, to care as he could for, as Johnson put it, "Not one race, but the human race." [8]

Arthur O. Wesley, a school principal in Jefferson, observed that Hall ultimately made fairness the key issue in the whole matter in Harrison County and Marshall, and so probably got a better balance of community support. Wesley compared the Harrison County integration program to the more difficult Marion County process that had to deal with a federal court challenge; it was good that Marshall avoided the rancor associated with resolving the integration issue in court. [9]

Hall had friends on both sides of the color line. In this, he was not unique, for personal friendships between blacks and whites were common, even if blacks and whites as classes stood separately. But hardly any relationships enjoyed as much mutual respect and friendship as those Hall had. Hall earned respect because of his fairness, and because of the long-term positive way that he treated blacks, personally and professionally. He also drew from the qualities for which his father was best known: the ability to speak to both sides of an issue, to relate to both sides. Judge Sam Hall Sr., though a segregationist, had a reputation as an impartial judge for all citizens, dealing equally with blacks and whites. Yet segregation remained a barrier to genuinely equitable treatment. In following his father's personal example of equanimity, Sam Jr. had an even greater advantage in his generation to move toward equality.[10]

During the years when racial hatred simmered just out of sight and people bristled about the changes they feared or the changes delayed, Hall was a civic leader who listened well. Marshall attorney Franklin Jones Jr. noted that Sam Hall "was where we would like to be if we were to transform ourselves back to that environment. He had the ear of people far to the right of him, but he was not a hater. He was a peacemaker. Believe you me we needed peacemakers in those days. There were plenty of haters. God knows what the city would be without him and folks like him." [11]

Black citizens who suggested that he did not listen evenly, thought differently. Many black citizens saw their ultimate goals frustrated; however, school integration, coming as it did in the distant wake of national civil rights legislation in the 1960s, produced real, though incomplete, progress. On the other side, Hall had white acquaintances who refused to speak to him out of resentment for his role in school integration.

Hall had other involvements. Dr. Isadore Lamothe, a local black physician, noted his and Hall's role with the "human relations commission" in the 1950s, which was formed out of the anticipation of possible confrontations, or any kind of trouble between white and black. Black perceptions were that the commission was a way of preventing racial confrontation on issues. [12]

Hall had positive, long-term friendships with a number of concerned black businessmen and leaders in Marshall. He participated, perhaps from the beginning, in a men's breakfast group that met at least monthly for years beginning in the late sixties and continuing into the early seventies. They had no charter and no written records, as an informal group. The wives of the breakfast club members typically did not attend except on special occasions. Jewell Young (afterwards Mrs. U. S. Gray) teased her husband, Price T., and the others that they were "sort of like the ladies' sewing circle." Frank Johnson arranged for the meeting place. Public locations were limited for a racially mixed group such as theirs. They usually met at the Ramada Inn; a few times, they met at the Gables Restaurant on Pine Crest Boulevard. At the core of the group were five or six men who were constant members: Dr. Noland H. Anderson was a physician, Robert J. Hall was in the elderly home care business, Frank L. Johnson was in real estate, Garfield A. Rosborough was a school principal, and Price T. Young, also a principal. Fred E. Lewis also participated, as did Samuel L. Birmingham on a few occasions. Birmingham communicated well with the group but took care not to identify so strongly as to have a conflict of interest with his political responsibilities in Marshall. He sat on the city council and became the first and only black mayor of Marshall in the twentieth century. The group discussed ways to work on both sides of the racial divide with people amenable to change and compromise, to achieve what reasonable people on both sides wanted and what people believed to be genuinely needed. The breakfast meetings allowed roundtable discussion on urgent community issues, "bouncing it off the wall," to work out problems, in advance if possible, and to facilitate clearer and more equitable communication between whites and blacks in the community about significant events and decisions in the community. They often counseled parents of children who were having behavioral or academic problems. All agreed they could do their best work as individual change agents who worked quietly, effectively, and cooperatively, drawing others into their efforts whenever they could. Jewell Gray recalled,

> They tried to see if we could substitute something else, or if we could meld how we thought things should be with yours—not to give us everything, or not to take everything, but to sort of reach a happy medium. And there were those on both sides, I felt, who were amenable to being fair. I never knew any of the members of the club to express any turbulence that they felt when they would have had a session with any of the powers-that-be to get anything settled. And in some ways we got some things settled that some groups hadn't even thought of getting settled—hadn't thought about. [13]

The breakfast group believed Hall had people's interests at heart apart from any racial considerations, hidden agenda or political motivations. The African-Americans endured accusations of being "Uncle Toms" too closely associated with and accommodating to white leaders and the status quo. There was no fanfare, no publicity, but rather quiet effectiveness. Their efforts and conciliatory stances attracted genuine conversation with other black and white community leaders. That they did not achieve every objective that members of the black community wanted and deserved was no failure. That they prevented animosity and conflict speaks well of their conciliatory spirits and their ability to deal directly with problems, some never known publicly then or thereafter, and to help people focus on long-term community goals. [14]

The public schools were among the breakfast club's many topics of conversation. Before and during the integration process, they discussed equitable treatment and access to programs and privileges for all schoolchildren in the district. During the time when the Marshall hospital did not extend staff privileges to African-American physicians, they discussed how and when to correct that dilemma. Blacks also were not getting equal access to medical care, and so they worked to change hospital policies. That would change the longstanding practice whereby blacks had to wait until all the white patients had received service and treatment in doctor's offices; it would mean the blacks would not have to settle for the inferior facilities downstairs and to the rear of the hospital complex. During the 1960s, Sam Hall Jr., Don Rives and other members of the hospital board recognized the need for changes, which they achieved through persuasion. Dr. Noland Anderson and Dr. Isadore Lamothe were the first two black physicians to have regular staff privileges at the Marshall hospital.

Evaluating Hall's participation with the breakfast club, Jewell Gray said, "We can make it easier for everybody to live together in harmony. We would have suffered more if it had not been for his interest in people. We are better off because he lived." [15]

Judge Phillip Baldwin characterized Hall's role from another perspective that placed him at the same time in both the traditional society and the society that was changing because individuals wanted to make a difference. "He was always a friend with the struggling black person who at that time had to really fight to find his place in this world," said Baldwin. "It doesn't seem possible, but it really hadn't been that many years ago that the slaves were freed—over 100 years ago—and just now, just in Lyndon Johnson's age, they got the right to vote." There were leaders such as Martin Luther King, but whites also had to help in order to make such dramatic changes for blacks. "I mean, if they hadn't been out there fighting for them, then they couldn't have made it. . . . They've got to get some outside stimulation, an awful lot of stimulation, and that's where Sam came in. He was a great man." Baldwin considered Hall to be middle-of-the road politically regardless of his professed and apparent conservatism, because of his desire to put people first. It was a matter of people before principle, and principle before politics. [16]

In September 1980, Hall was present with his colleagues on the school board and other dignitaries and the community to dedicate the new Marshall High School and athletic complex. He exclaimed, "This is a far cry from Adams lake," the swampy pond that was on the spot before construction. It was also a far cry from the segregated high schools that it replaced. [17]

The South Central Regional Director for the Federal Bureau of Prisons before retiring to become and administrator at Wiley College, O. Ivan White Jr. regarded Hall his mentor, and summed up an opinion shared by many in the Marshall African-American community:

> Judge Hall was a visionary leader, a humanitarian with an immeasurable sense of fairness. He possessed the foresight to realize that the future was arriving in Marshall before some in the community were ready for it. Lines of color were deeply ingrained, in the people, in the melting-pot culture of the community we knew as Marshall, Texas. In the height of the Civil Rights Movement, Sam Hall demonstrated his visionary capacities in a powerful way. As a leader in the community, he was instrumental in guiding Marshall and her people through the difficult process of school integration.
>
> Change came slowly and painfully to Marshall and certainly with much personal growth and struggle on everyone's part, including Sam Hall. He made known his commitment to the equality of all people and expressed through his words and actions his recognition that diversity provides a richness of ideas, a variety of insights, and many opportunities for invaluable interactions.
>
> As he impacted Marshall through the painful struggles of the integration process, Sam Hall served as public servant and community supporter in the truest of senses. He grew to be comfortable with and related well with all people, qualities which were amplified by his common sense approach in all situations. Most importantly, he was comfortable with himself. He unceasingly demonstrated the presence of God within his life, exemplifying the strong moral values which he advocated in all facets of his life. [18]

7

Four Elections: The 1976 Congressional Race

In 1976, shortly after he announced that he would not seek reelection, Wright Patman died, vacating the seat for the First Congressional District of Texas. A series of elections followed in order to determine who would complete Patman's unexpired term and who would win the Democratic Party nomination for election to a full term later in the year. In the May 1 primary race, Sam B. Hall Jr. placed first among ten candidates, afterwards winning the June 5 runoff election, defeating Dr. Glen Jones of Jacksonville, a minister and professor of government. Various prominent newspapers in the district strongly endorsed Hall and his "common-sense" conservatism. He would represent East Texans faithfully, and the public would be pleased with his strong moral and ethical convictions and proven record as a civic leader and servant. Hall received the backing of Abner V. McCall, the president of Baylor University—as he had in 1962— and Dr. H. D. Bruce, President Emeritus of East Texas Baptist College. [1]

Perhaps as important as any endorsement was that of the Wright Patman family. The son of the late Congressman, Connor Patman recommended Hall because he had extensive experience in public service and supported the values and policies that would keep America free and strong. Hall would be a good Congressman, "effective, fair, judicious, and compassionate." Patman declared that despite the political difference between his father and Hall, he would be a "good Congressman, for this district—effective, fair, judicious, and compassionate." Mrs. Benny Patman Ford, the sister of Wright Patman, endorsed Hall, emphasizing the importance of "an open mind, mature judgment, and a proven record of service to his fellow man," qualities she found present in him. She noted the respect and friendship her brother and Hall had despite their political disagreements, and focused on the respect Hall had gained for his love of working with people and his extraordinary efforts as a civic servant. [2]

A reasonable person, knowing Sam Hall Jr., his love of working with people and his habit of civic service, would easily understand why he ran for Congress in 1962 and 1976. Hall responded eagerly to the challenge and excitement of politics. He knew his own capabilities and believed he could do the work of a Congressman. He wanted to be a useful public servant as a U.S. Representative. The opportunity to prove it, starting with voter confirmation, unfolded during mid- to late 1976. [3]

Because of his work as a lawyer for the Marshall School District and his subsequent long-term service on the Board of Education and board of the medical center, Hall understood the workings of federal laws and guidelines at the local level, which would prove valuable as he tackled the job of a congressman. He stood for election as a lifelong Democrat from a traditionally Democratic region of Texas, which actually was a one-party state for most of Hall's years. Texas had many "yellow-dog" Democrats, who, it was said, would "vote for a yellow dog before they would vote for a Republican," or "vote for a yellow dog if it was a Democrat," and whose political sympathies usually lay to the right of the state Democratic leadership. Sometimes the conservative Democrats talked and voted much as Republicans did anyway. Hall's constituents sometimes identified themselves as "Sam Hall Democrats," genuine conservatives allied with the Democratic Party, different from voters who in other parts of the state would be neither so traditional nor conservative. Conservative Texas Democrats differed from Democrats nationally even as they did from mainstream Texas Democratic politics; Hall was such a conservative, though he once declared of his party loyalty, "I don't have an iron collar around my neck." Many Harrison County voters had supported the States' Rights Democratic Party ("Dixiecrat") candidate, Strom Thurmond, in the 1948 presidential election. Running as a Republican, Dwight D. Eisenhower got strong Harrison County support for the presidency in 1952 and 1956. Despite Lady Bird Johnson's family background at Karnack in Harrison County, Lyndon B. Johnson barely edged out the Republican Barry Goldwater in the 1964 election. Most Harrison County voters supported Alabama Governor George Wallace in 1968, the founder and first presidential candidate that election year of the American Independent Party. [4]

Hall also ran for election in a district that had experienced mixed changes during his lifetime. In 1928 when Wright Patman was first elected, the district encompassed eleven counties; by 1976 there were twenty counties plus parts of Hunt and Rains counties, a district with appreciable variation between town and country, but still distinctively "East Texas," and still distinct from other regions of Texas, culturally, socially, economically, topographically, and otherwise. The area ranging from around Clarksville in Red River County southward to Marion County displayed cultural and political similarities to southeastern Oklahoma, a region largely settled by Texans during the nineteenth century and still often called Little Dixie. Traditionally Democratic, it was the home of Speaker of the House Carl Albert. Yet southeastern Oklahoma and to some extent northeastern Texas belonged to a boundary region between the South, the Midwest and the Plains states. Thus, there were subtle distinctions, traditionally, between towns in the north and towns farther south in the First District. Observers have found it curious, too, that Wright Patman hailed from Texarkana, a cotton and railroad town on the periphery of the First District, divided between Texas and Arkansas. [5]

In late 1975 or early 1976, Wright Patman decided not to seek reelection and to retire at the end of his term. He called Hall to tell him first. Patman's health and vitality had declined for several years, and in 1975 he had been voted out of his congressional Banking and Currency Committee chairmanship by the House Steering and Policy Committee, a sign that his decades of leadership were coming to an end. After suffering influenza and pneumonia in early 1976, Patman died on March 7 at the age of eighty-two, having served forty-eight years in the Congress. [6]

Hall's desire to serve in Congress had not changed except as it was deepened and tempered, becoming more realistic with maturity. He presented himself as a better candidate than the determined young man who had run for office in 1962. Madeleine Hall's recollections presented how she understood his love for people and activity as motivations to serve:

> He thought he could serve the people and that he could make a difference. It's hard for one person to make a difference, but it takes one person to start making the difference. He really, really enjoyed that. He enjoyed driving up and down these highways, getting with people at meetings or at coffee shops. He just enjoyed it. He didn't mind the long hours campaigning and driving back from somewhere at one or two o'clock in the morning. I remember that he was driving back from Mt. Pleasant one night and encountered cows were on the road. He stopped and drove those cows back into the fella's pasture. That man never got over it. . . . He had a lot of cattle. I think he raised sweet potatoes because they used to send us crates of sweet potatoes. I don't know how he knew who put those cows back. But that was fun to him. He enjoyed that. [7]

Sam Hall had more years of experience in law by this time, more leadership experience in various civic organizations and on community boards, and his daughters were largely grown, with Becky, the eldest, married, the middle daughter, Amanda, working in Dallas, and the youngest, Sandra, finishing high school. He and his family had a clear view of the work it would take to win the election. Hall went about assembling his campaign staff, calling on friends he had developed over many years throughout East Texas, including many who had supported him in the 1962 campaign. He wanted Ray Lawson of Marshall to be his campaign manager. Lawson recounted how Hall asked him to take the position:

> When Sam approached me in January 1976 and asked if I would be his campaign manager, I said, "Sam, I'm not sure I know Harrison County that well to take on a job like this." There was a pause, and he said, "Ray, I'm not talking about only Harrison County. I'm talking about the First Congressional District of Texas which encompasses 21 counties and parts of two others!" After I swallowed real hard and gathered my composure, I told him I would give him my answer the next morning. I consulted with my wife, Mona, and my business partners, and told him we would do our best to get him elected. There were eleven Democrats in the primary race and they all wanted to be a congressman as did Sam. With the help of my wife, Mona, and Sam's secretary, Sue Jordan, we set off on the trail to towns and villages in East Texas that we didn't even know existed. But for every adult in this district, there was a potential vote. [8]

Hall drew on the support of old and new friends in the campaign, relying on experienced people such as George Christian, a public affairs consultant who had served as press secretary to Texas governors Price Daniel and John B. Connally and to President Lyndon B. Johnson. Christian was impressed with Sam's intelligence and commitment to win in order to serve, of course, but there was more. Hall possessed "an innate sense of fairness, a determination not to engage in dirty politics, and complete comfort in who he was, how he related to his family, and how he was governed by his God." [9]

A Marshall lawyer, Don Rives had worked with Hall in the 1962 campaign, helping with publicity and other matters and traveling extensively with him throughout the First District. In 1976 after Wright Patman died and Rives was working in Austin, Hall sought his help again, going to Austin where he met with Rives and George Christian over lunch at Mike and Charlie's Restaurant. Christian's advice contributed to Hall's success, and he managed Hall's subsequent campaigns, being responsible for developing campaign issues. Christian soon found that Hall knew what he believed and why he was running, with no questions or doubt. "Sam appreciated ideas but had his own views on how the country should be run domestically and internationally." No ideologue, Hall "applied his conservative, faith-based philosophy to the controversies of the day and never wavered." Christian recalled how in a television spot, Hall looked into the camera and promised to work in Congress with an attitude "as tight as a new pair of shoes." [10]

Lon Bates, Hall's fellow alumnus of the College of Marshall, managed the campaign in Titus County. Later, when Hall served in the Congress, Bates marveled at the effective, personal way he dealt with people who came in to speak with him in Bates' office, which he used whenever he visited that county. [11]

Hall got more local help from Bishop B. Curry Jr., who had come from Sulphur Springs to Marshall in 1968 to work for Wiley College. Soon after arriving in Marshall, he followed the recommendation of his friend B. D. "Boy" Maddox of Sulphur Springs that he meet Sam Hall. Hall and Curry quickly developed a solid bond. In 1976 Ray Lawson approached Curry for help in the campaign, and so Curry, Sam Birmingham, and Ruie Mathews made it their objective to take the Hall campaign to every black community in the First District. Curry took Hall to meetings throughout the district, amazed at his stamina, and Hall enjoyed and respected the energy and effectiveness Curry showed. Curry made no bones about it, "The tougher and closer the race, the harder we must work." Later he became the district liaison officer for Congressman Hall. Many people complimented Hall about Curry's work. Curry had been highly involved in various professional and civic organizations in East Texas, and his contacts helped the campaign considerably. Hall asked him how he had come to have such a good rapport with "so many people—black and white alike." Curry replied, "Mr. Hall, I have always been honest, willing to help in worthy undertakings with mouthy presence wherever I have been!" [12]

Arthur O. Wesley, a school principal in Jefferson, Texas, supported Hall "heart and soul," knowing that he could be trusted and that he had the best interests of all the citizens of East Texas in mind. In his local and East Texas career, Hall had built the confidence of many members of the black community in him, and he had many black friends, Wesley prominent among them. They responded well to someone who spoke, and then acted, on the premise that fairness and honesty toward all people was a non-negotiable virtue. [13]

The opinions of black East Texans were important in the campaign and counted a great deal toward the support Hall received as a candidate. It helped that Dr. R. D. Douglas of Jefferson emphasized how Hall had been active not only in Marshall community affairs, but had served also on the Board of Trustees of Wiley College, with the Human Relations Committee, and had been honored by the Bethesda Baptist Church, a black congregation, for his service and leadership in human relations. [14]

The campaign opened with a grand chili supper in Hallsville. Albert Agnor of Marshall brought massive chili pots and fed his special recipe to a crowd of five or six hundred. The Hallsville mayor, Tex Hatley, was Master of Ceremonies, and Robert Newhouse of the Dallas Cowboys, a native of Hallsville, came to lend support. [15]

Hall's family entered the 1976 campaigns wiser and more experienced than they had in 1962. The oldest daughter, Becky, was reluctant to see her father repeat the pain of the 1962 defeat. Besides, she had one young child and another on the way, and they filled her days. However, on one occasion she and Amanda did some campaigning:

> Amanda and I did go to Gilmer, and all the way up there, just the two of us, we were talking about how are we going to do this to where we don't have to do anything. We decided when we got there that she would take one side of the square, and I would go around the square—she took all the businesses. The first person I asked to vote for Daddy was Welby Parrish's secretary. He [Parrish] was one of the many running against him at the time. She was very nice and said that if she weren't working for Welby she'd certainly vote for Sam. I thanked her and went on to the next person, and he was Welby's campaign manager. So after that, I found Amanda. We went to Dairy Queen for lunch and came home. That was it! [16]

Even so, the Hall campaigners enjoyed promoting their candidate; Ray Lawson considered it more fun than work. The campaign rented the Sunshine Sam Special, Rex Brown's motor home, to travel throughout the district—the women during the day and the men at night. Mona Lawson, Madeleine Hall and Florine Miller put aside other duties. Sue Jordan balanced her duties and legal secrtary with preparing campaign paperwork and brochures with help from Lynda Lundy and Florine Lundy Miller, among others. It was a high pleasure to make new acquaintances, to discuss their concerns and Sam Hall. Ray and Mona Lawson went to Texarkana one evening early in the campaign. A certain man remarked how persuasively they came across for Hall. It was also their wedding anniversary, which could not be allowed to hinder the campaign. [17]

Silly or not, campaign slogans and songs captured people's feelings about Hall and reinforced the main point: vote for Sam Hall. A June election-eve sing-along featured light verses sung to popular tunes: To "Yankee Doodle" it was "Sam's the man for Congressman / He needs to be elected / If you vote for him on the 5th / You'll never be neglected." Others started with "Sam, Sam, Sam's the man . . ." and "For Sam's the right man for Congress . . . ." To the tune "You Are My Sunshine," it was "Sam is our sunshine / Our only sunshine / He is the best man for this job / He is so honest and so truthful / He's the man for Congressman." [18]

At San Augustine in the far south of the First District, Hall's long-time friend John Luther Smith worked with his political organization. A member with Hall of the first postwar law school class at Baylor, Smith knew that Hall had long since set his cap toward Congress, and that objective was foremost again in 1976. [19]

On the May 1 election night, after news of the Hall victory came, Hall declared how good it felt to have his friends and supporters gathered together to enjoy the victory. He asked his father to come to the microphone, and so Sam Sr. did, saying,

> I don't know a thing to say that would add to what about 25,000 people in this district have said today. It'd be useless for me to tell you how I appreciate this august occasion. I never dreamed fifty-two years ago—I lived down by the jail and he came into existence—that I would ever be confronted with this kind of a victory this soon. But I want you to know that I'm proud of him, and I just hope and pray that when he goes to work he won't make the kind of record that some fellas have made up there the last few weeks. And if he does—I want to say this—if he does, I regret being there about fifty-three years ago! Now, I can thankfully say that up to now, he may have been guilty of some unbecoming conduct, but it has never reached his mother and me, and I hope it never does. And I want to say, Son that my prayer is that God's richest and choicest blessings will rest, be and abide with you now and forevermore. I want you to live the kind of life, that when you lie down at night to go to bed, you can look up to the Father and say, "Yea, though I walk through the valley of the shadow of death, I will fear no evil, for thou art with me; they rod and thy staff, they comfort me. That's my parting remarks to you. Thank you. [20]

Sam Jr. responded to his father's admonitions and prayer, saying, "It's just a tremendous feeling that I have right now after having heard what my dad just said about me and what he expects of me. I appreciate so very, very much what the people of this district have done, especially the people of Harrison County." He promised to do his "dead level best" to live up to his father's creed. Hall also responded to the election results, declaring that he read them as a message from the voters who were looking for positive changes in government that would reduce the burdens of excessive government and taxation. [21]

The May 1 and June 5 elections established Hall as the Democratic nominee for the November election. Nevertheless, the special election on June 19 held significance also as a reliable gauge of support for the coming November election. Hall faced three other candidates in the special election. Fred Hudson of Center was a Harvard graduate, a banker, and a former district attorney for Shelby and Panola counties. After advising Hall of his intentions, he withdrew from the race and announced his recommendation that the voters support Hall. He considered Hall the most likely winner in November and thought his own withdrawal might help prevent a runoff after the November election. Hudson had finished well, but behind, Wright Patman in 1972 and 1974, and he recognized that Hall would be hard to beat. Hudson also thought that since he had run twice before, the voters might be weary of hearing about him again. Another consideration was his hometown, which was located away from the center of the First District, perhaps too distant from the center of district concerns, politics, and most of constituency. [22]

The other candidates competed for what could be only a brief term of service as Hall was already the Democratic nominee for the next full term. Dr. Glen Jones remained in the race. The Republican opponent, Dr. James Hogan of Atlanta, a dentist, expressed his hopes that Hudson's withdrawal would mean more votes for himself. Something of Hall's perceived assets for the job is found in the observation of the *Atlanta Times* that Hall and Dr. James Hogan as senior candidates were the only truly viable candidates.[23]

Hall got 72 per cent of the vote in the special election on June 19, a strong performance promising good prospects for the November election, especially as his Republican opponent, Dr. James Hogan of Atlanta, had won only 1,394 votes to his 20,556. With the district's long history of Democratic Party dominance, any Republican congressional candidate faced long odds against winning. [24]

Following the special election victory, and exhausted from the campaign effort, the Halls took a few days to recuperate in Florida as they usually did for a vacation, never thinking that Sam would be expected to fill Patman's vacated seat immediately. Congressional Administrative Assistant Baron Shacklette called their hotel in Fort Walton Beach and asked directly whether Hall wanted to take the oath of office or not. The Halls returned home and arranged their flight to Washington. Sue Jordan immediately sent out invitations. There were older guests who did not want to fly, so Brian Williams drove them to Washington in a motor home. [25]

The Halls invited about 75 friends to witness the swearing-in ceremony in the House of Representatives. Charlie and Louise Walters came from Bowie County, flying with other Hall supporters from Shreveport. Hall's Army Air Force buddy Bob Wainscott and his wife Florence came from Durham, North Carolina. Sam and Jean Birmingham took turns driving with Mr. and Mrs. Clifford Cole during the nonstop trip to Washington. Jean Birmingham recollected that the trip was well worth the effort, and their new congressman appreciated their efforts to attend the ceremony. In later conversation with the Birminghams, Hall recalled his gratitude for their presence as he took the oath of office and confessed how good he felt standing there with Representative Barbara Jordan to one side and Speaker of the House Carl Albert to the other, knowing, too, that his family and friends looked on from the balcony. [26]

At fifty-two years of age Sam B. Hall Jr. was sworn in as Representative of the First Congressional District of Texas. Besides Representative Barbara Jordan, the Houston Democrat, and Carl Albert of Oklahoma, George Mahon, the new dean of the Texas Congressional Delegation from Lubbock, was present. It so happened that Speaker of the House Carl Albert represented the Oklahoma Third District, adjacent to the Texas First District. A veteran of fourteen terms in office and Speaker since 1971, he administered the oath of office to his fellow Democrat. The regional significance was great, and Hall was the only new representative from the Texas First District that Speaker Albert ever swore into office. [27]

Having won a special election, Hall was the only congressman to take the oath of office on that Monday, June 28, 1976. The scripture and prayer offered by the House Chaplain, Rev. Edward G. Latch, aptly suited Sam B. Hall Jr.'s character and mission. Chaplain Latch quoted Deuteronomy 6:18, "Thou shalt do that which is right and good in the sight of the Lord." Latch prayed, "O God our Father, let Thy Spirit come afresh into all our hearts that with a keen perception of right and wrong we may strive earnestly to live by the high principles of our holy faith. Illumine our minds and quicken our consciences that we may see the way to take and with courage walk in it, keeping our minds clear, our hearts clean, and our hands strong. So may we serve our country with the best we have to give. In the spirit of Christ we offer this our morning prayer. Amen." [28]

For convenience the new representative, his wife, many family members, and friends stayed at the new Hyatt Regency Hotel downhill from the Senate side of the Capitol. The large reception after the ceremony included many Texans and the news media. By the next day nearly everyone had left, and Sam and Madeleine's youngest daughter, Sandra, returned to Marshall with her sisters while her parents quickly found an efficiency apartment to use as a temporary home in the District of Columbia.

The special election victory allowed Hall to complete the remainder of Wright Patman's term of office and to campaign for the November election as an incumbent. Hall was to gain experience during the remainder of Wright Patman's term that would put him ahead of the new Congressional freshman class. His lack of experience in elected politics could have been considered a drawback, but it was not. His strong background in public service contributed to his task-oriented attitude as he went to work on issues affecting his district.

In the *Shreveport Journal*, August 6, 1976, Joan McKinney reported how Hall had tackled the reading necessary to prepare for legislative voting decisions and his committee assignments. His age and experience gave him a more realistic view of what he could achieve in the Congress, though his high ideals made him want to accomplish a great deal. Hall was to experience frustrations with the processes of negotiation and behind-the-scenes dealing on legislation: he recognized that he was not going to remake the Congress.

Hall's law career experienced only a partial disruption during his first campaign for congressional office in 1962. Since then, he had become an established attorney with fourteen additional years of professional and civic leadership experience. He had learned in 1962 that timing often trumped desire and qualifications, especially after the Patman campaign and image defeated his congressional bid. Hall settled into his career and community involvement and waited for another opportunity to run. When victory came, his active career as an attorney ended, as did his formal association in the law firm of Smith, Hall and Huffman. By then the firm included a son-in-law, W. F. "Pinkie" Palmer, who had met Becky Hall at Baylor and who came from Baylor Law School to join the firm in 1972. A West Texan with roots in Wichita Falls and Olney, Palmer accepted a position when he graduated. Ernest Smith left the firm to have his own practice in 1972, just before Palmer arrived, an inexperienced but well-trained lawyer. He took well to what he considered the big city of Marshall and the forested beauty of East Texas. [29]

In running for Congress in 1976, Hall had to turn over his legal work to the others in the firm. In law, there always is a problem of having just the right balance of work, and he had just thrown the balance off for Palmer and Bill Huffman. Whenever it was he decided he was going to run for Congress, Palmer recalled, "He came to tell us he was going to run for Congress and then basically says, "Oh, by the way; all those files in these file cabinets are yours. Y'all have to take care of those things." And so, but for Bill Huffman I don't know that we would ever have got out of that stuff." [30]

Bill Huffman took Hall's leaving hard, being disappointed that he was to leave the law office behind in order to seek national office, but understood completely because it would be good for the United States. What to Huffman had been a dream partnership was ending, and his close association with Hall would never be the same again. "I could count on him as a friend and a law partner twenty-four hours a day seven days a week," Huffman said. "Sam's leaving the firm would create a void and I would miss seeing him on a daily basis. My feelings were much like those of his father." [31]

Hall also gave up a thriving practice. He had among his clients the power company, Darco, handling all manner of legal work, including land transactions related to expanding lignite coal mining operations. In 1976 Hall was at a pinnacle in his legal career. The decision to enter congressional politics meant that the prospects for developing that career further would have to wait. As it turned out, the delay was permanent. He was at the point where the most financially successful lawyers typically see their practices surge. A large client base and a reputation for effective legal work assured more opportunities to handle potentially lucrative cases. Hall's lack of ambition to pursue gain for its own sake was a factor. His son-in-law, Pinkie Palmer, said, "Sam was like the guy who carries the ball down to the three-yard line, and then somebody else is sent in to carry the ball across the goal line. He was at that point where he didn't have to worry about trying to go out and foster relationships for client business. All he had to do was open the door and people would come in. People never will understand the financial gain he gave up to go to Congress." [32]

After Hall was sworn into office as representative for the First District, Sue Jordan worked with the district offices to prepare for work under Hall. In the Marshall office were Alice Thomas, Harold Taylor and Jim Muckleroy; in Paris, Doris Bryant; and in Texarkana, Nell King. Later, Hall kept an office to use for occasional visits in Jacksonville.

Sam Hall knew that his three victories before November, 1976, could not guarantee a November election victory, and he had a strong Republican opponent. Thus, after Congress adjourned in the fall he campaigned intensely. He had gathered a corps of supporters for the 1976 special election, and these helped with the campaign. He drew more people to himself because they liked what they saw and wanted to take part in his election. He did not have to beg or cajole, there were no reciprocal deals or arm-twisting. There was instead a groundswell of help from across East Texas as people volunteered for his campaign. [33]

Hall positively impressed East Texas voters, who appreciated his commitment to hold government spending and to oppose liberal and inflationary lawmaking. Given his pro-business attitude, small business owners responded well to him. He promised he would not disappoint them once he went to work in Washington. [34]

The Hall campaign managers across the First Congressional District scheduled daily meetings at civic clubs such as Rotary International and the

Kiwanis, the Farm Bureau organizations, and the chambers of commerce. The typical day began between 6:30 and 7:00 o'clock with breakfast in a restaurant such as the Blossom Grill in Lamar County or the Ponderosa Restaurant in Atlanta. It was a good hour to meet with farmers, and Hall loved the fried bologna and eggs served at the Blossom Grill. There would be a coffee meeting later in the morning, and then a luncheon, all at different locations. People attending these meetings registered, and each of them got letters from Hall's office, every one with the candidate's personal signature. Sue Jordan supervised the flow of correspondence and requests for campaign materials such as flyers and placards. Supporters such as Bill Murphy and his son, Pat, David Lindsey, and others in Lamar County and beyond gave enthusiastic support. Harlan and Flovice Craig of Hopkins County were in the dairying and cattle business and lent a hand with campaigning. Harlan provided Hall a big hat and a spirited horse to ride in a rally. Worried that Sam might not be able to handle the horse, he asked how long it had been since he had ridden. "Just this morning," Hall replied. [35]

Randall and Mary Maddox were new supporters in 1976. Randall took time from his business as a Chrysler dealer to campaign for Hall. [36]

In Marion County Bonnie Spellings hosted coffees and dinners. A longtime restaurateur in Jefferson, Spellings had run the Colonial Coffee Shop, the Sherry Inn, and the Galley Pub. Sam and Madeleine Hall, like so many other Marshall residents, were regular patrons. Hall also had represented Spellings and other private school clients in a court case, so Jeffersonians knew him well. Hall's way of getting people's names as they entered the restaurant for a political meeting amused Spellings. He quizzed her, and she helped by calling out names. [37]

The old College of Marshall classmates threw in their support. Charlie and Louise Ayers Walters lived in New Boston, Bowie County, near Texarkana. Louise knew Sam and Madeleine during the 1941-1942 academic year. Charlie met Sam after he and Louise married; they lived in Marshall until 1948. They helped with the 1962 and 1976 campaigns in the northern part of the district, participating in barbeques, fish frys and coffee meetings in Cass, Titus and Camp Counties. [38]

Hall made new friends during the campaign, none better than Bobby Johnson, the owner of B&J Collision, an auto body repair shop between Marshall and Jefferson. Johnson told how he came to know Hall:

> I first met Sam while he was out shaking hands and running for Congress. He stopped by our business north of Marshall and shook hands with every employee at B&J Collision. Sam asked for our support, listened, and asked questions! Sam was very interested in my background in the Army Special Forces (Green Berets) and he looked at

> my photographs from Vietnam made in 1967-68. He was interested in the Purple Heart medal I received for wounds in 1967, and he did something no one else had ever done—*he thanked me for serving my country*! That statement by Sam really made an impact on me. This man really appreciated veterans, and that was important to me. Before Sam left that day, he told me he served in the Army Air Corps during WWII. My father also served in the Army Air Corps in Europe and North Africa. The more Sam and I visited that day, the more I liked this tall, big man running for Congress. I made a decision that day that was a first for me—I made a political contribution to Sam B. Hall's campaign. That one contribution was well spent, and I never had a single regret with Sam representing my family. [39]

The Halls attended fund-raising dinners throughout the district. Representative Jim Wright of Fort Worth, the congressman for the Twelfth District, spoke at the fund-raiser in Mount Pleasant on October 25. The Halls, including their three daughters, and Judge Sam Sr. and Mrs. Valerie Hall, attended, with Ray Lawson serving as Master of Ceremonies. Approximately 500 people attended the occasion, and Hall took the opportunity to thank his wife, parents, and Baron Shacklette for their support. Shacklette had been Wright Patman's Administrative Assistant, and had remained to work with Hall, which was a great help during the transition of offices.

From late January to mid-April, 1976, Hall traveled some 14,000 miles throughout the First Congressional District, making new friends and developing other political supporters such as David Lindsey, a honey producer in Lamar County; Rick Palmer, a barber from Sulphur Springs; Bill Bradford with radio station KSST in Sulphur Springs; and Bill Taylor, a dairy farmer in Hopkins County. Infused with energy and stamina, Hall did not need much sleep, which served him well in the campaign. But once, having become sleepy behind the wheel, he sang into his portable Dictaphone in order to stay alert. He had not done such a thing before, so the next day Sue Jordan reviewed the tape and got a surprise. Once home, though, even after a long day, Hall kept to his habit of reading awhile, in bed, with the light on. Madeleine declared she learned early in their marriage, especially during the law school days, to sleep with Sam's reading light on. The bedtime reading ritual revealed his ability to focus on those things, and persons, most important to him. As with other rituals in his life, such as church, family vacations, frequent socializing with friends and his relationship with Madeleine, he used it to concentrate on the central priorities of life, even in the midst of an intense political campaign. [40]

8

Representative Sam B. Hall Jr., 1976-1978

Sam Hall, Jr., lived most of his life in the small-town environment of Marshall, Texas. In small towns, the residents know nearly everything about each other. It is difficult, under these circumstances, for an individual to conceal personal faults—particularly if he or she is in public life. It is highly significant, then, that in Marshall and Harrison County, Sam Hall, Jr., was almost universally esteemed as a person of high moral character, keen intelligence, and, as well, an able and effective lawyer and leader. His forceful, yet amiable and witty, personality endeared him to his community. In later years, when he served as a United States Representative, these same characteristics were made evident to the inhabitants of East Texas, generally. Their response was to re-elect him to his position term after term. It is not surprising that Sam Hall, Jr., was so revered, for he mirrored the ideals and beliefs of his fellows in these locations. As a United States Representative, he voted the way the vast majority of the voting population of his area would have liked for him to vote."—U. S. District Judge William Wayne Justice [1]

Richard F. Fenno Jr. wrote about politics and politicians in his book *Home Style,* giving insights about the members of Congress and what it takes for them to gain and to keep office. Above all else the representative must have and convey the sense of belonging to the people and the home district. He must identify powerfully and closely with the constituents, making sure people believe their congressman is one of them and that his agenda and priorities match theirs. The people recognize a true representative; they cannot be fooled, at least not for long. They must continue to trust their representative, and they must be reminded who is representing them. Of course, once the member of Congress has established qualifications and credibility, keeping to a regular schedule of visits around the home district is a good way to increase the chance of reelection. Sam B. Hall Jr. was to serve in the Congress for just over nine years and participate in few significant, historic pieces of legislation. He went to Washington bearing moral, religious, and social convictions most citizens from his district wanted in a representative; he was no indecisive congressman tossed and turned by political waves and wind. East Texas voters re-elected Hall by overwhelming majorities in successive terms, several times without opposition. [2]

In 1980 Hall was asked whether he ever got homesick for Texas while serving in Washington. Surely, he did, but he declared, "The fact is I've never really left Texas." That statement revealed, first, his sincere attitude about where his true place and only enduring influence lay, and, second, his understanding that he must always think of home the same way the voters did. Hall never allowed himself or his staff to think of or refer to Washington, D.C., as home. He never felt at home in the capital, and he did not want people back home to think he could ever consider anywhere but East Texas as his home. His feelings and his public stance about "home" were true to his deepest desires not only to represent the people "back home," but to be among them and with his family as often as possible. [3]

Hall spoke out in the district frequently, which he enjoyed because his trips around East Texas allowed him to be out among the people. He championed patriotism and the flag with unequivocal sincerity. Beyond discussions about politics and policy, Hall emphasized the special relationship he enjoyed with his constituents and the pleasure he got serving as their representative in Congress. Blessed with the common touch, he made people feel comfortable. Hall did not seem the "politician," but instead simply epitomized respectable leadership. People responded well to his commitment and liked to identify with him. To be known as a constituent in the First District of Texas was to be identified with a representative who attracted near-universal respect and admiration, despite the political differences to be found among voters in the district and elsewhere. East Texans knew, as Washington, D.C., political society recognized, that Sam Hall held clear principles. He held them honestly and did not compromise on basic issues. Perhaps that characteristic was a political hindrance, but it gave Hall a reputation for firmness, stability and consistency, which voters found reassuring.[4]

Judge Lanny Ramsay commented on Hall's unquenchable desire to interact with people and to build them up, recalling the time Hall honored the Ramsay children when he participated in a panel discussion and reception in his honor in Mt. Vernon at the home of State Representative Neal Solomon:

> Sam knew our children, Whitney, a fourth grader, and Will, a first grader. At the reception he asked about Whitney and Will. We told him that they were at school and not far from where he had been. He said, "Do you mean that we were in the same building for the panel discussion that they were in and we didn't go see them?" We said, "Yes." Sam said, "Let's go back up there and see those kids.
>
> Kitty, Sam and I left the reception and the important dignitaries, got into his car, and drove back to the school. We went to Will's class, and then to Whitney's class to see them. Sam walked right into both those classes to see Whitney and Will. Needless to say, it was an honor for Whitney and Will, the teachers and the students, to have a United States congressman visit their class.
>
> To Kitty and me, it was a small thing done by a great man that showed the type of statesman and man Sam Hall was. Whitney, Will, Kitty and I will never forget that event or our friend, Sam Hall. [5]

Like others, Jewell Gray observed that Hall was a counterexample to a popular stereotype about politicians. People were not tools for political advancement, but valued friends whom he sought to serve whether he acted as a private citizen or as a congressman. [6]

Sam Hall energetically advanced policies he believed would most benefit his district and the nation, and his constituents approved. He could not be manipulated to forsake his beliefs. A firm personal standard of right and wrong governed his decisions, and he was sincere in this matter, thoroughly consistent in believing and living the principle. Thus, he was noted for his responsibility to commitments, and to let anyone down was never an option for him. He dared not bring reproach upon his family or upon his home district.

In defeating Dr. James Hogan of Atlanta with 83.7 per cent of the vote in November, 1976, Hall secured his first full term in Congress and returned to work in January, 1977. The *Henderson Daily News* emphasized the principled approach Hall had toward budgets and responsible spending. The *Daily News* editorial noted that people already admired how, even after raising contributions and spending some of his own funds, Hall won four elections in one year. He also set a noble example by opposing an automatic congressional pay raise—at the time the annual salary was $44,800. He thought that congressional salaries were too low, but Congress itself, not the executive branch, should be responsible for monitoring salaries. That matter was a major issue for him in his first term, along with a constitutional amendment to keep a balanced federal budget, and his strong opposition to relinquishing United States sovereignty over the Panama Canal. He also wanted to protect the interests of retirees and businesses essential to the economy in his district. [7]

As a new congressman, Hall characterized himself mostly as a conservative but in some ways a liberal because putting issues and people first often contradicted labels. He saw clearly what needed to change in the capital, what needed to be preserved, and what would best serve the people. By going to Washington, he hoped to join a movement to create positive changes. Perhaps he had a simplistic, naive view of government and legislative politics, a novice representative's excessive optimism, but none could question his sincerity and zeal. Hall was to show himself equal to any representative in his capacity to manage legislative details in his committee assignments. He proved to be diligent, knowledgeable leader. He adjusted well to the new tasks and routines, and his dedication to work commended him to his colleagues and those he represented.[8]

Soon after arriving in Washington, Hall offered an early analysis of its problems: the government bureaucracies dominated and stifled accomplishment. Even the best-designed laws produced mischief in the hands of government agencies. Not one to deliberate unnecessarily over a decision or project, he considered the intricacies and complications in congressional bills unnecessary. It was too hard to pass good laws, and lawmakers typically thought too little about what new laws would cost the taxpayers. Bad fiscal policies were bad for the nation. In one interview, he compared the national capital to imperial Rome: people needed to recognize the danger of assuming all was well when it was not. A few months later, in a speech before the East Texas Chapter of the Texas Association of Business, Hall spoke harshly about unnamed congressional colleagues whose lack of patriotism disappointed him. "We have people in the Congress of the United States who could care less if the flag stood or fell," he declared. "They could care less about us having the right to gather here tonight and peaceably assemble." But they were a tiny minority, as most congressional representatives genuinely cared about the country and showed they did through their hard work.[9]

Starting his first full term, Hall chose not to attend the two seminars, the Congress's provision for the unusually large freshman class in 1974, intended to acquaint first-time Congressmen about legislative procedures and issues. His six months of experience sufficed, and the time required to participate would distract from work in progress. Hall's performance suggests he lost nothing by missing the seminars. Asked about his lack of experience in the Texas State Legislature and Senate, he replied that he considered it an advantage to his work in Washington, "because you [would] have to unlearn, so to speak, a lot of the things you learned there—procedures, the committee line-ups in the House and Senate, that sort of thing."[10]

In his first newsletter to constituents, Hall repeated his vow to serve faithfully in the best interest of the people of East Texas. They "share my pride in the United States as well as our deep concern that we continue to be a strong Nation, eternally dedicated to our Constitutional principles." He was committed to those principles, and all people needed for proof was to see how he voted to promote fiscal responsibility. He also observed how hard it was to get money for business startups in the United States from the Small Business Administration; why then should the Congress be giving money to finance construction and business in other countries?[11]

Hall's outspokenness made a strong initial impression in Washington. Invited to participate in broadcast debates, in April, 1977, he appeared with the noted lawyer F. Lee Bailey on the ABC television network's *Good Morning America* program. They debated whether it was possible to get a fair jury in American courts. Bailey doubted it, but Hall insisted that jurors usually responded toward trial evidence in a reasoned, balanced way. Bailey contended that attorneys often rejected able, analytical jurors. Jurors sometimes misunderstood the jury process and courtroom testimony, he claimed. Commenting on how easy it was to avoid jury duty, especially for upper-class people and professionals, Hall and Bailey believed exemptions from jury service should be harder to get. On a July *Good Morning America* program, Hall and Ralph Nader, a leading consumer and conservation advocate, debated the need for and possible location of the Alaskan oil pipeline. A month later, Hall appeared on ABC's *Good Morning America* again, and proposed that lethal injection would provide an antidote to the "carnival spirit" of executions. He reminded viewers that in order to have a secure society, the death penalty was necessary as it deterred repeated serious crimes. [12]

During the second half of 1976, while Hall finished out the term of Wright Patman, and during the first year of the next Congress, he lived in Washington without Madeleine, who came from Texas for special occasions. He flew home every weekend he could, both to be home with family and to be available for activities in the district. This pattern lasted until their youngest daughter, Sandra, graduated from high school and became, like her sisters, a student at Baylor University. He and Madeleine then occupied a small apartment in the District of Columbia, and later rented an apartment in Crystal City, Alexandria, Virginia, which provided easy access to the

Capitol and to National Airport. Hall's administrative assistant Sue Jordan took the District apartment as it suited her needs and was close to the office. The Halls then found a larger townhouse in Arlington that allowed better hosting and entertaining. Don Womack recalled how Hall complained to his father about the inflated real estate prices in northern Virginia, and how much he had to pay. Sam Sr. said he hoped Sam Jr. had also gotten the mineral rights at that price. Sam told Don Womack, "After thinking about it, I believe I should have held out for them!"[13]

Representative Ralph Hall of the Texas Fourth Congressional District recalled a mix-up based on the shared Hall name in Washington. During the first week of Ralph Hall's first congressional term in 1981, an intensive search for suitable lodging had yielded nothing, until his wife found condominiums under construction and reserved one at 310 East Capitol Boulevard. Ralph Hall wrote,

> They asked her what her husband's occupation was, and she told them he was a Member of Congress. They checked, and their records showed only Sam B. Hall as a Member. Thus, they drew the contract of sale up in the name of Sam B. Hall, Jr., and my wife, Mary Ellen Hall. They first sent the papers over to his office for signature. Sam, being one of the sharpest men I have ever known, knew immediately what had happened and intended to have a little fun with the situation. He called me and told that he would go ahead and sign for the condo with Mary Ellen, but she was going to have to cook for him some while she was in D.C. We finally got the situation straightened out and we bought the condo and still live in it."[14]

Madeleine and Mary Ellen Hall spent considerable time together. Dorothy Runnels, whose husband Harold Runnels was a representative from New Mexico, had a Virginia farm, where the Halls enjoyed visiting on an occasional retreat from the capital.

The life in the nation's capital of course differed greatly from life in Marshall. Like other newcomers to Washington, the Halls soon learned there was no way to accept all the numerous invitations to receptions. Congressional activities alone provided more invitations for meetings, dinners, and receptions than anyone could reasonably accept. Those functions sponsored by business or industry or trade organizations were so plentiful that the representative might go only if there was some relevance for the home district.

Madeleine Hall said one could "only drink so many Cokes in a night." The initial newness and excitement of the capital scene faded after so many receptions and parties to which she and Sam were invited. Yet, there were numerous opportunities for personal and political relationships to grow, and the Halls took reasonable advantage of that over the years. Madeleine's favorite events included a "Texas Buffet" supper of chili and cornbread at Texas Second District Representative Charlie Wilson's apartment, or attending the Congressional Awards dinner at the Hilton hotel, with Phyllis George Brown of Kentucky as the Mistress of Ceremonies, Dinah Shore, and the U. S. Army Chorus. The annual White House Christmas Party was always a high pleasure. She was impressed that at the White House barbeque in 1982 President and Mrs. Reagan were present to greet all the guests and remained for the whole event, dressed smartly but informally. As the spouse of a representative, Madeleine got copies of her husband's weekly schedules and fit herself into them where appropriate. [15]

Sam and Madeleine enjoyed the Texas State Society, one of myriad political and social organizations in the nation's capitol. Comprised of the representatives and senators of Texas, its membership included judges, businesspersons, and, quite simply, anyone with a stake and interest in Texas. Madeleine served as the Society's delegate to the National Conference of State Societies in 1978 and 1979. The Halls' daughter Sandra was a Texas Princess for 1978. The annual Texas State Society barbeque was the big event. In 1978 and 1979 Hall was first vice-president of the society, and president for 1979 and 1980. [16]

The Congressional Club helped ease adjustments to the frenzied mix of social and political life in the capital. The wives of congressmen planned and attended social events, and were involved in some civic and social service opportunities. The Texas Wives also met for lunch. On occasion, Madeleine accompanied Sam whenever the congressional committees met for conferences beyond the capital itself. There were opportunities to visit interesting places; Madeleine always enjoyed Williamsburg, Virginia. The best experiences, though, usually involved inviting staff members, the student interns or friends to their home for dinner or out to a special restaurant. Ken Black sometimes joined the Halls at home for dinner, bringing with him his captivating sense of humor.[17]

The "trip to Washington" to meet with a friend and favorite congressional representative stands in the memory of many Americans. Sam and Madeleine marveled at how many East Texans visited Washington. There was a constant flow of constituents to greet from the First District. Ann (Mrs. Robert) Hall and Jewel (Mrs. Price T.) Young took time after attending the Top Ladies of Distinction Convention to visit with Sam and Madeleine, as he had insisted they do while they were in Washington. Sam and Jean Birmingham and the Lane Strahans of Marshall once met the Halls at the Texas Municipal League reception and the Texas Chamber of Commerce

Reception and Dinner.[18]

Long-time friends like Ralph and Verlin Watson, and Earl and Betty Rhoades found that Sam and Madeleine and Sue Jordan bent over backwards to assure they had the best possible visit. Hall also made sure to minimize added expense such as rental cars or taxicabs. He was delighted to take people on tours himself if he could. Madeleine often arranged White House and other special tours, so that the parts of the White House accessible to the public became familiar to her. She enjoyed numerous opportunities to visit the presidential mansion.[19]

Ralph Watson relished the Capitol tour when Hall ushered his friends into the Speaker's Sitting Room. Hall said Ralph was sitting where Sam Rayburn had sat, and declared that Earl Rhodes was seated in the chair Harry Truman occupied when the news came that Franklin Delano Roosevelt had died and he was to be president. He took the Watsons and Rhoadeses to Arlington Cemetery and displayed memorable anger when a cemetery clerk said there was no time to help them find the grave of a Harrison County native, an aviator, who had died in military service. Taking none of that, Hall identified himself as a member of the Congressional committee responsible for the cemetery budget and the clerk's salary. If the Arlington staff did not have time to help locate graves, for what did they have time? They saw the grave. Arlington National Cemetery topped Hall's list, and no matter how many times he visited, he always had energy and enthusiasm for it. He always went to watch the changing of the guard at the Tomb of the Unknowns, and he returned repeatedly to particular gravesites, taking his guests along in order to tell them about the special persons buried there. [20]

Hall also preferred to tour the State Department headquarters building. After renovations in the 1970s, it was an attractive and exciting place to tour, especially the top floor, which had been furnished with antiques and the memorabilia of former presidents and secretaries of state. [21]

Wayne Elizabeth Emery attended the College of Marshall with Hall and graduated in 1943. As a teacher, she brought and chaperoned students of the Oklahoma Future Business Leaders of America to their national convention in Washington. Scheduled to meet with their congressman from Oklahoma who did not meet with them, "He stood us up!", Emery took her students to Sam Hall's office nearby. Emery wrote, "Although it was July third, the last day before the Congressional summer recess, he took the time to visit with us, see that we had our picture made with him, and gave us all a goodbye hug. Duncan, Oklahoma, students returned home very impressed, telling the hometown, "Mrs. Emery knew a congressman well enough that he called her 'Wayne.'"[22]

Regular churchgoers, attending twice on Sunday and the Wednesday service when at home in Marshall, Sam and Madeleine continued their habit of regular church involvement when they were in Alexandria, first attending a Church of Christ in Arlington, and then attending a church in Falls Church, Virginia, one their daughter Sandra enjoyed. Hall enjoyed the congressional prayer groups and the annual prayer breakfast.[23]

The youngest of the Hall daughters, Sandra worked in Washington with the Texas office of State and Federal Relations from 1981 to 1983. "I made many friends there," she recalled. "Daddy would run into people all over the city, and they would tell him that they knew me. He asked me one day if I just stood around on street corners and introduced myself to people."[24]

Sandra became ill in the middle of the night and called her parents. Hall took her to a pharmacy. Recounting the incident, she said, "At midnight he had on his Stetson hat and leather jacket—what a Texan! As he walked in, I noticed something hanging from under his jacket—yes, there was the Honorable Sam B. Hall Jr. with his gold silk pajamas hanging from beneath his jacket!"[25]

Like her sisters, Sandra recognized the lack of privacy being the daughter of a public figure, but there were compensating opportunities, such as the barbeque party on the White House lawn hosted by President and Mrs. Carter, and the White House Christmas Party hosted by President and Mrs. Reagan. She noticed her father made a point of visiting with the police and Secret Service agents wherever he went, and when he showed guests around the Capitol he was never a stranger to the Capital Police and Secret Service, who often helped make a tour all the more special.[26]

Hall's hat and boots had always caught attention outside Texas, as when the family visited Harold Taylor, a vice-president with Texaco in Europe. At a border checkpoint someone asked, "Are you the sheriff?" Hall decided to let the man think so and said that he was. The Texan identity wore long and well. During their years in the capital the Halls had a big black car with a Texas license plate that read "#1 Texas," indicating the First Congressional District. People sometimes thought it was the governor's car, and few places were off-limits to it. Madeleine recalled Sam's claim, "if you get in this car, I can get you in anywhere. And we went up there and spent two weeks and it did. I mean they would look at that license number and take us right on through."[27]

The Hall's middle daughter, Amanda, had a roommate at Baylor University, Joann Diggs, who dated a U.S. Marshal who was also the son and brother of U.S. Marshals T. P. and Parnell McNamara. At the McNamara farm near Bosqueville and Waco, Deputy U.S. Marshal Mike McNamara helped Joann practice shooting skeet for her physical activities course at Baylor, which she was taking with Amanda. The Parnell brothers taught the young women to shoot machine guns there, using junked automobiles as targets. Confessing that she enjoyed the shooting, Amanda sent her dad a photograph, and he displayed it in his office. Remembering her dad's eventual response to the photograph, Amanda said, "I got a phone call sometime after that, and he said he believed he was going to have to "retire" that picture for a while. They were in the middle of a gun-lobbying bill and he just hated having to tell people it was his daughter in the picture with the machine gun."[28]

A representative's work in Washington centers around committee assignments and attendance on the floor of the House to participate in debate and to vote. At the time of his death, Wright Patman was an influential senior member or chair of several committees. [29]

When first elected, Hall served briefly on the Education and Labor, and Science and Technology Committees, until he had completed Wright Patman's unexpired term. Thereafter he requested and got assignments to the Veterans' Affairs and Judiciary committees, remaining there throughout his terms as both a committee member and chair or vice-chair of several subcommittees. Later on he described himself as being typically the lone conservative on the liberal Judiciary committee. [30]

Hall wanted to serve on the House Judiciary Committee, knowing his legal experience had prepared him for the work, and explaining that federal gun control laws and the welfare of veterans were important issues to him. Years later he revealed that when he ran for Congress he had hoped to serve on Veterans' Affairs. His friend and longtime chair of the committee, Olin "Tiger" Teague, Representative for the Texas Sixth Congressional District, encouraged him to serve there. Teague was the second most highly decorated combat soldier after Audie Murphy during World War II. Hall said, "Tiger Teague was one of the greatest friends the American veteran ever had, and I considered it a great honor to serve on the Committee that he had once chaired." [31]

G. V. "Sonny" Montgomery of Mississippi chaired the Veterans Affairs Committee. Sam Hall was fourth among twenty-one Democrats there, serving on the Oversight and Investigations subcommittee that Montgomery chaired, on the Compensation, Pension, and Insurance subcommittee directly under Douglas Applegate of Ohio, and on the Select Committee on Narcotics Abuse and Control, chaired by Charles B. Rangel of New York. [32]

Hall's committee assignments benefited from his strong background in committee and board work, his knack for getting to the gist of the crucial issues, and the decisiveness, if not ease, with which he worked through the minutiae and implications of legislative proposals. Committees routinely met to hear witnesses about proposed legislation. Thus informed, the committee members could debate and decide whether to propose the legislation to a higher committee, which could present it as a bill on the House floor. Witnesses, published documents, and opinion papers furnished the facts that committees needed. Hall observed to Ray Lawson of Marshall that as a congressional representative he had to read a lot in order to do his work, but claimed to enjoy the reading as he always had. [33]

Hall earned a reputation for diligence, contrary to the counter example of some representatives, even committee chairs, who routinely missed or arrived late for meetings. He often told about the time only he and the janitor showed up for a particular subcommittee meeting—his first with that committee. Sam Hall Sr. told his son it was probably the committee's most productive meeting ever. Committee members might notice the "job performance" of a representative in committee, but committee staffers, the people responsible for the essential administrative and clerical tasks, knew when unreliable members hindered the progress of legislation. Hall attended not just to be counted present on the record. [34]

Assigned to the Judiciary and Veterans' Affairs committees in the 95th Congress of 1977 and 1978, Hall joined the Immigration, Refugees, and International Law subcommittee chaired by Romano L. "Ron" Mazzoli of Kentucky. They routinely reviewed individual suspension of deportation appeals from the Immigration and Naturalization Service and saw many examples of the human side of immigration problems. Hall chaired the Administrative Law subcommittee that was revising the United States Criminal Code for the first time in a century or more. That particular project was a long-term work of the Congress. In the aftermath of the Watergate crisis, the same committee was working to create the special prosecutor law. [35]

Congressman Hall had numerous opportunities to speak his mind on issues of national and regional importance. He scorned any lack of patriotism and anyone who scorned patriotism by refusing to serve when their country called. In late 1976 he co-signed a bi-partisan letter to President Gerald Ford disapproving his pledge to grant Vietnam-era draft evaders a blanket pardon. He considered the pardon a national insult to veterans and families of servicemen injured or missing in action. When President Jimmy Carter pardoned the draft evaders, Hall declared the pardon a "mockery of those who served honorably and well," and a "damnable disgrace." [36]

Hall invoked an even greater principle. During House debate, he declared that draft-evaders had

> violated the law and should be brought before the bar of justice to answer for their actions and receive judgment. This is both a privilege and a responsibility incumbent upon them

> and upon us. They must explain their apparent violation of the law and we must listen with open minds to that explanation. We both must accept and abide by the impartial judgment of our judicial system. [37]

By his report, Hall's constituents overwhelmingly opposed amnesty. For him,

> The word, "Amnesty" itself means forgetfulness. It is like a strange and dangerous ailment of the body politic; it is a selective amnesia. We are asked to forget distasteful incidents of the past and reflect only upon what is pleasant, forgetting that we live in a hostile world environment. More than a billion people on this earth are dedicated to the total destruction of our way of life. Draft evaders, in my opinion, are the epitome of selfishness. In the name of personal freedom, they undermine and threaten the only system that allows the human spirit to be free.
>
> The United States of America is a republic in which the will of the Democratic majority is made effective through its elected representatives. In this context, amnesty is anarchy. It substitutes the willfulness of the individual for the lawful judgment of the majority.
>
> Blanket unconditional amnesty would be bad for America. To me, it is as unthinkable as adopting for the State of Texas a new slogan, "Forget the Alamo." [38]

Few things perturbed Hall more than the proposal that the United States relinquish ownership of and sovereignty over the Panama Canal. The Panama Canal Treaties, "the most inglorious give-away in the history of our country," should not be approved by the United States Senate. "As the Naval hero, Admiral Farragut, no doubt would have said under these circumstances if he were alive today, 'Damn the torpedoes—keep the Canal.'" He co-sponsored a bill (H.R. 8790) to require passage of the canal treaties by both houses of Congress, based on Article IV, Section 3, Clause 2 of the United States Constitution, which placed that power with the Congress alone. He co-sponsored House concurrent resolutions to keep U.S. sovereignty in the Canal Zone, and to have the president withdraw ratification of the Panama Canal treaties. Hall also opposed the presidential disposal of lands in the Canal Zone without approval of both Houses of the Congress. [39]

The canal giveaway was bad enough, but it was all Hall could do to believe, much less tolerate, the associated requirement that the State Department prepare a Draft Environmental Impact Statement to protect wildlife in the Canal Zone. The process would take years to complete, just

On the night of a successful election in 1976, Sam B. Hall Jr. receives congratulations from his proud father.

Representative Hall speaking to a meeting of the Northeast Texas Health Systems Agency, Marshall, Texas – Wednesday, April 13, 1977.

Sam Jr., Madeleine, and Amanda watch returns on the Texas First District congressional race, 1976.

as it had to do the same for the Cooper Lake Project in the First District of Texas. [40]

Hall provoked rebukes with his response to the Public Television broadcast, "Death of a Princess," the story of Mish'al, a Saudi Arabian princess executed along with her lover for adultery in 1977. The young woman's grandfather ordered the princess shot in public and the man hacked to death. The broadcast in the United Kingdom had already produced the British ambassador's expulsion from Saudi Arabia, and the Saudis were pressing the U.S. State Department on the issue. Congressman Hall lodged a complaint with the Chairman of the House Committee on Interstate and Foreign Commerce, expressing his disappointment that the United States would allow the broadcast of a film so offensive to Saudi religious and cultural convictions. He called the movie "a gratuitous slap in the face of a proud and honorable people," a "blatant example of official churlishness and mockery" sure to achieve only ill will and damage business relations between the United States and Saudi Arabia as well. [41]

His personable nature, enthusiasm, dignity, and approachability impressed people. Blessed with the common touch, Sam B. Hall Jr. made people feel comfortable.

A *Marshall News Messenger* editorial objected to Hall's protests and the pressure he introduced, emphasizing the broadcast's accuracy about what was clearly the execution of the princess. The Saudis were understandably reluctant to have the execution broadcast as a revelation of the dark side of their society. But, wrote the editor, "It does surprise and shock us that Sam Hall Jr. holds American liberty and tradition in so low regard as to suggest government interference in public television, because of a program he and the Saudis dislike." The tension in the Middle East already constituted a problem, but "Hall's suggestion [that the Saudi's will in the matter be respected] is an appalling affront to American ideals and freedoms, the very ones he is sworn to protect." [42]

The Members of Congress have opportunities to participate in congressional delegations as a part of their committee responsibilities. Delegations may have general purposes associated with international trade and business relationships, defense considerations, and may be amicable

Left to Right: Sam B. Hall Sr., Joe Lovelace of Linden, Sam Jr., Margaret Lovelace, and Valerie Hall (Mrs. Sam B. Hall Sr.)

Sam and Madeleine Hall on the Capitol steps.

Sue Jordan, personal secretary, and Representative Hall

W. H. (Harold) Taylor of Arlington, Texas, and Congressman Hall – Hall's Washington Office, July 19, 1978.

Representative Hall during House Veterans Committee hearings.

Congressman Hall, President Jimmy Carter, Congressman Beryl Anthony of Arkansas, and Lieutenant Governor Bobby Freeman of Louisiana, aboard Air Force One from Waco, Texas, to Texarkana, Arkansas-Texas, on October 22, 1980.

President of Egypt Anwar Sadat, Speaker of the House of Representatives Thomas P. "Tip" O'Neill Jr., and Congressman Hall, at the time of the Camp David Accords between Israel and Egypt, September 1978.

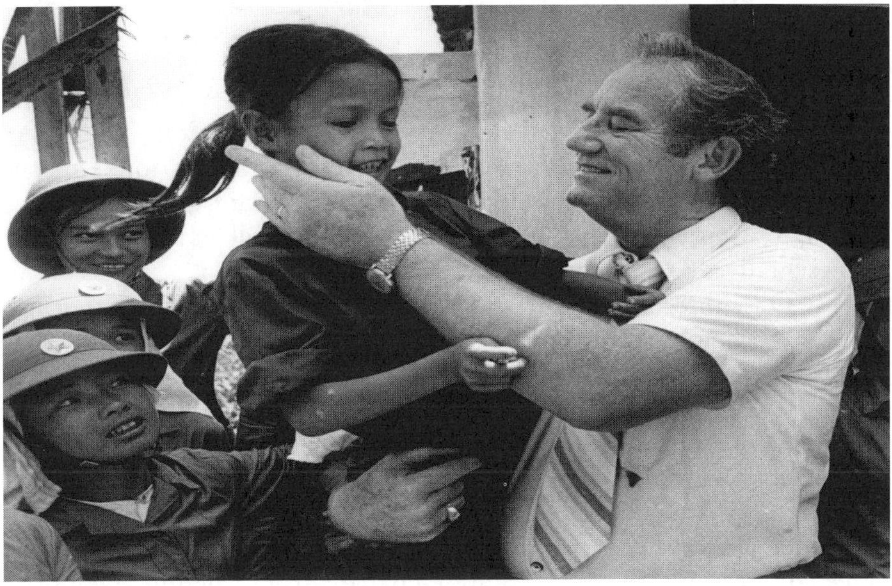

As a member of a congressional delegation to Southeast Asia in August, 1978, Hall visited Hanoi, toured a refugee camp in Laos, and saw the remains of American servicemen Missing-in-Action.

visits with friends and allies as a complement to diplomacy. Representative Hall took several such opportunities, some of which dramatically influenced his awareness and understanding of international issues.

A resolute and vocal patriot, Congressman Hall believed veterans deserved honor and respect and he considered his work on the Veterans' Committee to be crucial. Disturbed that personnel matters remained unresolved though years had passed since the United States had withdrawn from Vietnam, he believed the United States should seek to account for every possible prisoner of war or person missing in action. In 1977 he participated in his first congressional delegation to Southeast Asia and afterward considered it one of the most significant experiences of his life.

For many years during and after the war, families lived in limbo as they sought answers from the government about their loved ones listed as Prisoners of War or Missing in Action. Many accused the government of withholding information, engaging in a conspiracy of silence. Organizations such as The National League of Families of American Prisoners and Missing in Southeast Asia urged the U. S. government to persuade Southeast Asian governments and China to release information about missing or imprisoned service members. But the war details were sorted out only in the middle to late seventies, after the restoration of normal diplomacy; however, some questions remained unresolved. [43]

Americans wanted a full investigation of the POW/MIA problem. The House introduced many resolutions, including H. Con. Res. 331 of August, 1977, which recommended that a "United National special investigatory commission should be established to secure a full accounting of Americans listed as missing in Southeast Asia." Hall and eighteen other Representatives co-sponsored the resolution. [44]

Only three or so years after the United States withdrew its armed forces from South Vietnam, Hall received an unprecedented opportunity to join a delegation of congressional representatives to Southeast Asia. In August 1978 he accompanied James Broyhill, a North Carolina Republican; George Danielson, a California Democrat; G. V. "Sonny" Montgomery, a Mississippi Democrat; Henson Moore, a Louisiana Republican; John P. Murtha, a Pennsylvania Democrat; and Ike Skelton, a Missouri Democrat. Tony Won Pat (Antonia Borja), the delegate from Guam, three congressional staffers, a State Department interpreter, seven press representatives, and a U.S. Air Force escort for the delegation's plane completed the entourage. [45]

The delegates were to visit with Vietnamese and Laotian officials in order to locate and return the physical remains of Americans missing in action. As a member of the Veterans Committee, Hall was thought to have the right sympathies for the trip. Glenn McCasland of the *Terrell Tribune* wrote that "Hall is one of those 'square' American congressmen who believes in God, Mother, Country and, oh yes, apple pie." Hall made the trip out of duty: "Sam would go anywhere to do a job for Uncle Sam." [46]

Representative Sonny Montgomery expressed hope that the trip could end once-for-all the question of MIAs and POWs. The group's Boeing 707 left Andrews Air Force Base at eight o'clock, Friday morning, August 18, 1978, stopped at Travis Air Force Base in California, and proceeded to Hickam AFB in Hawaii. The first day ended with a reception and dinner at the Officers' Club with the Commander-in-Chief of the Pacific. After a Saturday morning tour of the Central Identification Lab where servicemen's remains were taken for analysis and identification, the delegation continued to Guam for refueling, then to Manila for a Sunday evening dinner hosted by Ambassador Murphy at the U.S. Embassy. On Monday, August 21, they flew from Manila to Hanoi, and then to Ho Chi Minh City. The delegation was to be in Hanoi only 36 hours. [47]

Family members stayed behind; the trip would be hard and conditions might be primitive. Tensions remained after the Vietnam war. Travelers have routine difficulties, and the delegates were no exceptions. The Asian food was a shock to their systems; as Hall put it, "It was hot, atrocious." [48]

Ike Skelton described how the Vietnamese honored the group with a state dinner in Ho Chi Minh City, writing, "We were served whole chickens with the head and neck feathers still attached. When Sam saw these platters, he pushed his plate back and ate nothing else all evening. When we got back on the Air Force airplane to return to America, the chefs prepared good old American steak and potatoes for the members of the delegation. I well remember Sam Hall eating heartily for a few minutes, then getting sick on the American food." On August 23, 1978, UPI correspondent Dick Growald gave Hall an airsickness bag with a cartoon, two men talking, and the remark on it: "No, not a Ho Chi Minh City shopping bag—this is Sam Hall's thank you barf bag." [49]

Hall described the primitive conditions he witnessed on the trip, both in Vietnam and in Laos. Evidence of the destruction of war presented itself at every hand, including the day he entered a shop to buy a comb to replace one he had lost. Told that the metal comb he bought was made from the aluminum salvaged from an American B-52 bomber, he bought another and took both home. He saw boys and teenagers carrying weapons as members of the Vietnamese military. He observed that the Vietnamese under Communist rule were compliant to authority and resigned to their living situations, but there seemed no feeling of liberty; the people seemed oppressed. [50]

In Hanoi, the delegates disagreed whether some POWs-MIAs might still be alive. Sonny Montgomery and most of the others believed there were no survivors, but Hall and Henson Moore hoped some might still be found, despite the low probability of it. Hall said, "I just have a gut feeling that one of these MIAs will show up someday. Sonny, I wish I shared your view but I don't." The delegates balanced logic and the improbability of survivors being found with the sense of responsibility to investigate thoroughly, while not giving the families of POWS and MIAs false hope. Antonio Won Pat of Guam said, "I believe we should close the chapter on hope." [51]

Based on the Vietnamese government's treatment of the congressional delegation, the committee report to the Congress noted that finding MIA remains could take years, and, without any particular fault of Vietnam, it could be an enormous undertaking. As for diplomacy, the Vietnamese seemed to want to resolve differences. Thus, the delegates recommended that the Department of State investigate the prospects for diplomatic normalization with Vietnam. Sam Hall and Ike Skelton dissented from the committee report, opposing the normalization of relations with Vietnam. They insisted that when the State Department commenced negotiations with the Vietnamese, they should remember that Vietnam is a "dedicated Communist country" whose interests were contrary to the interests of the United States. Rep. Henson Moore did not sign the report because he wanted neither to validate nor to recognize the Vietnamese government, nor support foreign aid for Vietnam. [52]

Traveling to Laos, the delegation visited a camp where an estimated 9,000 refugees had gathered from the Khmer Rouge turmoil in Cambodia. Hall told stories about women whose husbands had been hacked to death and beheaded with hoes before their eyes. The older people in particular carried the signs of the holocaust from which they had escaped. Hall said, "The older people tell the story of the horror they've been through in their eyes . . . I can't forget that look in their eyes, just like black agates." [53]

The delegation received the remains of eleven service members missing in action from the Vietnamese authorities and four from the Laotians; some 424 service members were missing in Laos. The Vietnamese government had identities for the remains of eight MIAs: six from the Air Force and two from the Navy. Three of the identifications were presumed accurate. They took the skeletal remains, which the Vietnamese and Laotians presented in individual plastic body bags. Hall later noted he could not help then but think of the families to whom they had been lost for so long. [54]

The delegation took the remains, having placed them more properly in coffins, to the Joint Casualty Resolution Center in Honolulu, Hawaii, for analysis and identification. In Honolulu, Hall saw the still unidentified remains of a number of service members from the Vietnam conflict. Perhaps he saw the very remains of an Air Force lieutenant later identified. As a senior member of the House Veterans' Affairs Committee, Hall was present in the Rotunda of the Capitol Building to see the casket bearing the same remains brought in for a three-day lying in state. [55]

Congressman Joe D. Waggonner Jr. remarked about the powerful impression he and others got from Hall about the congressional delegation to Asia. Hall talked about it a lot after he returned home. [56]

In his September, 1978, congressional newsletter, Hall stated that if more remains were not found in Southeast Asia, the deaths of American servicemen would still remind Americans to resist Communism. He refused to support economic assistance to Vietnam, explaining, "Our experience with Communist nations teaches us that billions donated for relief end up buying ammunition for our destruction." [57]

Hall suspected the Vietnamese were trying to play on American sympathies for the death and destruction that attended the Vietnam War, but he was not opposed to emergency food aid in 1978, particularly because of the one-two punch of a drought and a major monsoon that reduced food supplies. As long as the people who needed food the most got it, he would approve. [58]

Hall's concerns were reasonable, given the enmity between the People's Republic of China and the Soviet Union. The Vietnamese undoubtedly recognized the value of American influence in Southeast Asia as a counterweight to Soviet intentions there. One could not presume that the Vietnamese would act in good faith politically or protect human rights in ways acceptable to the Carter Administration and the Congress. Hall's experiences with the congressional delegation did nothing to diminish his mistrust of communist regimes, but helped him to comprehend the desperation present among the people living under those regimes or trying to recover from war. His disgust with the inefficiencies and short-sightedness of such governments was not diminished during his successive terms of office. [59]

9

The Ninety-Sixth and Ninety-Seventh Congresses, 1979-1982

In May, 1978, Sam Hall entered the Democratic primary election unopposed, a clear indication that his constituents were largely satisfied with his work on their behalf. Ranked the twenty-second most conservative member of the House of Representatives in 1977, nine times out of ten he had voted with the conservative coalition in Congress, but did verge into "populist" voting where his constituents stood to benefit; only rarely did he vote with liberals. The lack of primary election opposition also revealed either that he was considered unbeatable, or that the effort and cost to unseat him discouraged potential contenders. [1]

Hall's Veterans Affairs Committee service was among his most important contributions as a Member of Congress. In the late 1970s a bipartisan spirit ruled in Congress. There was little controversy. In connection with his service on the Veterans Committee, Hall was one of 103 House cosponsors for the bill by John Hammerschmidt of Arkansas proposing the Vietnam Veterans Memorial Fund and a memorial to be erected in Washington, D.C. He also supported making a Veterans court of appeals separate from the federal system of courts. Such a court was implemented by public law in 1988, after he had resigned from Congress. Hall and Rep. Don Edwards of California worked with Judiciary Chairman G. V. "Sonny" Montgomery to make the compromises that allowed creation of the Veterans Court of Appeals. [2]

In 1977 when Hall was still new to Congress, Southern Democrats and East Texans hoped he would be elected to the highly influential House Ways and Means Committee; after all, Wright Patman had served there. Petroleum and gas industry issues ranked high in Texas and in the deliberations of Ways and Means. Moreover, East Texans considered his nomination fully proper considering the talents he showed in his work and thought his brief service to date should not disqualify him. [3]

The Democratic Steering and Policy Committee nominated Hall in early 1979, but the Democratic Caucus denied his nomination. The next year a non-Southerner, Marty Russo of Illinois, was selected for a new opening. Hall considered asking help from the Conservative Democratic Forum, but decided to remain with the Judiciary Committee in the Ninety-Seventh Congress rather than be nominated again to Ways and Means. East Texas constituents considered his exclusion from Ways and Means a "slap in the face" and a repudiation of the true criterion for service: that Hall served his constituency and voted faithfully on their behalf, conservatively and consistently. They had little regard for Democratic Party leaders who criticized him, such Bill Alexander of Arkansas, who said Hall voted too much like a Republican. Tracy Messler in *The Atlanta Times* praised Hall for refusing to be a sheep, and for supporting the sentiments of the fellow Texans in his district rather than the Democratic Party caucus. [4]

In a January, 1980, *Texarkana Gazette* interview, Hall explained that his disagreements with the Democratic leadership prevented his assignment to Ways and Means. "I just put principles above what they wanted me to do and I will continue to keep that frame of mind as long as I am in Congress." He asserted that the voters wanted him to do right by them, no matter what the high-profile political leaders in Washington might think of it. A *Longview Daily News* editorial echoed Hall's promise that "he would never sacrifice a principle for personal aggrandizement, and he has not done so." [5]

Fred Pool, a foreign trade consultant from Hallsville, expressed what many constituents thought about Hall and his relationship with the Democratic leadership:

> Tip" [O'Neill, the Speaker of the House of Representatives] didn't elect you and he couldn't if he wanted to. Jim Wright didn't elect you, and you could never make me believe he is "for" you either! Dangling the bait in front of a congressman is as ancient a ploy as has ever existed, and the so-called "leaders" are saying to themselves, "Oh, it will take time, but we'll bring him around." The First Congressional District is yours for as long as you want it given the kind of performance you have turned in thus far. And no matter who runs against you next year, or in '82, or whenever, you are SOLID with your constituency. I just wish you could go around with me and hear all the great compliments I'm getting on you; and when I travel in other districts, I hear: "Fred, I wish we had a congressman like

> Sam Hall in our district! . . . The most fatal error any congressman could make is to forget who put him where he is, and too many, I fear, have failed to remember that very important lesson. Hang in there! It is a joy to hear—all over your district—the very great satisfaction everyone seems to be expressing as to the job you are doing. And believe me, it is also amazing when you learn how many people keep up with those voting records. [6]

During his second full term in the Congress, Hall expressed his dismay about the "euphoria" over the not-yet-ratified Strategic Arms Limitation Treaty (SALT II). "It is absolutely incredible to me that the Senate of the United States would even consider ratification of a SALT II treaty, given the current intensification of Soviet aggression around the world." It could mean less money for military defense, which Hall could not justify. Reductions would compromise the United States' ability to defend itself against the Soviets. Not to be trusted in view of their lamentable human rights record and international aggression, the Soviets would honor the treaty only while it was convenient for them to do so:

> Soviet troops and so-called 'technicians' are so prevalent on the continent of Africa that every moderate government there is trembling with fear. The list is endless and it should be out of the question to reward this aggression with a Salt treaty that, like every treaty entered into by the Soviets, will be broken by Moscow when it becomes 'Convenient.' [7]

Asked in a radio interview by Bill Bradford of Sulphur Springs, Texas, whether he was re-evaluating his views on the Russians, he responded,

> Well, I've never—I don't have to re-evaluate the Russians. I didn't trust them before; I don't trust them now. I think that one of the things that has come out of the Afghanistan matter is the fact that Russia is going to do what it wants to do regardless of what people think about it and what they may have thought about the Russians in the past. No, I don't; I think it is going to make us reappraise our entire situation. Of course what they are trying to do—it's to grab a few of those oil fields over there. If you would take a look at a map, and I'm sure people have; if you look at that map you will see that if they can get through Afghanistan—that leaves them 250 miles from a "warm-water port" as they call it. That's what they've been looking for all these years, for generations, a way down there to it. Of course it gives them an access that they have never had before. I think that, I don't think that they are going to leave Afghanistan.

> I don't think they are going to leave at all.

Frustrated, the Soviets eventually did leave, but only after leaving a ruinous legacy in Afghanistan. Until then, Hall believed that the United States must have a stronger military presence in the region in order to deter the Soviets. By 1984 Hall had not altered his suspicion of the Soviets. In his weekly radio message he reminded listeners of Soviet willfulness in "violating every international law and humanitarian ideal known to decent people," so much so that the Soviet army brutalized its own and was riddled with corruption. [8]

Hall consistently opposed sending foreign aid to countries he considered false friends, and whose leaders squandered the money on themselves while their own people lived in misery. Evaluating his congressional role in January, 1979, Hall confessed that

> I never dreamed three and a half years ago that I'd be concerning myself on an intimate basis with SALT II, the Iranian Question, Afghanistan, the national defense posture as it respects the Navy, the Army, the Air Force and the Marine Corps, you know. You knew you would be dealing with those matters but not to the standpoint of talking face-to-face or one-on-one with an admiral in the Navy or a general who just tells you what we need or what we must have to exist as a nation. It's a very, very enlightening position to see all of those things happening and you are becoming involved as a part of it. [9]

Reductions in military spending were one thing, but Hall thought anemic increases for national defense equally dangerous. Modest budgetary increases did not replace losses from inflation, so the United States could not guarantee that adequate weapons systems could be developed. Hall thought the Congress needed to be vigilant so that the "anti-defense establishment" did not weaken the military by diverting funds for social programs—the increased risk to the nation was unjustified. [10]

In late 1979, Hall and five other representatives (Tom Corcoran of Illinois, Richard Gephardt & Ike Skelton of Missouri, Dan Glickman and Jim Jeffries of Kansas) visited the *USS Saratoga* during a three-day inspection tour of the Navy to evaluate East-coast combat readiness. Hall was already alarmed at the rising power of the Soviet navy as a possible tool for Soviet expansion; moreover, the Iran hostage situation also made a strong, flexible United States Navy even more important. [11]

In October, 1980, Hall spoke at the Red River Army Depot near Texarkana about the need to increase defense initiatives due to the curtailment of the B-1 bomber and MX missile programs, the greater numbers of Soviet conventional weapons in Eastern Europe, and the threat of submarine-launched nuclear ballistic missiles. Said Hall, "It is time to build a fire of patriotism, Americanism and belief in God and country, the likes of which we have never seen in our lifetime." He opposed the attempt to stop funding nerve gas production, which proponents saw as a strategic deterrent, and voted against an anti-MX missile amendment. [12]

In late 1979 Hall cosponsored legislation to prohibit Social Security abuse by prisoners who got disability payments while in prison. Possibly 30,000 or so inmates were receiving Social Security disability payments; the resulting federal outlay was about $60 million per year. It galled him to know that prisoners used the money to buy personal items such as stereos and televisions or to make investments in the stock market. Hall also supported reducing, or better, removing the outside earnings limitation on retirees receiving Social Security. The modest changes in regulations that came from these discussions resulted in higher earnings limits for retirees, but did not eliminate the penalty. [13]

Among other matters during his second full term, Hall supported the Hospital Cost Containment and Reporting Act of 1979 and supported energy development. He refused to support a moratorium on construction permits for nuclear power plants after the Three-Mile Island incident in March, 1979, when radioactive steam had been released from the nuclear powered generating plant during an accident and partial meltdown of a reactor core. He supported reducing Federal Trade Commission powers. His vote to approve a federal loan for Chrysler Corporation confirmed his reputation for support of business. He always opposed any variation of the so-called windfall profits tax, both the idea and every provision of it. "It won't produce a gallon of oil or a foot of gas," he said, and it would produce a daunting burden for oil and gas investments because of the intrinsically high risk and cost of exploration and development. Hall supported extending Most-Favored Nation trade status to China. [14]

By 1980 Representative Hall found himself rising in recognition, popularity and seniority. Voters considered him diligent in pursuing issues important not only to his district but the nation. He was an active legislator, in terms of committee work and sponsorship and co-sponsorship of bills and resolutions. He continued to consider government incursions into free-enterprise processes as threats to individual freedoms and to the operation of democracy; his was a "philosophy of positive conservatism" [15]

In 1980 Hall became more closely identified with business interests; after all, he and his family had a few oil and gas investments and owned real estate. He understood business and how government policies influenced it. The February, 1980, issue of *Texas Business* magazine named Hall Texas' "Best Conservative" in the Congress, a fact that businessmen appreciated. The magazine hinted that some Democrats were adopting a more conservative position, that is, in a direction similar to that of Hall. Later in 1980 he received the "Guardian of Small Business Award" from the National Federation of Independent Businesses. [16]

The Iran Hostage Crisis of 1979 and 1980 kept Americans distressed, and the failed attempt to rescue the hostages worsened the situation while damaging Carter's presidency. Hall was one of fifty-four congressional representatives who considered Iran's taking of hostages an act of war and supported a resolution for military action if the American hostages had not been released by a certain date. The House Foreign Affairs Committee declined to act in accordance with the resolution because it might be unwise to implement such a strategy as long as Iran held hostages. Representative Hall thought that after months of American patience with the Iranians, the attempt to resolve the situation by force was understandable, and that Americans should support the president. But the military strike to free the hostages turned disastrous. Some representatives denounced the president for failing to consult Congress first as required by the War Powers Act. Hall disagreed because the consultation might have compromised American security. After the helicopters crashed and eight servicemen died, he was convinced that the equipment failures on the helicopters emphasized the need to put first priority on building national defense by strengthening the armed forces. In late April Hall and Representative Ray Roberts of Texas opposed an attempt in the Congress to require the Carter administration to turn over information about its dealings in Iran. [17]

In his 1980 re-election campaign, Hall stayed true to the themes that had gotten him elected in the first place. Announcing in January, he declared,

> No one can deny that these are perilous times for our great nation. The decade of the Eighties will demand strong, moral leadership, forthrightness on the part of all elected officials, and a commitment to put the welfare of America ahead of selfish, vested interests. At stake is our freedom and the future of Western civilization, and I pledge, if re-elected, to champion this just and proper cause in the Congress." [18]

In the primary and general elections, Hall ran unopposed and still got many votes throughout the district. Ronald Reagan won the presidential election, and the Republicans and conservatives became a greater force in the House and had a majority in the Senate. Responding to the 1980 election results, Hall observed that voters wanted to reduce the government bureaucracy and taxation, and to achieve a balanced budget. With his failure to get votes in Texas as a factor, President Carter's defeat did not surprise Hall. Among the reasons was the Carter administration's windfall profits tax, which most affected the petroleum industry. Hall looked ahead optimistically to the conservative administration of Ronald Reagan, the prospects for a stronger economy, and a more positive outlook in Washington. [19]

Hall usually had voted against matters that President Carter supported. At the start of the Carter administration, he had expressed his personal approval of the man, noting his patriotism and religious faith. "This kind of dedication is not really understood by observers and opinion makers in our Capital City," he wrote. "Much of the mystery and some of the fear with which they are viewing the President apparently stems from a belief that Jimmy Carter is either hopelessly old-fashioned, or playing a Napoleonic game of winner-take-all. I believe we are witnessing a return to simple dignity without pomp or ceremonial formalities and to plainspoken honesty rather than double-talk. No wonder President Carter has them confused." [20]

After a time with Ronald Reagan as president, Hall revised his views on President Carter, not concerning his Christian faith and patriotism, but rather his conception of the presidency and conduct as president. He compared the two, saying of Carter, "I'm not sure that he ever understood and had a full grasp of what it meant to be president of the United States." Hall judged that Reagan had taken charge decisively, providing stronger and clearer leadership. Earlier, he had perceived a flaw in Carter's leadership. Carter, of whom Hall said, "He will go the last mile before changing his mind," needed to communicate more effectively with the Congress instead of failing to express his intentions. [21]

Only a month after the 1980 elections, Hall was on the published list of sixty-six Congressional representatives and five conservative Senators whom the National Committee for an Effective Congress wanted to see defeated in the 1982 general elections. They took their cue from the tactics of the National Conservative Political Action Committee, which had wielded considerable influence in the 1980 elections. [22]

Hall's conservatism placed him and other representatives of similar stripe in the position to support the agenda and policies of Ronald Reagan. The landslide Republican electoral victory in 1980 presaged a major turn from the policies and attitudes of the Carter Administration. [23]

In the Ninety-seventh Congress, though he did not co-sponsor the legislation, Hall supported the Reagan budget proposal, the Gramm-Latta Balanced Budget and Deficit Control Act of June, 1981. It received Hall's vote two days after he opposed a question blocking a vote on the bipartisan package, signaling his general support of the Administration's "Economic Recovery Program," which entailed "reduced inflation, lower taxes, diminishing interest rates and a return to economic prosperity." His vote matched one the previous month to support the Bipartisan Budget Resolution. In July he supported the Conable-Hance bipartisan tax bill. Later in 1981 he co-sponsored a failed resolution designed to force adherence to a balanced budget for the government. [24]

Hall approved the Reagan budget reforms in the Omnibus Budget Reconciliation Act, though the budget reductions excluded reductions in the largest portions of the budget in social security, Medicare, and other entitlements, which most Congressmen considered inviolable. He approved the fiscal and tax policies of the "Reagan Revolution" as they reduced taxes on personal incomes, businesses, capital gains, gifts, and inheritances. The focus of Reagan's philosophy on income and capital gains taxes during his first term was the Economic Recovery Tax Act of August 1981. [25]

In these measures the Conservative Democratic Caucus (the Boll Weevils) and other conservatives supported the Reagan administration. Congressman Charles Stenholm, a Texas Democrat and member of the Boll Weevils put the developments in context:

> Ronald Reagan won a landslide victory in November of 1980 and, in January of 1981, the Senate came under Republican control for the first time in years. It was no mystery to me why this happened; the leadership of the Democratic Party was left of center, and the American public had seen enough. I decided it was time for conservative Democrats like me to make our voices heard, and Hall would play an important role in that process.
>
> I founded the Conservative Democratic Forum (CDF) to bring like-minded conservative Democrats together to formulate policy and legislation and bring another perspective to the Democratic Party. We were also known as the "boll weevils." In any event, the so-called Reagan Revolution would not have been possible without the support of the CDF, and Sam Hall was an active and effective member of the CDF. [26]

However, "Reaganomics," as critics called it, aroused intense debate, for it put questionable controls on spending, particularly in the military, during a period when Reagan was emphasizing the need to fight communism, chiefly the Soviet "evil empire," through military strength and a revival of the Cold War policy of containment. Hall differed from many congressmen by supporting President Reagan's second-term policies against the Soviet Union, including the Strategic Defense Initiative, derisively called the "Star Wars" initiative, that was to involve a computerized system of satellite tracking and defensive firepower against enemy intercontinental ballistic missiles. [27]

Nonetheless, in his support of the administration's budget proposal of 1981, Hall displayed his commitment to fiscal conservatism and to decreasing governmental spending and debt, which in turn prompted complaints of lost faith with the Democratic Party and the certainty of retribution in committee assignments from the party leadership. Hall was unconcerned about the future of the Democratic Party and said so. Surely he was not worried if the Democratic leaders thought he betrayed the party. [28]

Hall in fact played a decisive role not forgotten in Congress. In January, 2001, Senators Trent Lott and Phil Gramm debated a resolution to encourage bipartisanship in the nation's first "50-50 Senate." Lott recollected the tense voting on the 1981 Reagan Budget, reminding the Senate that in 1981 the Speaker of the House of Representatives, Thomas P. "Tip" O'Neill, fervently opposed the Reagan proposals; nonetheless, he pursued the ideal and reality of bipartisanship. O'Neill approached Hall, urging him not to vote in favor of the budget. Lott urged Hall otherwise, and Hall, with O'Neill and Lott present, placed his voting card in the slot, making an affirmative, and decisive, vote on the legislation. Recalling Hall's vote, Lott said, "That required an act of courage. Did the Speaker get mad at him?" No, he explained, because colleagues must preserve respect for one another despite differences, and must focus on the nation's long-term good, even when votes do not go their way. Using that story, Lott urged the Senate to get beyond the divisive partisanship of the 1990s, recognizing that only the will to cooperate could assure progress in a Senate evenly divided between Democrats and Republicans. [29]

Yet, Hall decided to support the Reagan program tax bill only after careful deliberation, even second-guessing himself after the fact. Late one evening, intern Michael Sandlin entered the congressman's office to find him at his desk reviewing the budget provisions, wondering if he had done the right thing in voting as he did for them. [30]

Hall's consistent record with Republicans, especially regrading the Gramm-Latta budget reduction legislation and the Reagan budget, led to incessant speculation and a news report that he would switch to the Republican Party, as would Phil Gramm. Hall denied the rumor in the strongest terms, declaring, "That story hit East Texas in big banner headlines, and I just want to try to stop it once and for all. I'm not joining the Republican Party. I haven't contemplated it and I don't intend to. I have a lot of friends on both sides of the aisle, but I have no intention of leaving the Democratic Party. I'm just trying to put to rest this rumor that's gotten wilder and wilder all across the country. It's just not true and I want to let that be known." [31]

Just as they had other conservative Democrats elsewhere, Texas

Republicans did indeed ask Hall to consider changing parties. Hall responded that he was accustomed to voting according to his conscience and principles; other congressional representatives and the president learned Hall was unmovable. Was he too rigid on certain issues? At least he resisted the politics of persuasion. Becky Hall Palmer explained that people knew "that if he made a stand in an area, he was going to still be standing there when it was over. They weren't going to entice him to do something else. He always tried to do the right thing. Whether that was the popular thing or not was never on his mind. But he wasn't raised that way. He was raised that there was a right and a wrong and that is the way he lived." [32]

Hall's service on the Veterans Affairs committee took him to Southeast Asia a second time in 1981 as part of a congressional delegation comprised of nine representatives (and two spouses), eight members of the press, and five Air Force escorts. They toured refugee camps in Hong Kong and Bangkok, Thailand. Asked about the issue of refugees and immigration upon his return, the congressman forthrightly said that despite the terrible conditions of the camps, the United States could not take everyone in who might want to: "We have no place to put them, and they will not mesh into our society." [33]

As to the refugee camps, Hall insisted that sovereign nations must bear responsibility for the welfare of their people. The camp problems, including starvation, were properly Asian problems and Asians should seek to solve them. He worried that immigrants might bring diseases into the United States. Then there were the Hmong people of Vietnam, who belonged to such a radically different culture Hall thought they could not possibly be assimilated as Americans. [34]

The *International Herald Tribune* quoted Hall as saying that "the United States can't serve as a depository for every person in the world who wishes to leave his country. Word must be sent back that the United States is getting ready to draw the line." An American panel led on a twenty-five-day tour of South East Asia by former Assistant Secretary of State Marshall Green found that most Vietnamese refugees were legitimate, and not everyone wanted to come to the United States. [35]

In mid-year 1982 conservative Democrats cooperated with the Republicans to protect the budget and tax cut programs begun two years before, battling strong Democratic Party support for military spending reductions and increased taxes for funding domestic social programs. In the Ninety-Seventh Congress Hall supported an initiative to improve national defense and approved the sale of defensive weapons to Saudi Arabia, a contentious issue in the House and Senate. The Reagan Administration argued that the measures were necessary to promote stability and peace in the Middle East and stronger arms control agreements with the Soviet Union. Hall supported the Broomfield-Carney-Stratton arms control resolution in August 1982, which would freeze arms numbers at their current limits. He also joined in a resolution to promote and preserve peace and a decisive foreign policy by keeping the military strong. [36]

In the debates on civil defense funding, Hall emphasized the importance of a well-coordinated and funded civil defense program for the United States, particularly as offensive weapons development had overshadowed civil defense. He explained his doubts about American superiority over the Soviets, saying,

> We no longer have the luxury of assured force superiority over the Soviets. Those days are long behind us and it is questionable today whether or not a balance of strategic military power—often referred to as a "rough equivalence"—exists. At best, we can say that, for the present time, the real strength and preparedness of the U.S. strategic Triad remains credible to the Soviet Union. However, the future of relative United States-Soviet strategic balance is cloudy. United States development and deployment of modern strategic weapons just are not keeping pace with the Soviet Union and our defense capability, in the eyes of the Soviets, may be waning. [37]

Hall cited the aging 1950s-era B-52 bomber fleet and the inability of the Intercontinental Ballistic Missile (ICBM) system to counter advances in Soviet missile technology. It was not enough that the submarine-launched ballistic missile force alone was being renovated while the Soviets updated and expanded all of their forces. Although the U.S. had the edge in technology, they were not deploying it, thus giving the advantage to the Soviets. These considerations compelled Congressman Hall to urge American civil defense program expansion because a stronger passive civil defense program would increase the deterrent strength of the entire U.S. defense program. [38]

In his Washington newsletter and elsewhere, Hall lamented the sorry state of American foreign policy and the low regard he saw other countries giving to the United States, as if it were a weak nation, saying,

> If the economy has top priority, then foreign policy can only be a percentage point behind as the Reagan Administration takes office. The state of our foreign policy is in shambles. Pious platitudes, Olympic boycotts and meaningless sanctions are no substitute for strength, resolve and forthrightness in foreign policy....While our State Department badgers and harasses friendly nations about so-

> called "human rights" violations, the Russians destroy human rights, human values, and human lives with everyone they come into contact with. If a nation is perceived as weak it will be treated accordingly....The solution is strong national leadership with emphasis on standing up to aggression, convincing allies of the sureness of our word, and rebuilding our military strength." [39]

Hall was especially contemptuous of policy decisions that made the United States responsible for the disposition of Cubans "boat-lifted" to the United States, many of them prisoners released by the Castro regime. The government proposed an internment site in East Texas, and the prospect of having those former prisoners in Harrison County angered him. His colleague from the Texas Fourth District, Ralph Hall, remembered Hall's response to the government. "One of the first problems I faced as a member of Congress was shoulder to shoulder to Sam," he wrote. "Some parts of our government wanted to put some dissidents from another country who were dangerous criminals, station them in this area of East Texas, and we had a meeting right here in Marshall, Texas, out here on the Interstate. I sat there by Sam as he looked across at the agents and representatives of our own government and said, 'I'm not going to waste any words on you. I'm going to give you three words. You'd better not.' And they didn't." [40]

Hall gained national attention in spring, 1982, when he denounced the atheist Madalyn Murray O'Hair for her opposition to the public funding for chaplains in the Congress. Standing in the House of Representatives, Hall declared, "It's a terrible thing to have to be faced with a creature like Madalyn Murray O'Hair. But I would like—with all the force that I can command, as it be within the power of my being able to say on the floor of this body—to request that Mrs. O'Hair, since she does not believe in hell, immediately go straight to hell and make what determination she can as to what she believes in is true or false." Stunned, the House sat in tense silence. After his comment sank in, the members applauded Hall, thereafter voting 388-0 to approve having a House chaplain to offer prayer. Hall's constituents approved too, among them a Bowie County resident who wrote, "It is a very gratifying feeling to know there are Christian leaders in this country that will stand up for God and for the people that are fighting for the right to believe in our Supreme Being." People with similar convictions easily associated the issue of prayer before the Congress with the exercise of prayer in the schools and the free exercise of faith elsewhere—convictions in complete agreement with Congressman Hall. [41]

In 1981 at the beginning of his third full term of office as a Congressman, Hall became chair of the Veterans Subcommittee on Compensation, Pension, and Insurance, a committee responsible for overseeing a $13.8 billion budget for fiscal year 1982, a significant part of the third-largest government agency in the United States. Hall regarded the assignment a great responsibility and honor. [42]

He continued his service on the Judiciary Committee and the subcommittees on Criminal Justice and Immigration, Refugees and International Law. By 1982 he chaired the Administrative Law subcommittee. On the Immigration Subcommittee, Hall opposed criminal penalties on employers who hired illegal aliens, and failed to get the legislation ejected. On the Judiciary Committee, he supported extension of the Voting Rights Act and endorsed a failed amendment that would grant more authority for voting rights decisions to Southern district judges. He also wanted to eliminate funding for the Legal Services Corporation, which he believed often went beyond its charter responsibilities. A number of bills emerged under his leadership, including one to revise the post-Watergate special prosecutor law, providing higher standards and tighter guidelines for appointment of the special prosecutor. [43]

In mid-1982 Hall became chair of the Judiciary Subcommittee on Administrative Law and Governmental Relations. In June, amid a large slate of deliberations that included bills for appropriations for the Office of Government Ethics and updating the authority of the Secret Service, Hall presided over hearings to determine how to develop a better system of debt repayments to the federal government. The committee also set hearings on government regulatory reform, seeking ways to reduce paperwork and official procedures, especially for small businesses. Hall said, "People are fed up with the number of regulations, government interference, and the enormous costs of regulation." Such reforms were a large part of the Reagan administration legislative program; Hall's committee handled the Regulatory Reform Bill. [44]

Sam B. Hall Jr. had entered office in 1976 inheriting his predecessor's unfinished business, some of which remained unfinished at the end of his own tenure as well, though finally underway in the case of the Cooper Lake project. The major water projects either developed slowly or had been bypassed in Washington. As a new representative, Hall had stated his goal to support the continuation of the Red River Waterway from Shreveport, Louisiana, to Daingerfield, Texas, and the funding of an authorized project that had been delayed twenty years: the "channelization" project from Cooper, Texas, to Texarkana. [45]

The Cooper Lake Reservoir Project was authorized in August 1955 while Wright Patman served in Congress, but in 1978 a court injunction halted the process that had already been prolonged over twenty-five years. Population growth in the region around the Cooper Lake site assured rising water demands, and the various city councils and the Sulphur River

Municipal Water District sought relief from the injunction in the early eighties. [46]

The Committee to Save Northeast Texas filed a class action suit against two environmental groups opposed to the Cooper Lake development—the Texas Committee on Natural Resources and the Sulphur River Heritage Society. Flooding problems, extended local costs on the delayed project, and the loss of taxes provoked the lawsuit. In July, 1982, Congressman Hall testified before the Congressional Subcommittee on Water Resources about the Cooper Project and other water resources projects in his district. He noted the years of delay, the appropriation of $30 million for the project, and the delays since 1971 based on environmental litigation. The Cooper Lake project aroused frustrations. Speaking later at Commerce, Texas, Hall declared everyone had been talking about Cooper "since Judge [William Wayne] Justice was a child." Referring to his earlier comments around the district, he reminded people that he had said, "We're going to build that lake if it hairlips [sic] every dog in Texas." He continued efforts to get the government to fund the Cooper Lake project throughout his successive terms of office, leaving with the project incomplete, but with actual construction soon to come. The transfer of authority for the project from the New Orleans to Forth Worth office of the U.S. Army Corps of Engineers facilitated its start. He had local support from Walter "Punk" Helm, the president of the Sulphur River Municipal Water District. [47]

As Sam B. Hall Jr. approached the 1982 election, he had the overwhelming support of East Texas voters. Especially during difficult political times when conservative areas of the country had felt ignored, Hall's emphasis on service, along with the hope conservatives placed on the Reagan leadership, bolstered his political capital. His supporters held a campaign fund-raising dinner and rally in March, 1982, at the Marshall Civic Center. It included twelve congressional guests: the Texans were the House Majority leader Jim Wright, J. J. (James Jarrell) "Jake" Pickle, Charles Wilson, Jack Hightower, Marvin Leath, Jack Fields, and Charles Stenholm; the others were G. V. "Sonny" Montgomery of Mississippi, Bill Nichols of Alabama, Bill Hefner of North Carolina, and Charles E. "Buddy" Roemer of Louisiana. As was typical of many political gatherings, there was a heavy dose of levity and plenty of commentary: Marvin Leath played guitar with the Cypress Creek Band and dedicated a song to Hall: "O, Lord, It's Hard to be Humble." Bill Hefner of North Carolina revived his professional career as an entertainer, telling well-received jokes, and singing a variety of traditional and patriotic songs, including "Dixie" and "Amazing Grace." After the event, Congressman Hall got media criticism in what Roger Cramer of the *Marshall News Messenger* called "the nonstory of the week," about gifts to the fourteen congressmen who attended the Hall appreciation and fund-raising dinner.

Having received mementoes and gifts when he attended similar events for other congressional representatives in their districts, he reciprocated by giving each of his colleagues a rifle. The gifts were legitimate campaign expenses, given as a "common courtesy," and Hall had already checked with the Federal Election Commission before he acted to purchase them with campaign funds, which, said Cramer, were entirely to be spent at the discretion of the candidate as they were private, not public, funds. [48]

Typically, the turnover in Congress is high, with some representatives staying but one term as voters' preferences and other factors discourage long tenures, though many representatives stay for several decades. The real continuity in congressional work thus comes from the staff; strongly put, the work requires enormous cooperation, and the representative can accomplish little without their help. In mid-1976 Hall inherited the Patman office staff and later began his first full term with that staff mostly intact. After Hall won in the November election, his long-time secretary Sue Jordan came to Washington, arriving in December. She drove from Texas, pulling a U-Haul trailer, and among the first things she did was to go shopping with Madeleine for a long coat and boots, items she had not needed in the relatively milder East Texas winters. [49]

In 1977 Hall's staff included Administrative Assistant Baron Shacklette, Legislative Assistant James H. Muckleroy Jr., Secretaries Dorothy Councill and Sue Jordan, and other staff members Adrienne Anderson, Dennis Braddock, Susan Driggers, Linda McKee, Mary Jane Merritts, Albert Oetken as a legislative assistant, Joanna O'Rourke, and Sue Ann Ray. The district office in Marshall had Alice Thomas and Bishop Curry; the Paris office, Doris Wright, and, in Texarkana, Nell King. James Muckleroy moved to the Marshall office in 1978. Ken Black was the Administrative Assistant in Washington by 1979, and Ann Strickland had joined that office. By 1981, Barbara Cart was working as a legislative assistant, and Janet Dameron and Cindy Levings were caseworkers. Kathleen Tobin handled legislative correspondence, and Patti Byford dealt with government projects. W. H. "Harold" Taylor had joined the Marshall office as a field assistant. By 1983, some staff members had moved on, and others replaced them. A string of congressional interns passed through the office as well. Clearly, Hall's staff expanded by a few persons by the time he had been serving five years, and they stayed busy. [50]

Hall's congressional office revealed distinctive traits of his personality and character. It started with the selection of his staff and his loyalty toward them, continued with his personal secretary, Sue Jordan, and extended to those who spent the least amount of time with his office, the student interns. The interns were responsible to Sue Jordan, whom they called "our mother." She took them on as friends and charges, making sure they were properly housed, fed and occupied. [51]

The son of Ray and Mona Lawson and a neighbor to the Halls in Marshall, David Lawson described Sue Jordan as a proactive administrator who often anticipated Hall's requests and activities, inquiring about various matters in order to complement the congressman's preparation. Jordan always prepared well for her congressman; some have said that Hall would have been nothing in the Congress without her. [52]

Jordan was a top-notch secretary and office manager, though she served primarily as Hall's personal secretary while Dorothy Councill managed the office. She was kind, but firm, as in one instance when a well-known network television anchorman came to interview Hall about his role as a Boll Weevil and his voting as a Democrat for the Reagan tax reform bill. When asked to wait, the anchorman insinuated that a person of his stature could not be kept waiting and demanded to see the congressman. Jordan responded that Hall was dealing with an important matter—the newsman would have to wait his turn. Apparently regarding his schedule more important than the interview, he left in a huff. [53]

Hall's office habits set a high benchmark. On principle, he personally signed all outgoing correspondence. If there was a return address, even the hundreds of post cards sent out by lobbying organizations got a response letter acknowledging the card, stating that Hall was taking note of their concerns and considering his response, if necessary. Interns for other representatives marveled that Hall personally signed all his correspondence instead of having the staff members use automatic signature machines. He proofread his letters and added handwritten comments. Inefficient, perhaps, but he considered his personal attention to correspondence the best kind of responsibility to his constituency. [54]

Congressman Hall was both compulsive and principled about making sure he had completed the day's work before he left the office each evening, at times in the early morning hours. He kept up with meetings and daily issues using five-by-seven inch note cards prepared for him. He managed his correspondence and other matters as he could throughout the day, often late into the evening. There were four mail deliveries per day, each averaging between 25 and 75 pieces of mail. The interns ferried mail and his responses between the office and House floor during sessions. In the evenings Hall also made telephone calls and studied proposed legislation or committee matters, not leaving before his desk was cleared for the next day's work. [55]

Most congressional offices hire interns for short-term work. Hall's interns confessed their excitement about being able to serve, but also about the particular attention they received. Hall liked to involve college interns between their freshman and sophomore years who had an interest in politics and law, though that was not mandatory. Interns generally considered service with Hall desirable because he treated them well and took a personal interest in them, making sure they had a positive and challenging experience. As an example of his fairness, Hall actually used the funds appropriated for the internship program to pay them, which not all congressional representatives did. Some diverted those funds to other purposes, using students who would work for the privilege and experience without pay, which eliminated students of modest means who could not afford to live and work in Washington on their own or their parents' money. Students from modest economic backgrounds had a chance with Hall's office. [56]

Other conditions made service with Hall a coveted thing. He routinely took one or two interns home for dinner and conversation. They accompanied him to functions not typically available to interns, such as lunch caucuses to which Members of Congress could bring political contributors, and to parts of the Capitol typically restricted to the representatives and select staff members. Walt Sears, Mike Coker, Mike Sandlin, and perhaps another intern accompanied Hall to the Texas Democratic delegation luncheon—they were the only interns there. They went on special White House tours and to Arlington Cemetery for closed session ceremonies, which were rare and coveted opportunities. They attended subcommittee meetings, and Congressman Hall made sure that each intern's name was entered into the *Federal Record* at least once as having attended these meetings. The point was not lost: Hall considered them important people. They should learn by doing far more than clerical and filing work, and they should receive proper respect and appreciation, as they and their parents ideally would want them to be treated. He personally taught them what was important about his work, the capital and the nation. [57]

David Lawson of Marshall, Texas, enjoyed watching the political processes in Washington during his internship. Even making the numerous daily mail runs and conveying messages between the office and Congressman Hall allowed new experiences that made strong impressions. His duties took him in and out of rooms where committees met before a full audience; the Judiciary Committee hearings were most memorable. He met numerous influential people. One day the congressman handed him the keys to his car and sent him and Sue Jordan to National Airport to pick up Abner McCall, who was president of Baylor University in Waco, Hall's former law professor at Baylor Law School and a longtime friend. He remembered the day Senator Strom Thurmond of South Carolina mistakenly entered a meeting of the Texas congressional delegation and commented that he must be in the wrong room but thought Texans were great, second only to South Carolinians. [58]

Hall expected the interns to taste the calling to greater public service. Years after his internship, Michael Sandlin met Hall, who asked what he was doing to make things better, "What are you doing for the public; what are you doing to make things better for everybody else?" Hall understood that service was the criterion for significance. Hall's predecessor, Wright Patman, had excelled in the *quid pro quo*, the give and take that lubricates the political process. Hall's friends and supporters believed Hall was capable of such give and take, but only to the limits of principle, friendship, and service. Consequently, his constituents honored him as a real friend who shared common concerns with them. Those who never met him supported him because of his reputation for representing what they valued and admired. [59]

Judge Robert Parker assessed the Congressional service of his longtime friend with these words, "If you take the entire makeup of what Sam Hall Jr. was, he more naturally fit the role of Congressman than any of his other careers. He had a wonderful way with people. He had a wonderful way of instilling confidence in people. He was philosophically attuned to the people of the First Congressional District." Hall was not elected to be a leading legislator and party leader. His district "wanted a congressman they were comfortable with and somebody who was approachable and that they could contact. They could get a response and feel like the congressman was interested in them. Hall certainly filled that role." [60]

10

Ninety-Eighth & Ninety-Ninth Congresses, 1983-1985

I still get mad at people when they refer to "all those crooks in Washington." When I tell them they don't know what they are talking about, they just smirk and ask me how I know any different. I just tell them that I used to know a Congressman that wasn't a crook. He voted his heart and not his party. If he thought you were wrong, he would try to convince you he was right, whether it was popular or not. Had he voted with the Democratic Party more often, he might have had a more "prestigious" Congressional career. He might have been placed on a more powerful committee or he may even have been chairman of one of those committees. But Pop wasn't there for that. He was there so the people in Harleton and New Boston would have someone fighting for them. He didn't just preach Patriotism, he lived it. — Chase Palmer [1]

Having won the 1982 election with 98 per cent of the vote over Libertarian John Traylor, Hall returned for the Ninety-eighth Congress declaring that the new Congress had to correct the mistakes of the old one. The gasoline tax bill that discriminated against the trucking industry had to go. The IRS should not be able to direct financial institutions to withhold 10 per cent of interest dividends for income taxes; he had always rejected that. The Members of Congress should not have received a pay increase. On the other hand, President Reagan's proposals to build up the military during the next five years deserved support, though more liberal Democrats worked to limit increases in military spending. Hall supported the Fiscal Year 1984 Defense Authorization Bill, and continued to support any measures that would influence weapons negotiations with the Soviets at Geneva. Hall was at odds with the House Democratic Party leadership in his vote against the Wright-Perkins amendment to the Fiscal Year 1984 Continuing Resolution, which he believed would increase inflation and the deficit. [2]

Hall thought the new GI bill within the 1984 Defense Authorization Act would help to attract the best enlistees in the All-Volunteer Force. Apart from the Middle East in United States foreign policy and immigration policy, budgetary matters always concerned Hall, who still considered the government un-businesslike and wasteful. A more immediate evil was the drug problem, and better funding of drug enforcement programs was crucial because of the immensity of the law enforcement efforts that would be required. [3]

Hall's appointment to the House Select Committee on Narcotics Abuse and Control in March 1983 was appropriate to his emphasis on keeping illegal drugs out of the country, "clamping down on the filthy vermin who make their living pushing those drugs, especially to our young people." He attributed the high crime rate and the pressures on law enforcement to the rise in narcotics and other illicit drugs. [4]

By 1983 the Boll Weevils appeared to have lost influence, as moderate and liberal Democrats gained twenty-six seats in the House in the 1982 congressional elections, taking influence away from the Conservative Democratic Forum. One consequence was that the Democrats won by a significant margin in the January budget vote. [5]

During the 1983 session, Hall dealt with a perennial economic issue in East Texas. Lone Star Steel, a major employer in the First District, experienced setbacks due to trade policies limiting imports of tubular steel like the kind heavily used in domestic oilfields. Tubular steel imports were less heavily limited than other steel under trade rules and agreements, and Lone Star had to compete against tubular steel imported from Europe. After decreased demand for several years, the Europeans had not significantly reduced their exports to the United States, thus the domestic steel business was being depressed, and East Texans were losing jobs. In September 1983 Hall introduced The Fair Trade in Steel Pipe and Tube Products Act of 1983. Not a protectionist bill according to Hall, "it simply restores a measure of fairness to an area of our trade policy which is currently open to abuse by our European trading partners." He urged legislation to allow enforcement of existing and recently completed trade agreements between the United States and the European Community. Before adjourning in late 1984, the Congress ultimately passed a comprehensive trade bill that afforded protection to American industry, though not as much from Asian steel producers. [6]

On June 12, 1984, Representative Hall saw his two amendments to the Simpson-Mazzoli immigration bill (The Immigration Reform and Control Act of 1983) passed in the House of Representatives. These were positive votes, but he still wanted to remove provisions that would reward "illegality over legality with the current amnesty provision," making it too easy for illegal aliens in the United States before January 1, 1982, to apply for citizenship. He wanted to toughen employer sanctions for hiring illegal immigrants. Hall warned about the probable high costs that would be created as many illegal aliens became citizens and thus eligible for welfare assistance. [7]

House partisanship ruled in January 1983 when the Democratic Steering and Policy Committee dropped Representative William Philip "Phil" Gramm of Texas from the House Budget Committee. Always outspoken, Gramm had boldly supported the president's economic policies. Hall considered the Steering Committee decision bad policy; the leadership would "rue the day they did it." Gramm considered either changing parties or resigning and running for reelection as a Republican. Hall hoped neither would be the case. Gramm disappointed the other thirty-eight Conservative Democratic Forum members by resigning and seeking reelection as a Republican. Representative Charles Stenholm observed that Gramm had charted his own course some time previous: "He chose to paddle his own canoe and now he has chosen to change boats." Gramm found vindication in his district, however, winning re-election as a Republican in 1983 and subsequently election to the Senate in 1984. [8]

In the same session of Congress, Hall gave heartfelt attention to the Veterans Administration as a member of the Oversight Committee of the House Veterans Affairs Committee. He was involved in an investigation of the Veterans hospitals and medical system, which he found "grotesquely inefficient and wasteful." [9]

The Soviet attack and destruction of Korean Air Lines Flight 007 in September 1983 incensed the Congress and prompted Hall to denounce the Soviets for their action. The plane crash killed 269 persons, 60 of them Americans. [10]

In the House of Representatives Hall declared,

> Mr. Speaker, Funk and Wagnalls Standard Dictionary defines "base" as low in sentiment, morals—low in rank, cheap, contemptible, degraded, despicable, ignobile [sic], infamous, low minded, mean, miserable, shabby, sneaking, sordid, squalid, vile, worthless, wretched.
>
> Those are only a few of the words that express my utter contempt and revulsion for the Soviet Union by reason of

> their dastardly and inhuman action in shooting down Korean flight 007. The Soviets should never be allowed to forget this illegal and cowardly act.
>
> I would hope that every Soviet leader in the United States and those around the world would read the CONGRESSIONAL RECORD of this Congress in order that they might learn firsthand just how low in esteem they are held by this Congress and by the people of the United States of America. [11]

Hall expressed his displeasure more strongly during the next session of debate on the House Foreign Affairs committee resolution of condemnation:

> I think that the first thing we should do in discussing and thinking about something of this nature is to think about the nature of the beast that is on the other side of this picture. The nature of the beast here is a murderer and a liar and a thug.
>
> Now you can dress them up, you can put them before a camera and you can have them sitting down and talking about peaceful means; but you must keep in mind that you are dealing with murderers, thugs and crooks. In my part of the country, you desire to deal with those people in a way that we cannot deal with them today, but we would certainly deal with them in a way different in many respects from what we are hearing.
>
> ... In my district [this] is all the people are talking about. They are mad, they are furious, they want us to do something, and they want us to know that they stand behind what this Congress does 100 per cent. I think that if we can galvanize that kind of public opinion against these thugs, murderers and outlaws, something good could come out of this. Now, I do not believe that anyone who has reached the age of accountability can come before this Congress and say that we do not have sufficient strength in order to combat what they have, because people who do what these people did raises the question—what will the second time around bring to the American people? [12]

With these matters in mind, in September 1983 Hall supported the defense bill containing approval for the MX missile, the B-1 bomber, the Pershing missile, and other weapons projects. He wanted to stand with other members of the Congress not only in denouncing the Soviets, but to show them that the United States planned to strengthen its defensive and offensive weapons programs.

International events hardened Hall's attitude about the Soviets and America's military strength. He considered the Soviet Union a continuing menace. The Korean Air Lines incident was in the background of Hall's support for a $187.5 billion defense bill for 1984, particularly the provisions for the MX missile and B-1 bomber. In April 1984 his commitment to strong national defense forces won for him the Leadership Award from the Coalition for Peace Through Strength, which was associated with the American Legion Auxiliary. [13]

During the Lebanese civil war, the United States Marines were deployed in Lebanon as part of a multinational peacekeeping force. The deployment was to be temporary, with no combat involved. Amid a cease-fire beginning in September,1982, American servicemen remained at risk and under frequent attack. On October 23, 1983, the Marine barracks in Beirut suffered a massive car bomb attack which killed 241 Marines and wounded eighty more.

In late October, 1983, Sam Hall joined ten other congressmen on an inspection tour of the Marine barracks site in Lebanon. Afterwards the delegation visited the hospital in Germany where the injured Marines were under care. Hall was angered that the Marines had been limited in their ability to defend themselves; the deaths of the servicemen bombed in their barracks weighed heavily on him. Hall considered the United Nations Resolution 521 regarding the Multinational Force to be a useless, failed agreement. It gave every advantage to the violent Lebanese factions and made the American forces "sitting ducks." He thought that the "mission to keep the peace and end the violence was destined from the beginning to end in failure." The United States needed to reconsider their participation in the Multinational Force and take wiser steps to protect American troops. The existing situation was intolerable, however, and Hall favored a gradual withdrawal of troops. The officers and enlisted men on duty in Lebanon had assessed their situation as "vulnerable," he said. "They are in an impossible situation."[14]

The diplomacy of the United States was a sore point for Hall because some nations evinced hostility or an unwillingness to cooperate. As before, he criticized the practice of the United States to send foreign aid to Third World nations he considered contemptuous of the United States. "I think we spend entirely too much money on these foreign countries that don't give a continental you-know-what about us. I say if they're not friends of ours—shut the money off."[15]

Hardly anything incensed Hall more than Cuba's manipulation of the drug trade and interference in Central America. He held Fidel Castro's regime responsible for using violence to export revolution, which included smuggling drugs into the United States. There was a connection with the Cuban release of numerous criminals from prison so that they could enter the United States with a wave of refugees, all at great expense to the country. The way to deal with the criminals was to deport them, returning them to Cuba. In addition, Hall supported holding the Cuban soldiers captured during the Grenada campaign until Castro took the criminals back, and he co-sponsored a resolution to that effect. He regarded Cuba and the Soviet KGB to be firmly behind international narcotics trafficking and the Cuban criminals in the United States a part of the system. The Cubans used drug money to sponsor Central American terrorism, particularly in Nicaragua, with the ultimate intention of bringing harm to the United States. He put it this way: "The next time you hear some national spokesman, including a Member of Congress or two, telling us that the Nicaraguan government is a bunch of nice guys, don't believe it. That government believes in violent revolution, and it is trying to destroy the moral fabric of our nation with dangerous drugs." Hall also linked Cuba to the Colombian drug business and to the use of Nicaragua as a staging area for communist guerillas under Soviet and Cuban sponsorship. He clearly supported the Reagan administration's efforts to deal with Nicaragua. As a member of the House Subcommittee on Narcotics and Drug Abuse, he also wanted to see the laws enforced stringently and the young people of the United States educated properly about the dangers of drug use. More than anything, he wanted the United States government to stand up against the Cubans, the Soviets, and any other countries involved in the drug threat.[16]

Representative Hall held a deeply conservative view regarding prayer in the public schools. Citing a formidable public majority supporting a constitutional amendment to allow prayer, he approved vocal prayer in the schools and in 1984 voted for a constitutional amendment to permit it. [17]

With the Democratic House leadership confining the amendment to committee, Hall signed a discharge petition to force the amendment to the floor of the House for a vote and participated in an all-night session in which representatives expressed their support for a constitutional amendment. His sentiments were expressed in his view that,

> Frankly, it is absolutely incredible that we should even be placed in the situation of having to argue for a right that so many have fought and died for—namely—to pray to the Almighty. Acceptance of a Divine Being is a principal basis of our development as a nation, and it is offensive for any court of law to arbitrarily strike this core of our existence from the national purpose.

The Constitution of the United States guarantees

> freedom of religion. It does not prescribe freedom from religion. The Founding Fathers in their infinite wisdom were justifiably concerned about state-established denominations. This is why the debate at the Constitutional Convention leading up to the establishment clause of the first amendment was among the most important of the entire Constitution. The foresight and genius of the establishment clause has truly given us religious freedom. If any nation in the history of the world ever had freedom of religion, then certainly it is the United States of America.

The founders of the United States were not neutral about religion, Hall insisted; moreover, they consciously sought divine direction in establishing the nation, saying, "If anything is clear about our early days as a nation, it's the proposition that God's blessing was constantly sought as we battled to become independent and free. The founding fathers wanted the American people to be one nation under God. Therefore, from the earliest days our mottoes, coinage, seals, courts, legislatures, civic functions, and, yes, our schools, all sanctioned the name of God and recognized His existence."[18]

With his arguments Hall struck at the contentious debates about identifying the United States as a Christian versus a secular nation. His claims for the pervasiveness and predominance of Christian culture and belief in earlier America resonated with many Americans. Hall's sentiments on school prayer were sincere expressions of his faith in God and in the United States of America, which he considered the remarkable product of the "infinite" wisdom of the founding fathers and the Constitution.

Hall castigated the 1962 Supreme Court decision in *Engel* v. *Vitale* because he thought it replaced genuine freedom with a legal restriction on religion, while ironically permitting any other conceivable exercise of constitutional freedoms. "The High Court started this business by blatantly making law, by failing to exercise judicial restraint, and by establishing a bad precedent in law that has given rise to all sorts of frivolous court suits dealing with the mere mention of providence in our ordinary lives." He denounced the Supreme Court for granting the demands of a minority while revoking an essential right of the majority, establishing in fact a "tyranny over the majority" such as the Constitution had never allowed. *Engel* v. *Vitale* had negative consequences for American schools and school children, and the nation needed the prayer amendment "to rekindle respect for authority in schools. It is needed to remind us all that faith, devotion and adherence to a higher order is to be desired over adherence to the temporary materialistic whims of the times." The Supreme Court had "legislated," and now was the time for the Congress to legislate, "to give democracy a chance to work."[19]

In view of the mandate for a prayer amendment from the majority of Americans, the Congressman Hall considered prejudiced the "dilatory" obstruction of debate and a vote on the matter. He held that the amendment would not establish any religion, but would reaffirm "the establishment clause of the First Amendment by confirming what the forefathers had in mind. It represents a return to the legal norm that kept us in good stead until that norm was thrust aside by bad law and bad precedent."[20]

In a radio message, Congressman Hall told how the communist government of Poland had prohibited prayer, telling the Polish people "that the United States Government does not allow prayer in American schools. Therefore, no prayer is needed in Polish schools." He found it an "unbelievable irony" that in "the citadel of liberty and freedom" children were "denied the right to recite a prayer in public schools." It was painfully ironic that a Communist government was able to use the American example as a means of repression. He declared, "instead of hope and inspiration, our federal courts, and yes, our Congress, set a bad example for Poland and other nations who are in chains." Hall doubted the prayer amendment would be passed. [21]

The amendment did fail in the House of Representatives, 215-194, but the House did subsequently vote to approve "voluntary, silent, non-official prayer." And Hall supported the measure for equal access of religious groups to the use of school facilities, which passed overwhelmingly in the House. [22]

At the midpoint of his last full term in office, the media recognized Hall as the Texas representative most successful in getting his bills passed in the House. Eventually, six of the thirty-nine bills Hall sponsored in 1983 and 1984 became law. The Senate passed another, the Ethics in Government bill, in another form. Three of his bills came out of the Subcommittee on Administrative Law and Governmental Relations and concerned claims settlements from the government. [23]

In November, 1984, Charles Stenholm, others in the Texas delegation, and the Conservative Democratic Caucus, the Boll Weevils, organized an effort to unseat Tip O'Neill as Speaker of the House of Representatives. It was a clear attempt to achieve a more conservative direction for the Democratic Party. Hall was considered a possible nominee for Speaker. Ralph Hall had asked him to consider it. He refused but supported Stenholm's candidacy. He added, "I love Tip, but he and I just don't see eye to eye. He doesn't speak for Democrats." [24]

The Conservative Democratic Caucus also disliked the Democratic Party's presidential and vice-presidential ticket of Walter Mondale and Geraldine Ferraro in 1984. Among other things, Ferraro's support for natural gas deregulation alienated Texas voters and prompted opposition from Hall and others. About the Democratic platform, Hall said, "I'm a Democrat, but they've got some things that are far and away against the best interests of Texas. I want to support them, but I've got to tongue-in-cheek it for a while." He disagreed with the Democratic Party stance on windfall profits taxes, defense, and the gay rights issue: "They support lesbian and gay rights, and I don't think those people ought to be recognized." He gave the national Democrats little hope for support in the Texas First District. [25]

In his final term before resigning to take the federal bench, Hall continued with his committee assignments, staying in fourth position on Veterans Affairs, rising to fourth on the subcommittee on Oversight and Investigations, and keeping the same position on Compensation, Pension, and Insurance. The Immigration and Naturalization subcommittee continued to debate the question of government compensation for Japanese Americans interned by the government during World War II. Hall considered better monitoring of military defense spending an important part of assuring the efficient use of funds, especially in spare parts: "It's going to be a big job. After all, one military aircraft can contain thousands of parts. Think of the F-16 fighter as 75,000 parts flying in close formation." [26]

Hall enjoyed the endorsement of the U.S. Chamber of Commerce in 1984 because of his pro-business voting record in Congress. In early 1985 Texas Republicans considered the First District a possible target for their party. The Democratic State senator from Texarkana, Ed Howard, was thought to be a possible challenger in the 1986 Democratic primary, but he declared he had no intention to mount a challenge to Hall. The Republican challenger Edd Hargett would be a more viable candidate along with others such as Judge Ed Miller from Bowie County and Jim McWilliams, the Democratic state representative from Marshall.[27]

One can get some sense of Hall's manner of speaking in the Congress from the tape of a speech he made in association with a Crime Bill:

> I've been listening to this debate for 4 years, going back into the time when Father Drinan headed this subcommittee [Subcommittee on Criminal Justice], and what I've heard here today reminds me of two brama [sic] bulls looking at each other through a plank fence, jealously guarding their domain. I think what we have heard here today has nothing whatsoever to do with substance, and I think it is time for this body to act. If we stay here another 3 years [It makes no difference how long we stay (taped transcription text)] we will never come up with a bill that satisfies everyone.
>
> We have 24 items today that should be voted upon; [we've got twenty-four items that] we should not allow the American people to believe that we cannot, as reasonable

> men and women, come together and work out our differences.
>
> Now, everybody on both sides of the aisle knows that this bill is going to pass. It is going to pass by a big vote. So why sit here and quibble? Why sit here and look at each other through a plank fence and try to decide who is right and who is wrong? Let us get to the end of it. Let us vote [on] this bill. Let us go to conference and work out the differences. [28]

Legislation late in his final term included Hall's introduction of a bill that would put farm credit banks under local control, a proposal that drew criticism from Roy A. Seburg Jr., chairman of the board of the Farm Credit Banks of Texas. Among the latest resolutions Hall cosponsored was that to proclaim "Mule Appreciation Day" for October 26, 1985. He received the President's Award from the National Association of State Directors of Veterans Affairs for his exemplary work in support of Veterans issues and legislation. Late in May he received an award from the Federal Administrative Law Judges Conference, the Award of Merit, in recognition of his detailed and effective work as a member of the House Judiciary Committee. [29]

During the spring, Hall had consented to accept a judicial nomination. After his confirmation as a federal judge in early May, he set his resignation for May 27, 1985, in order to close his office in Washington and complete legislative responsibilities, thus unintentionally slowing the process toward the special election to fill his vacated seat in Congress. President Reagan's return from Europe and Senate business also had delayed the confirmation. Hall submitted his resignation letters to House Speaker Tip O'Neill and to Governor Mark White of Texas. [30]

Representative Hall thrived in the camaraderie of the Congress and added richly to the experience of other Members. One was Congressman Joe Waggonner who had worked closely with Wright Patman in the Texas congressional district just to the west of his in Louisiana. Sam Hall was just the right person to succeed Patman, and from the start Waggonner knew he was right to support Hall. "After I retired from the United States House of Representatives," Waggoner wrote, "I was asked from time to time, 'Who's your Congressman, Joe?' I always replied with a smile and a chuckle, 'Sam Hall.' People were confounded by my response since I am a lifelong resident of Louisiana and Sam represented the First Congressional District of Texas." [31]

Waggonner and the Halls lived in the same apartment building in Crystal City, Alexandria, Virginia. Waggonner and Hall often flew together between Shreveport and Washington, and their friendship grew with the hours of travel they shared. Hall once declared, "We wore out seats 3 and

Hall presents Texas cufflinks to President Ronald Reagan, June 3, 1981.

The Halls with President Reagan – The White House Oval Office, July 12, 1983. L-R: President Reagan, Representative Hall, Chase Palmer, Madeleine Hall, Rebecca Palmer, Amanda Wynn, and Becky Palmer.

Representative Hall extends his hand to President Reagan at the Joint Session of Congress on February 6, 1985. Other individuals in the picture are Congressman Bill Hughes, Supreme Court Justice Blackmun, Supreme Court Justice Rehnquist (portion of head shown in the upper right-hand corner), Senator Bob Dole, and Congressmen Mickey Edwards, Ralph Regula, Jim Wright, Bob Michel, John Porter, and Bill Whitehurst.

On May 23, 1985, Hall submitted his resignation as a Member of Congress to the Honorable Thomas P. "Tip" O'Neill Jr., Speaker of the U. S. House of Representatives.

In October 1981 Hall traveled with a congressional delegation to inspect the Marine barracks that had been bombed in Beirut, Lebanon, and to visit hospitalized Marines in Germany.

3-A on Delta going back and forth from Shreveport to Washington." The Hall family loved Waggonner. Hall told Waggonner that Sandra had declared if anything should happen to her parents, "Don't worry about me. I'll just go live with Joe Waggonner. Will me to Joe." Waggonner wrote, "Sam did not know it, but he just paid me one of the biggest compliments of my life." [32]

And there was Charles E. "Buddy" Roemer III. The businessman became a congressman for Louisiana's fourth district in the 1980s, after Waggoner retired. Later, as Louisiana governor, he left the Democratic Party and joined the Republicans. In his business activities Roemer had observed Hall's career and heard favorable comments about Hall from business people in East Texas. Consequently, he admired and respected Hall long before he met him in late 1980, soon after he won election to Congress.

Roemer flew frequently with Hall to and from Washington, so they became good friends and quite knowledgeable about each other. The younger Roemer found Hall to be a respectful conversationalist and listener. Their common geographical and philosophical concerns enhanced the relationship and helped to place them among the conservative Democrats called the "Boll Weevils." Roemer supported a conservative agenda and rather consistently spurned the positions of the national Democratic leadership. So there was a substantial base of agreement between Roemer, the greater group of conservative Southern Democrats, and Sam B. Hall Jr. [33]

Among the strongest leadership in the Boll Weevil caucus were Charles Stenholm, Roemer, Sam Hall, G. V. "Sonny" Montgomery, and Phil Gramm. The success of the caucus increased the Democratic Party pressure on its members, who clearly understood how the Party leadership exercised punishment by limiting appointments to choice committees or appointing people to committees not well suited to their backgrounds and talents. Roemer suspected that the leadership was reluctant to punish Hall as he garnered too much respect in the Congress. "They would jump on me because I'm new and I'm loud and to hell with them! That's my attitude. But Sam got his way without ever saying to hell with them; that's pretty effective in politics." [34]

The work of the conservative caucus added hours to each working day, which was already too full with committees, constituent services, speeches, and debates on the House floor, but Sam Hall made those meetings. "You find out who will work and who's just hot air," said Roemer. "And Sonny Montgomery was one of those who I put at the top of my fingers of a single hand list along with Sam." [35]

The attitude of respect others had for him was a measure of Hall's effectiveness as a congressional representative. As Roemer put it, "What the hall does when a member rises to speak is another clue. How many times did I see Sam get to his feet and the room quiet down? You don't have to fuzzy up what you are going to write about when it comes down to the respect that people had for him. It was real. It was genuine. It was across the board. It didn't have anything to do with what Sam had done for you politically. It had to do with the way Sam treated you personally. Sam was genuinely personal—very rare, very rare." [36]

Texas Breakfast Club, Thursday, September 22, 1977. L-R: Rep W. R. Poage, Rep. George Mahon, Rep. Ray Roberts, John Ben Shepperd of Odessa, Texas, Rep. Jack Hightower, Rep. Dick White, Rep. Jake Pickle, and Rep. Sam Hall.

Congressman Hall announced in November, 1984, as the candidate of the Conservative Democratic Forum, or "Boll Weevils."

Sonny Montgomery said, "Sam was down to earth, yet he was very intelligent and could analyze legislation and also analyze the Member that was handling the bill." Congressman J. J. "Jake" Pickle of Texas recalled Hall as an excellent representative who grew more valuable with each year of service, writing, "He grew into a deep appreciation of the individual member's personal life. He developed personal friends and learned to understand the member's background, training and experiences during life. He was as interested in the character and integrity of the individual as he was in the legislation being considered, although he was an outstanding student of the law. He made dear friends, and he liked to belong to his group of friends."[37]

Hall's friends in Congress were not a somber group. Kent Hance, in particular, loved practical jokes. He described a moderately elaborate prank he played on Hall:

> One day I called his office and disguised my voice, pretending that I was the manager of delivery for the bus station. I informed his staff that I had several boxes of baby chickens for delivery to Congressman Hall. I first visited with Sue Jordan, and she passed me on to some other aide, who finally let me talk to the Congressman. He quizzed me about the chickens, and I told him they had to be delivered either to his office or to his house. He asked, "Are they addressed specifically to me? Do they have my name, Sam

Sam Hall and Congressman Joe Waggonner of Louisiana.

B. Hall, on the box?" And I said, "No, but they're yours." He then asked me, "How do you know they belong to me?" And I said, "Because on the box it says, 'To the Biggest Chicken S— in Washington.'" At that time he burst out laughing and asked, "Who is this?" After that, we had a running joke about how his chickens were doing."[38]

Hall in fact recounted the story at the ceremony to unveil his portrait as a federal judge, adding an aftermath about how Tommy Whaley, a Marshall businessman, fell into Hance's conspiracy to follow up on the deed. About eleven or twelve years after the first event, Judge and Mrs. Hall arrived home late at night to find a dozen chicks, "a twenty-five pound sack of baby chicken feed, watering and feed troughs for the chickens." It was "from a friend," and Hall knew very well who the friend was. He decided to keep it quiet, gave the chickens and feed to a friend who could use them, and waited to see how long Hance could stay quiet. "Well, we didn't say a word about it," Hall said. "In about two or three days, Tommy Whaley walks in the office and he said, 'For God's sake, call Kent Hance. He's about to go crazy on those chickens—says he has heard nothing from you.'" Whaley admitted to buying the chickens for Hance and delivering them to the Halls' porch. [39]

Charles Stenholm of Texas first entered Congress in January, 1979, where he found Sam Hall already well established with a reputation as "a sound and reliable legislator. Stenholm wrote, "I realized early on that he was a man of great character and sound judgment. Primarily, Sam was a representative of the people and, as I was a freshman congressman from West Texas, he was an excellent role model for me. Sam Hall was the epitome of what a Member of Congress should be." [40]

After Hall became a federal judge, he loved to reminisce about his time in the House of Representatives. He explained to Arthur Wesley of Jefferson, Texas, how impressed he was that the black members of the House represented over three-fourths of the African-Americans who had served in that body in the twentieth century, and he kept emphasizing his belief that knowledge and decency were not matters of one's color. He left it perfectly clear he enjoyed all the relationships in the House, and one of his favorite relationships was with Barbara Jordan of Texas; they spoke the same language even if their politics differed. [41]

Congressman and later U.S. Ambassador Robert Krueger formed a high estimate of Hall during their time together in the House of Representatives. Krueger brought together his observations and recollections of Hall and his friendship with Jordan:

> When I think of Sam, the first picture that comes to mind is of a large, chesty, imposing figure, most often found sitting three or four rows down along the center aisle of the House of Representatives. Sam sat either next to the aisle, or one seat in. Whereas some members of Congress choose to spend a great deal of time either in their committee meetings or in their offices, Sam spent considerable time on the floor of the House. And the seat he occupied most often was either next to, or immediately behind, Barbara Jordan of Houston, who had won national fame as a member of the Judiciary Committee that undertook impeachment hearings against President Richard Nixon. Her richly sonorous voice and Southern Baptist eloquence were respected and remembered nationwide, as was her observation that the Constitution when written did not include her. She reminded Americans of the important advancements that our nation had achieved and the important civil rights challenges that remained before us. She was arguably the most "liberal" of the 22 members of the Texas Democratic Delegation in the House. Sam was arguably the most "conservative" of that group. Yet he was one of the two closest friends that Barbara Jordan had in Congress, the other being the similarly conservative member from New Mexico, Harold Runnels, who could usually be found sitting next to either Barbara or Sam." [42]

Others commented on the closeness between Hall and Jordan. Ron Mazzoli of Kentucky wrote that

> They spent many an hour on the House Floor sitting side by side with heads tilted toward one another for better

> catching the *sotto voce* comments of the other during the course of debates taking place just a few feet in front of them in the well of the House of Representatives. Both Barbara and Sam had large and expressive faces to go with their imposing physiques, and it was a picnic to observe from a respectable distance these two important political people, these two very dynamic personalities and these two very different political philosophers 'chew the fat'.[43]

Jake Pickle noted that Hall's colleagues used to tease him after his solid victory in 1976 that he was just "appointed" Congressman. He recollected observing Hall in the House:

> Sam took his seat in the House Chamber, toward the back near the center aisle. Seats are unassigned in the House of Representatives, but habit caused him to sit near or around a group of Congressmen who enjoyed the informal relationship of their fellow members. It was a generally conservative group—many Southerners—but they were Democrats who personally enjoyed being together and engaged in conversation with their colleagues and Republicans across the aisle. [44]

These Democrats included Sonny Montgomery of Mississippi, Joe Waggoner of Louisiana, Harold "Mud" Runnels of New Mexico, Barbara Jordan of Texas, Carlos Parker of Mississippi, Jack Hightower of Texas, and Phil Gramm of Texas. Kent Hance and Charles Stenholm frequently were in the group, and, on occasion, Martin Frost. Ralph M. Hall of the Texas Fourth District and a member of the Boll Weevils consulted with Hall on votes, noting that "Usually, if our votes differed, I had cast a bad vote." [45]

J. J. "Jake" Pickle of Texas remembered how earnest a friend Hall was, writing,

> Sam literally fell in love with his comrades. He liked to swap stories, to listen to and understand the joys, apprehensions and disappointments of each member. He appreciated their philosophy and commitment to public service. If something happened to any one of his group, Sam would take the sadness—or joy—as a part of his own life. It wasn't a matter of conservatism; it was a matter of personal involvement and appreciation. If you attended one of his fund raisers, or made a visit to his district, Sam would remember it forever. He would give a special gift to one of his colleagues just because he wanted to show his approval and thanks for their loyalty. Personal friendship meant more to him than just the office." [46]

Jack Hightower and Sam Hall accompanied each other many times to the unending series of receptions held in the capital. The first time they went in Jack's car because he knew the way better, and went to the first reception. Said Hightower, "We went in and shook hands and I turned to him and asked him if he was ready to go, and he said 'yeah.' So we went to the second one and did the same thing. After the third one, when we left, he started laughing and said that I was a man after his own heart. He said that I knew how to go to a reception. I said, 'That's the way to do it. You go in and shake hands with whoever you're supposed to see and whoever is the host or hostess and eat a Ritz cracker and leave.' That's what we did."[47]

Ike Skelton, a Missouri Democrat, often sat on the House Floor near Sam Hall. "Sam enjoyed poking fun at Missouri, my home state, because [during the Civil War] the seat of government left Missouri and settled in his hometown of Marshall, Texas." The Texan mentioned it several times, always making sure a sizable group of colleagues was present to hear. "Sam, being a typical Texan, enjoyed this bit of Texas lore at my expense."[48]

Harold S. "Hal" Sawyer, a moderate Republican from Michigan, came to the Congress when, like Hall, he was in his mid-fifties. Their previous business and life experiences enhanced their influence in committees, though they did not rise in their respective party hierarchies. Sawyer described his relationship with Hall, saying,

> While we were both lawyers, of course, we were of opposite political parties, but we had much more in common than we had in difference. While all members of Judiciary were required to be lawyers (I understand that Congressman Bono of California is presently our exception) Sam and I were the only "real" practicing lawyers. All of the others, while being lawyers and having had somewhat insignificant quantity and quality of practice, were primarily career politicians serving in state legislatures, etc., before coming to Congress. Sam and I both interrupted very busy and successful legal careers. [49]

The relationships between peers extended to care in a crisis, as when Representative Harold Runnels of New Mexico died. The death of her husband in 1980 put Dorothy Runnels into a new and confusing situation that she very much needed help with. "Sam didn't wait for me to ask, he volunteered. He was a presence to be reckoned with. At the funeral, he represented the Congressional part of Harold's life and delivered a eulogy that brought tears to everyone's eyes."[50]

From his vantage point in Texas, Judge Tom Reavley observed that as a Congressman Hall "seemed to get bigger, more forceful, and sturdier.

He thrived at that extremely demanding work. One day he came unexpectedly to visit me in my Austin office. His handshake hurt, his voice was commanding, and he carried a force field about him. He was the warm friend of old, but his body and personality had somehow been infused with great vigor." [51]

Despite his sometime appellation of Washington, D.C., as "Disneyland East" and the frustrations he felt working in a highly politicized environment, Hall nevertheless relished being there. Buddy Roemer opined that "Sam always looked at those periods in Congress as maybe the best part of his life. Maybe I am wrong about that. I always kind of sensed that he enjoyed, he counted those years with high regard."[52]

Hall's experience in Washington, D.C., was sweetened through associations with friends outside the congressional ranks. Daryl Arey, a Secret Service agent, had a mother and grandmother in East Texas, and he took the trouble to read Hall's speeches given in the House. Arey liked Hall. As one who worked in Washington and risked becoming cynical about the politics and scandals he observed, Arey found when he visited with Hall that "before long you'd be running your flag back up the flagpole" because of his inviolable faith in the United States of America. [53]

Hall nurtured positive working relationships with his peers even if they rarely, if ever, voted as he did. He admired Albert Gore from Tennessee. He sought common ground and friendship with everyone, even those considerably to the political left of him. Representative Don Edwards said, "He never pushed in an offensive way his conservative beliefs. He was comfortable with them, and they were very decent ideas that he had. I liked Sam Hall a lot. We all did." [54]

Buddy Roemer asserted that the number of representatives like Sam Hall could be numbered on the fingers of one hand: in his time there were not to be found "more than a handful" like him among the 435 members of Congress, "strong, deep, honest, consistent, country first, easy to work with, political, but non-political. It's like there's a season for politics, but when that season is over, let's help the country, and that's a pretty rare find."[55]

Political consultant George Christian matched Roemer's assessment, using an experience with Hall and Jack Hightower to praise both men:

> Once on a visit to Washington I had seafood dinner with Sam and another Texas Congressman, Jack Hightower of Vernon. Jack was a longtime personal friend, and I had helped him in all of his political races. He and Sam got along because he had the same values as Sam. During the course of the meal Sam referred to Jack a time or two as "Preacher." When I asked him later why he applied that nickname to his colleague, he replied, "Oh, he doesn't really

preach to me or anybody else. He's just so pure." It was nice to have at least two men of that stripe in the Texas delegation.[56]

Judge Phillip Baldwin seized on an aphorism that described Hall's image and credibility in every arena of service and relationship. As he had been in his civic life in East Texas, so he was in the Congress. As Lyndon B. Johnson often liked to say, Hall was the kind of man who would "Go to the well with you." The expression recalled those times when "renegade" Indians were a threat in Texas, and one never went alone to the well; there had to be someone who could be counted on to risk his own life while protecting another's. On the Texas frontier there was no higher compliment. As an observation about the reliability and trustworthiness that people imputed to Sam B. Hall, Jr., Judge Baldwin's observation was just right. [58]

11

Named to the Federal Court

Sam Hall is the only man I have known that quit one lifetime job for another with the same tenure. For surely Sam B. Hall, Jr., of Marshall, Texas, if he chose to do so, could easily have been returned biennially to the House of Representatives as long as he wished to serve the people of this country, his state, and his district.... His family, upon whom he doted, was the apple of his eye, and came first in his life decisions. —Judge Howell Cobb, United States District Court, Eastern District of Texas, Beaumont/Lufkin Division [1]

I served with him in the Congress where he proved that he was not only a patriotic American of sound judgment, but that he was a Texan with nerve enough to vote his own convictions. That is the kind of man I want in our federal judiciary and I think Sam Hall will go a long way in instilling confidence and respect for our Federal Judges. —Congressman W. R. "Bob" Poage [2]

Sam Hall gave the strong and accurate impression that he could do the work of a federal judge. After twenty-six years as a practicing lawyer he served in Congress on the Judiciary Committee and other committees that required extensive analysis, application, and revision of the law. It did not hurt that Hall had brought his legal skills and capacity for the extended hours and effort required in committee work. He pulled his full share of the legislative load and got a comparatively high percentage of his bills passed into law. His legislative accomplishments were capped with an Award of Merit from the Federal Administrative Law Judges Conference in May 1985, in recognition of his exemplary work on the House Judiciary Committee and the Subcommittee on Administrative Law and Governmental Relations. These things enhanced his qualifications, and so the federal judicial nomination seemed patently fitting. He was thought to fit squarely in the best tradition of American jurists as "an exceptional person with extraordinary native and acquired talents" and earned the prestige of a judge. [3]

On taking office in 1985 as a Republican and former Democrat, Senator Phil Gramm recommended Sam Hall, Howell Cobb and Paul Brown to judicial positions in the Eastern District of Texas. Gramm had been hesitant. Speaking at Paris Junior College, he said, "I wasn't too excited about the prospects when Sam Hall came to me after my election to the Senate and asked me to consider him for an appointment to the federal bench." It would mean the loss of Hall's influence in the House of Representatives, and, as Gramm put it, "I told him we needed him in Washington a lot more than we needed him on the federal bench." Hall had political and personal reasons for moving on: Gramm said, "He told me he was tired of having to work with Tip O'Neill and he was too far along in politics to change. His father and his uncle had been a judge, and no lawyer worth his salt doesn't want to be on the federal bench." The senator thought him well qualified because, first, Hall was a strict constructionist on the constitution; second, he believed "that federal judges ought to interpret the law and enforce that law not make the law;" and, third, Hall would put "the rights of law-abiding citizens" over those of criminals. President Reagan called on April 16, 1985, to inform Hall of his choice and to check personally on his willingness to accept; the White House announced the nomination the next day. [4]

Hall's nomination was no exception to President Reagan's systematic appointments of conservatives as judges. Reagan had the unusual opportunity to nominate enough judges that ultimately somewhat over half of the Supreme Court and the federal judiciary were his appointees. The president's preference for judges known for judicial restraint rather than activism matched the philosophy of the conservative Democrat Sam B. Hall Jr.

The 1980 Republican Party platform statement on the judiciary revealed a view congenial to Hall's political principles:

> We pledge... the appointment of women and men who respect and reflect the values of the American people, and whose judicial philosophy is characterized by the highest regard for protecting the rights of law-abiding citizens, and is consistent with the belief in the decentralization of the federal government and efforts to return decision-making power to state and local elected officials. We will work for the appointment of judges at all levels of the judiciary who respect traditional family values and the sanctity of innocent human life.[5]

Justices confirmed to the Supreme Court were Sandra Day O'Connor, the first woman justice and generally a constitutional conservative, and the conservatives William H. Rehnquist, Antonin Scalia, and Anthony Kennedy. Kennedy was nominated after the Senate refused to confirm Robert Bork, the former solicitor general during the Nixon administration who was rejected amid acrimonious controversy because many regarded him a doctrinaire conservative. [6]

It was a difficult decision to resign from the Congress in order to take the federal judgeship. Hall enjoyed the give-and-take in the Congress, whether on the floor of the House or in the office, in the halls or in the Capitol restaurant. "I'll miss the day-to-day camaraderie," he promised. "You may not agree, but there's just a day-to-day relationship that you never forget. On both sides of the aisle." However, there was considerable frustration that he could accomplish only so much in the House of Representatives. The congressional legislative processes deterred a sense of closure and accomplishment most of the time. Hall knew these limitations when he went to Congress; still, he believed he should be an agent of change. Nonetheless, when the opportunity arrived in 1985, he decided he might be of greater service in the role of federal judge. [7]

Representative Barbara Jordan expressed a common mix of thoughts and feelings about Hall's decision, writing, "Like you, I have mixed emotions about your leaving the House. While I know that our politics were often different, I felt you brought a necessary dimension to the Democratic Party, and I regret your loss in the House of Representatives." Her comments no doubt reflected their private conversations on the subject, and revealed that Hall confided with his colleagues about his decision. [8]

Other considerations influenced his decision, and he discussed them with family, friends and advisors. Colleagues and friends had recognized his dissatisfaction and occasional disenchantment with the work of the Congress. Former Congressman and Ambassador Robert Krueger recalled that

> In the 1980s Sam seemed increasingly dissatisfied with the developing partisanship which, he told me, took much of the pleasure out of serving in Congress. To him it was not the same as when we had served together in the Seventies. The Eighties brought deeper divisions; deeper partisan rancor; and deeper dissatisfaction with the job itself. To be able to serve the people of one's district and country is an honor and a source of abiding satisfaction. But to enter the Floor of the House, which never ceased to be thrilling to me because of the honor and responsibility that it imposed, and there to hear accusation, attacks, and sometimes near

> slanders perhaps from people who are usually no better than those they had scorned and slashed must have been wearying to a civilized, magnanimous man like Sam Hall. Sam chose to follow in the family tradition of becoming a judge, a position to which he was appointed by President Reagan, a sign both of Sam's innate conservatism, his close rapport with Republicans as well as Democrats, and his ability to be non-partisan. [9]

Apart from the frustrations of congressional processes, the opportunity to be home with his family on most nights appealed to him, and the fact of not having to run every two years and to engage in fund-raising was an attractive factor. Attorney Franklin Jones Jr. observed that

> Sam really did a lot of "soul searching" because he liked what he did so well as a congressman. Some of the people he admired and respected so much were "men in a robe and on the bench." Men like his father, Sam Hall Sr., his uncle Reuben Hall, and many others that were actually role models for Sam. He was still agonizing that he couldn't serve as many people as a federal judge as he could as a congressman. I told him it was a lifetime appointment, and he wouldn't have to worry about running for a political office again. He could be with his family all the time. He could spend more time on the farm. I wish I could express adequately how happy Sam was when he was on his farm. [10]

Hall's former law partner Bill Huffman stated that Sam Jr. never disappointed his father except when he went to Congress, and that was only because they would be separated, though Sam Sr. was intensely proud of his son's election. The ability of family members to be together was not taken for granted; to do otherwise was painful. [11]

During Sam Sr.'s last years, Sam and Madeleine were in the capital most of the time. The two elder Hall daughters had more responsibility to look after Sam Sr. and Valerie. Hall told them he was sorry they had to bear such responsibility by themselves. They willingly took excellent care of their grandparents, but their father was torn. He agonized that he could not be at home to help with the father he revered. Sam B. Hall Sr. died in October 1982, and over the next few years Valerie's health declined. Eventually, the desire to return home permanently became a principal factor in his decision to accept appointment to the federal judiciary.

By accepting the appointment as a federal judge, Hall also honored his father in the strongest way, following in his judicial footsteps. He could be at home in Marshall and fulfill the lifelong ambition of his parents for him that he be a federal judge. It meant also that he could resolve the tension between a calling to high public service and the responsibilities of a son and father to parents and family. By choosing to return he allowed himself to resolve the loss he had felt while separated from his family and hometown. Sam Jr.'s feelings matched Sam Sr.'s feelings about "being away." For Sam Sr., Shreveport was far away though just 35 miles distant. In 1960 Sam and Madeleine had moved the family into town from the house next door to Sam and Valerie on U.S. Highway 80 West, just a few miles. It devastated Sam Sr. to be separated from the granddaughters by even that small distance. [12]

Apparently, some people harbored the misconception that Hall resigned from the Congress to allow a Republican to run in his stead. To be sure, the Republicans wanted to present a strong candidate for the First District. Senator Gramm, who nominated Hall, was a Republican. At the time of Hall's death in 1994, a *Marshall News Messenger* writer repeated the misunderstanding without checking the facts. Sam R. Moseley Jr. of Marshall responded in a letter, calling the assertion an insult and an "affront to the memory of one of the finest jurists ever to serve on the federal bench!" Moseley went on, "Judge Hall was appointed because of his excellent record as a lawyer and congressman and his demonstrated compassion, good judgment and conservative approach to the law. Sen. Phil Gramm would not have recommended him for any other reason and he would not have accepted for any other reason. To suggest otherwise is to malign them both." [13]

Before President Reagan signed the commission papers for the federal judgeship, he called Hall one more time. Unlike his predecessors, Reagan inquired with nominees by telephone, as was typical of his personal involvement in the selection process. The president preferred that he stay in Congress, but Hall's mind was set; he was going home to Texas.[14]

Senator Strom Thurmond of South Carolina chaired the final Senate committee hearing on Hall's appointment. Seventeen colleagues from Texas and seven from other states were present to encourage him. Hall testified to his commitment to the strict interpretation of the United States Constitution; he was not going to be a judicial activist. Senator Gramm described Hall as "the most respected member of the United States Congress," exuberant praise he no doubt meant seriously. Senator Thurmond declared, "I think you will make an outstanding judge. You are a man of common sense who has respect for the Constitution."[15]

The *Marshall News Messenger* editorialized about East Texas's "ideal representative in Congress," who was to be a judge: "When a man of Sam B. Hall's philosophy ascends to the federal bench, it is certain that laws will be respected and upheld, not made and remade, in his courtroom." It was a "sacred" distinction Hall would preserve, he said. "I want to interpret the

Constitution as it was intended to be and not try to amend it by placing on it an interpretation that maybe the Founding Fathers did not intend."[16]

G. V. "Sonny" Montgomery of Mississippi recalled that in his thirty years of service as a Representative, he had never seen as large a confirmation group in the Senate: "We had over fifty Members of Congress attend that hearing to show how much we thought of Congressman Hall. It was the most Members I have ever seen at any confirmation or as one group in the Senate." The Senate confirmed Hall unanimously. Representative Charles B. Rangel later wrote, "I find comfort in knowing that Sam Hall continues in public service in the Judiciary. I never did believe the myths of the greatest that can come from the sovereign state of Texas, but knowing Sam has forced me to reconsider." Former Speaker of the House Carl Albert wrote to Hall, "You showed outstanding promise to become a great Congressman in the tradition of Sam Rayburn and Wright Patman." Albert expressed his pleasure, though, at Hall's judicial appointment, saying, "You will do it honor and you will serve the ends of justice well. As one who was formerly your leader in Congress, I am very pleased. You have made me proud." Hall took the oath of office as a federal judge from U.S. District Judge Joe Fisher on May 28, 1985. The ceremony took place in the Harrison County courtroom where Sam B. Hall Sr. had presided as a state district judge for many years. Madeleine Hall and the Hall daughters stood with him as he took the oath, Madeleine holding the family Bible, and the daughters donning him with his judicial robe. Judge William Wayne Justice welcomed Hall to the district bench, delivered some cautionary admonitions about the duties of a federal judge, and noted the relief that this new judge would provide to the crowded Texas Eastern District court docket. [17]

A surprising turn of events absorbed the immediate Hall family for a brief period, when Texas Republicans courted Hall's daughter Amanda Hall Wynn as his successor. Among the Hall daughters Amanda most resembled her father in personality, and with Hall's resignation from the Congress the Texas Republicans pondered whether with her father's name identification she could enter politics on their side. Her identification as owner and operator of the Manda Jane Corporation, a children's clothng manufacturer, also commended her as a possible candidate. The loss of Hall and his conservative voting pattern was a loss of political influence for Republicans, so they considered a possible solution in Amanda. [18]

Soon after Sam Hall left Washington, and with the special election approaching, Amanda returned a call from Rep. Steve Bartlett, who told her he had already spoken with Hall, who responded that any decision was to be Amanda's alone; he would not interfere. Bartlett, Phil Gramm, Congressman Jack Fields, and others asked her to consider running for election to the Texas First District seat. She argued that she was not qualified.

No matter was the response; by election time, she would be. She knew the issues, had grown up hearing about them, discussing them, but the prospect of debating before the people was intimidating. Besides, her business experience and background helping with Hall's campaigns were assets. The Republicans would prepare her for that. What about the expense? They had a "war chest" ready to go. [19]

Texas Governor George W. Bush visited Marshall to speak at the Chamber of Commerce banquet. Madeleine introduced family members to him, and he asked which daughter was Amanda. He declared, "I have a message, and if I don't give this message to you, I'll have the devil to pay." Just the day before, Jack Fields had told him not to leave until he had reminded Amanda the Republicans still were "looking for you on the other side of the aisle." Wynn was surprised overall, not the least because she was being asked to run from "the other side of the aisle," as a Republican. Her husband Tom Wynn put the decision in her hands and pledged support, whatever she decided. Amanda recalled, however, "But I knew that it wasn't right at the time. I knew they wanted him back but they just wanted him dressed as a Republican. So I was the one and I thought about it a lot over the years, and I would have loved it. But at the time, I was so involved; I did love what I was doing—still do."[20]

Then and thereafter until redistricting and the election of Louis Gohmert in 2004, the Republicans failed to gain a representative in the Texas First Congressional District, though they gained seats elsewhere in Texas. Amanda Hall Wynn let the issue pass quietly, and afterwards few people knew about the matter.

Hall accepted an appointment to the United States District Court, Eastern District of Texas, to occupy the Beaumont bench Judge Joe J. Fisher was vacating in order to become senior judge. Beaumont's heavy court docket required another judge there. But the prospect of moving to Beaumont thwarted Hall's desire to stay in or within commuting range of Marshall. He simply would not agree to be based in the Beaumont court if it meant he had to make his home there. Therefore he resisted direction from Judge Charles Clark of the U.S. Court of Appeals for the Fifth Circuit to take Beaumont. Instead, he sought to encourage the recommendation and appointment of someone else to that position. His lifelong friend, Judge Robert Parker, was assigned to the Marshall division, and so would have to move elsewhere if Hall were to be assigned to Marshall. [21]

As it happened, Hall held court in Texarkana most of the time during the first two years he served as judge. He held court in Marshall less frequently and otherwise commuted daily between Marshall and Texarkana. Another district nominee, Richard Schell, eventually was appointed to serve in Beaumont, and Hall was involved in assuring that Schell would get the appointment. Schell recalled the process:

> From May of 1985 until January of 1988, Sam had successfully postponed his move to Beaumont, but pressure was building. The U.S. Court of Appeals for the Fifth circuit had weighed in on the issue and had insisted that Sam relocate unless an alternative solution to the caseload problem in Beaumont was found. The deadline for Sam to move was May 15, 1988, or as soon thereafter as the new courtroom in Beaumont was finished. Senator Gramm's recommendation of me to a seat on the federal bench presented a window of opportunity for both Sam and me.... My appointment and subsequent move to Beaumont would ensure that Sam could remain in Marshall. Sam always said he had nothing against Beaumont except that he could not move his farm there, and he and Madeleine loved their home in Marshall and living near their daughters. [22]

Hall kept up with every detail of Schell's confirmation process. Finally, Schell received formal nomination and notice of his scheduled confirmation hearing:

> Before I had a chance to call Sam to tell him of the scheduled hearing, I received a call from him in Washington on Monday, May 9. Sam had traveled to Washington, D.C., apparently over the weekend. He had gone there to visit with various members of Congress in order to tell them how important it was to him that my confirmation not be delayed. Sam knew many of the Senators and Representatives, having served with them in Congress for four terms....He urged his former colleagues to schedule my hearing as soon as possible. As it turned out, I did receive a hearing along with several other nominees, and I was confirmed about ten days later. Sam remained in Marshall, and I moved to Beaumont. [23]

For his part, Hall recalled his part in working out that process, "I said, "Mr. Chief Judge, if you'll let me go to Washington and spend about a day and a half, I'll get you two judges. I'll get you Sim Lake in Houston and Richard Schell for you in Beaumont. Well, I went to Washington and worked the House and Senate floors just like I was a member again and within a few weeks Richard Schell was sitting where he is now." [24]

Judge Thomas M. Reavley was with the Judicial Council of the Fifth Circuit at the time when Hall was resisting the move to Beaumont. Reavley met with Judge Charles Clark and the other judges. "Judge Clark and I were firm and adamant," Reavley said. "Judge Hall had to move. I can still see his face, and his eyes looking back into mine. I felt that he was thinking that I should have left it to others to talk to him as I did. And I also felt that we had not moved him even an inch toward Beaumont. Well, he never moved. He was not openly contumacious; he simply worked on the Beaumont docket without moving until a new judge took office to establish a Beaumont residence. Then he established permanent chambers in Marshall." [25]

Hall had to adjust to his new position and second-guessed himself at least once about taking the job. About six or so months after taking the federal bench, he commented to Phillip Baldwin, "Phillip, I'm afraid I may have made a mistake." Baldwin replied, "Sam, if you had come to me, I would have told you point-blank that you made a mistake!" Despite his initial doubts, he overcame them. [26]

Congressman Ron Mazzoli of Kentucky confessed to the impression that "when Sam came back to the House Chamber when he was in town for federal judicial conferences, that he might have had some slight second thoughts about his decision to accept President Reagan's judicial appointment. I always thought Sam's personality better suited the somewhat hurly-burly, shoulder-to-shoulder, down-in-the-dirt atmosphere of the House of Representatives than in the more hushed, solemn and genteel atmosphere of the Federal Bench." [27]

J. J. "Jake" Pickle of Texas echoed the sentiment, noting that after Hall became a federal judge, he returned to Washington when he could to visit his old friends:

> He would take a seat in that same section of the House which he had frequented so many years. He would talk and talk, rehash and rethink, laugh and laugh again about some legislative recollection. He said to me on one occasion, "You know, the biggest mistake I made in life was leaving this House. You can't imagine how much I miss exchanging confidences and opinions with you fellows. You were the joy of my life. Now, I'm proud to be a Federal Judge, but it is kind of a lonely life—you are the Judge; you must make a singular decision, and you have few people you can talk to about the decision. Here in the Congress, you could share confidences and opinions, likes and dislikes; you had the close friendships—men and women you loved. I sure miss being with you now." Sam had indeed fallen in love with his colleagues, not as Democrats, or Republicans, liberal or conservative, men or women, but people he knew and trusted and respected. Sam's House was its members, not

just the party or legislative issues.

Pickle expressed what former members of Congress frequently feel after they have left about the loss of the routines and relationships that add joy to the work. [28]

After the initial transition to his new role, Hall set distinctive standards for the work he had undertaken. Soon after becoming a judge, he told his friend, attorney Franklin Jones Jr., "Franklin, the only thing I don't like about this job is that seventy-five percent of the time you don't have anything to do." Franklin attributed this comment to Hall's work ethic and the probability he did not find the job as demanding as other work he had done, despite the case load in the Eastern District of Texas being quite high. [29]

Some time after Hall had left the House of Representatives, Congressman Jack Brooks of Texas remarked that when Hall returned to Washington on a trip he had lunch with members of the Texas Delegation one day. "Someone remarked that Sam looked like he had gained weight since his resignation from Congress. I told them that he was just wearing his judicial robe under the suit!" The remark symbolized how his former colleague recognized Hall's resolution to fulfill the federal judge's role. East Texas was again fully home, and the days of life and service in the nation's capital were a bright memory. [30]

Texas Fourth District Congressman Ralph Hall later summed up the transition for the Halls with a renovated story:

> Sam, our mutual friend and fellow Texan Jim Baker was ambling around in the desert a couple of months ago. I ran into him in Washington last week and he told me this story. He said he was ambling around on the desert and kicked on a bit of sand and a bottle appeared and a genie came out of the bottle and the genie said, "Aren't you Jim Baker, the Secretary of State? You represent the greatest country among all the countries of the free world." He said, "I'll give you one wish, any one wish you want." And Jim got all of his maps out and showed him where Libya was and where Syria was and where Saudi Arabia was and where Israel was and where Egypt was and he said, "I want peace in this area." And the genie just said, "Put the maps up. Put them back in the car. There's absolutely no chance of that. That's ridiculous. I won't even consider it." Then he said, "But since you are who you are, I'll still give you your one wish." And he said, "Well, I'd like for Madeleine Hall to ask Sam to please move back to Washington, D.C." And the genie said, "Let's take another look at those maps!" [31]

Sam B. Hall Jr. now could focus on the new federal judicial assignment, and to the luxury of serving his country in a particular way much as he had during his wartime service—without ever leaving Texas. As a U.S. Representative, he had insisted he thought always and only of Texas as home. This time, except for brief trips on official business or vacation, he would not leave Texas again.

The new judge and portrait of his father, State District Judge Sam B. Hall Sr., May 28, 1985.

L-R: Dr. Jesse Brooks of Atlanta, Texas, Mrs. Marguerite Ratcliff, and Congressman Hall

Hall with Marshall friends and political supporters Mona and Ray Lawson.

On the way to the Senate Judiciary Committee confirmation hearing, May 1985. L-R: Sue Jordan, Ken Black, Sam and Madeleine Hall, Veterans Committee staff member Janet Potts.

Madeleine and Sam on the day of his swearing-in as federal judge of the Eastern District of Texas – Marshall, Texas, May 28, 1985.

Federal judges of the Eastern District of Texas. L-R: Joe J. Fisher, William Wayne Justice, Sam B. Hall Jr., Robert Parker, Howell Cobb, Paul Brown, William M. Steger.

12

Federal Judge Sam B. Hall Jr.

"I often felt Sam Hall's talents as a judge were underused, and I strongly believe he felt that way himself.... I remember Sam Hall pointedly asking me, "What am I for?" —Ernie Metzger, Senior Lecturer, School of Law, University of Aberdeen, Scotland, and former Hall judicial law clerk. [1]

"If you called down to central casting and said, 'send me an East Texas federal judge,' they'd probably send Judge Hall. He looked like a federal judge. He talked like an East Texas federal judge should talk. There was no arrogance or pretension about him." —John G. Crews, Assistant U. S. Attorney, New Mexico District, and former Hall judicial law clerk. [2]

The True Gentleman is the man whose conduct proceeds from good will and an acute sense of propriety, and whose self-control is equal to all emergencies; who does not make the poor man conscious of his poverty, the obscure man of his obscurity, or any man of his inferiority or deformity; who is himself humbled if necessity compels him to humble another; who does not flatter wealth, cringe before power, or boast of his own possessions or achievements; who speaks with frankness but always with sincerity and sympathy; whose deed follows his word; who thinks of the rights and feelings of others, rather than his own; and who appears well in any company, a man in whom honor is sacred and virtue is safe. —The True Gentleman, *by John Walter Wayland*

I recited Mr. Wayland's famous words to Judge Sam B. Hall, Jr., the evening I ended my employment as his Federal Judicial Law Clerk, an evening that marked the culmination of the finest twenty months of my life. In retrospect, it is hard to believe that our Federal Government paid me to work for Judge Hall.

Knowing what I know now, and considering all that I learned, I would have willingly paid the government for that opportunity.
—Attorney Ed Hohn [3]

Judge Hall's judicial law clerks and attorneys who got courtroom experience with him often compared him favorably with other judges. His identity as an East Texan was important, especially to outsiders, but his deeper qualities prevailed even over that. He took his position as judge, but not himself, seriously. The black robe was the uniform; he disliked wearing it and wisecracked to his brother-in-law, John McLendon, "It's too hard to get my handkerchief." [4]

Hall took many cues from his father's example as a state district judge. Judge Hall Sr. maintained an even temper in court and was firm but not harsh with lawyers. Lawyers enjoyed the freedom to try their cases without being required to stay within the minutiae of legal procedure; the principle of right and wrong prevailed. One might not recognize all the elements leading to a judgment, but Judge Hall Sr. typically came to a just and proper decision, as the limited number of reversals for his decisions attest. In passing sentence, he spelled out the reasons for his decisions, seeking to make sure the one being sentenced understood the implications of the decision. Bill Huffman said of the senior Hall, "He could sentence someone to the penitentiary in the grandest manner." [5]

The father as mentor and model shaped the son's legal skills. Sam Jr.'s judicial style developed from his own experiences as a trial lawyer in his father's court. At the time of his death at ninety-four, Sam B. Hall Sr. had been hailed for his "strong judicial sense," and his son had it, too. Like his father, Sam Jr. had an uncanny ability to reach a reasoned judgment without undue deliberation and study, though he made sure to consider law and precedent properly. Also drawing on unshakable convictions of right and wrong, he was regarded as an instinctive judge who by and large arrived quickly at just and proper conclusions. Altogether, his respect for the intention and outcome of the law, his regard for proper conduct and mutual respect in the courtroom, and his reputation as a judge of proper gravity and humanity were his father's legacy. Marcus F. Vascocu was a lawyer of Sam Jr.'s generation who recognized the tutoring Sam Sr., "Judge Sam," provided them on law and trial procedure. He reckoned that Sam Jr. caught and learned the proper virtues of practicing law and being a judge from his father. [6]

Some people considered Sam Hall Jr. an exceptional judge. Few judges could surpass, or match, his temperament and competencies in court. Attorney Gilbert Adams considered him to be as free of inadequacies as any judge he had seen. His confidence and personality assured that everyone associated with a trial could contribute their best. Hall made it clear that everyone was present to seek justice. Additionally, his ability to use humor and cheer people up served to alleviate tension. It was as if he were welcoming friends into his home to solve a problem together, though the dignity of the courtroom was non-negotiable. Thus the secure, humane atmosphere of Judge Hall's courtroom enhanced the trial process.[7]

One of Judge Hall's earliest cases, indeed his first criminal case, the Fredeman trial in Beaumont, Texas, involved several defendants and attorneys from all over the country. It was a technically complex trial lasting almost six months, during which time two primary defendants died. John Crews likened it to "taking up jogging by running a marathon the first time one laced up the shoes. Prominent attorneys from around the country appeared on behalf of the attendants. They remarked what a true gentleman Judge Hall was during that entire trial." Indeed, when the trial began, with two-dozen or so attorneys, a sizable crowd, and the court officers present, Hall announced that this was his first criminal trial. He was a relatively new judge entering a high profile trial, but he conducted the trial in a way that exceeded the expectations of everyone involved.[8]

The trial produced at least one example of humor, as often happens when the human side of even the most formal situations cannot be stifled. The victim, Attorney Gilbert Low, recalled the incident:

> There were many famous trial lawyers, including the lawyer who had prosecuted Spiro Agnew, as well as the famous Houston lawyer [Richard C.] "Racehorse" Haynes. As jurors were questioned, they all had heard of many of these lawyers, and all would say that they had not heard of me. After about a day and a half of this, Judge Hall called me up to the bench and told me that he thought I was supposed to be a well-known lawyer and that none of these people knew me. Quite frankly, I had picked up the same point and was a little hurt by my lack of fame. The next day a gentleman from a small community near Beaumont raised his hand and told how he knew all the other lawyers and that he knew me. When asked how he knew me, he said, "Well, Mr. Low is just a famous man." Judge Hall motioned me up to the bench and looked at me and said, "How much did you pay that old boy to say that?" We all had a good laugh and went on about the business of justice. After that Judge Hall always jokingly referred to me as "that famous man. [9]

Hall's legal experience and knowledge distinguished him in the way that he conducted his court. He attented to the problems of lawyers, sometimes their need for discipline and direction in the courtroom. Consequently, he maintained strong court discipline and helped the lawyers feel confident in his court. His courtesy remained constant even when he perceived a lawyer to be serving the needs of his or her client inadequately by, for example, failing to keep the client informed about the trial. He kept any negative opinion of a lawyer to himself. Hall's attitude rested on his conviction that both persons and the law should be served, and that while a counselor might fail, the judge could not. [10]

The courtroom procedures and argument put pressure on a judge, and lawyers sometimes exert too much pressure in order to win a point, with tension as the result. If a lawyer was disrespectful or too pushy, Hall readily called him or her aside for a word of reproof or warning. [11]

Hall detested unneeded, time-consuming tactics, repetition, and delay. In one case he became perturbed that an attorney presented an unedited video deposition. In order to expedite the trial, he required the attorney to read written testimony into evidence rather than to show the whole video. [12]

In another trial, Hall observed that attorney Ed Merritt was unconsciously prompting a witness with subtle body language cues. He sent the jury out and instructed Merritt to stop it, declaring, "Mr. Merritt, I don't think I've ever seen you do this before, but your client is looking right at you every time there's a question asked, and you are nodding up and down or sideways depending on how you want your client to answer. I don't think that's appropriate, and I want you to keep your head still in the courtroom!" [13]

Hall became exasperated with attorneys, but quietly, or privately in chambers, and often with bemusement. A lawyer asked the judge's permission to approach the witness, and Hall said yes. After that, he handed a note to his clerk Ernie Metzger. It read, "Lawyers ask such silly questions. What do they expect me to say? What would they do if I said, "No, you can't do that?" [14]

In an era when civil cases usually were settled out of court and the pool of trial lawyers was relatively limited, judges might come with relatively less courtroom. Federal judges typically had more than adequate experience, but even then their demeanor sometimes reflected the nature of the legal profession as it had become in recent decades. The specialization of law and the decline of a culture of respect meant that courtroom conduct too often succumbed to expediency. In former days lawyers assumed their courtroom conduct toward one another would influence professional relationships over the span of a career, so they were careful to maintain respect even in the heat of disagreement. Many younger judges gained experience during a time when civility had declined and mutual suspicion increased among lawyers, thus influencing how some newer judges were predisposed to view the lawyers practicing before them in court. Hall belonged to an older generation whose members recognized lawyer's tricks and expected proper conduct in court, so he managed problems through direct, personal communication, correcting and chiding lawyers, but often praising them, in the meantime keeping their respect. Judge Hall's own preferred relational style also had been refined during his time as a U.S. Representative. As the judiciary became increasingly professionalized, he was one of fewer and fewer federal judges who had previous congressional experience. He was distinctive as a judge with both legal and legislative background, both influences having reinforced his bent toward fostering good working relationships. [15]

Ernest Metzger, who after clerking with Hall taught law in the United Kingdom, analyzed Hall's judicial approach, comparing it with a divergent trend in the United States:

> Sam Hall was a judge of the Anglo-American cast: he had an exceptional legal intuition and sense of justice. He could look at past examples and arrive at a just result. He was a model of the common-law judge. The problem was that America was moving away from the traditional model, and like Europe had come to prefer a system based on rules to a system based on examples. The reasons are complicated, and have a lot to do with the fact that judges (and especially federal judges) are now called on to preside over a broad range of intensely complicated cases. But in addition a large component of European-style mistrust of judges has come into our legal system. No one likes the idea that a judge's decision might depend on his education, or his biases, or what he had for breakfast. So we scribble down a lot of rules in the hope that we can settle in advance what the judge's decision will be. Hence much of a judge's job nowadays is to read and apply rules. If he had something bad for breakfast, it shouldn't make a difference. [16]

Hall's conservatism was a potential factor in decisions. In the middle 1980s when Hall was still a new judge, the issue of prayer arose in the Marshall public schools. The superintendent was surveying the laws associated with a number of challenges to prayer across the nation, questioning whether public prayer was permissible and what might happen if someone made a legal challenge. Hall declared privately that any such lawsuit was not going to get far in his court, regardless what a higher court might have ruled. Other courts might misapply law in their rulings, but he would not make any such prohibitive judgment on public prayer in his court. His opinion was as he had always expressed it during his congressional career. [17]

The Texas Eastern District federal courts, including Marshall, had a longstanding reputation for swift consideration of cases, which encouraged litigants to file cases in Marshall. Hall enhanced that reputation because of the way he ran his court. Consequently, major corporations that normally would have no reason for legal involvement in East Texas frequently chose the Marshall venue, seeking quick resolution to a case, such as a dispute in patent technology law with national or even global significance. The tendency to resolve cases efficiently and expeditiously had been set long before. The proliferation of lawyers and the number of national cases brought to Marshall came partly because of the oil boom in the region during the 1920s and the railroads' prominence in the region long before that. The high level of business and economic activity attracted lawyers who took plaintiff's cases, such as personal-injury lawsuits against major local and regional corporations. For example, earlier in the century, in the 1920s, Franklin Jones Sr. and his father, Sol "Soupy" Jones, established a national reputation for plaintiff's suits against the railroads. In the next generation, Franklin Jones Jr., F. Scott Baldwin, and several other lawyers developed national and international reputations for their success with personal injury suits and other kinds of cases often tried in the federal courts and associated with sizable settlements. Over decades of practice, both the bar and the courts learned the virtues of a well-oiled court docket—what was often dubbed the "rocket-docket." [18]

Political considerations applied, too. In 1962 the Marshall federal court belonged to the Jefferson division of the Texas Eastern District. Under legislation sponsored by Representative Wright Patman, the division was moved to Marshall, where the post office building was renovated to become the federal courthouse. This helped to balance the case load among the Texas Eastern District courts and enhanced the reputation of Marshall as a favorable venue for plaintiffs' cases. Marshall Attorney Michael Smith remembered Hall joking about the process:

> Judge Hall always said when I was clerking for him that they ought to name that courthouse for him. He believed Wright Patman moved the courthouse to Marshall in 1962 because a young Marshall lawyer named Sam B. Hall Jr. ran against Patman for Congress. So he always viewed that courthouse as something of a personal insult to him from Wright Patman, a way of essentially showing Judge Hall's hometown that Patman could "bring home the bacon." He felt pretty strongly about that even

when I was clerking for him. [19]

Judge Hall excelled at personal time management, a skill he had long since developed as a lawyer and as a congressman who had, ideally, to be decisive. The conduct of his court motions docket illustrates the point. He used the one-page briefs, draft orders, and strategically placed notes to manage the motions to come before the court on any given day. What could keep some judges up late at night he often handled in a few hours. Sometimes the court docket was too long to complete in a day. He sought to resolve the most pressing or difficult motions or cases as soon as possible. And so, like his father, Hall also gained a reputation for dispatching cases efficiently. [20]

When Hall first took the bench, he examined the backlog of cases in Texarkana and Beaumont where literally thousands of civil cases awaited resolution, mostly because there had not been enough judges to serve in the Texas Eastern District. He solved the problem by having his court schedule a hundred cases for docket call at a time. Perhaps fifty of those might be quickly settled out of court. Once the remaining cases got a scheduling order setting the dates for discovery, final pretrial, and jury selection, forty of the fifty remaining cases might be settled without trial. Ultimately the court oversaw jury selection in most of the remaining cases, but even then not all those juries were used in a full trial. Most civil cases could be settled without going to trial. That way of dispatching civil cases also helps to explain why many lawyers have more experience preparing for than actually going to trial. [21]

On a particular day, the court oversaw the selection of fourteen juries in a session lasting from court opening in the morning until 7:30 that evening. The process entailed selecting juries, giving fifteen minutes to a side, for case after case. At times when the jury selection process wearied everyone, Hall injected levity into the situation by reading from his collection of excuses from potential jurors. [22]

The matter of motions is crucial to the conduct of a trial, because unexamined or pending motions, which have a bearing on the case, can easily stop its progress. Former judicial law clerk Michael Smith reflected on Hall's expectations:

> My orders were when we had a management conference or we had trial, there better not be any pending motions. They had better be taken care of because it is so hard for the parties to prepare a case when you don't know what the judge is going to allow and what he isn't. The first time I went to a state court trial . . . there were ten motions that the judge hadn't done anything on! You don't know how to prepare your case because you don't know how much of your case is

> going to be left after the judge rules. We never could have done that working for Judge Hall. It reflected poorly on him, he believed, if the parties couldn't prepare their cases because he wasn't getting his work done, and so, he got his work done. That was something I was really proud of. [23]

Hall proactively expedited certain kinds of cases. Attorney Ned Dennis explained that he did not routinely have cases in the federal court, save for disability cases. Normally with Social Security disability cases, the federal judges would refer the lawyer to a United States magistrate to make a finding of fact, or note conclusions of law, in a recommendation to the judge as to the disposition of the case. Judge Hall preferred to take direct action, which meant a quicker resolution to the clients' problems. For example, unemployed and disabled clients with Social Security income alone got help more quickly. [24]

Judge Hall trusted his own abilities to the extent that he never worried that another court, the Fifth Circuit Court of Appeals, might reverse his decisions. He vowed to make the best decisions he could as judge and regarded a reversal as an instance of a wiser, more prudent court having for proper reasons found a more just decision. His friend and later a district judge, William L. Peek Jr., made a successful appeal to the Fifth Circuit Court of Appeals at New Orleans after Hall ruled against his client in a case. Hall declared to Peek, "You're the first rascal to get one of my rulings reversed!" [25]

Judge Hall's staff began with Sue Jordan. She had spoiled him from early on, taking care of the minute details of the Marshall law office, organizing receipts he had stuffed into his pockets, running errands, and routing records to the accountant. She was the personal secretary who covered the details so that he could do his primary tasks. In Washington Sue's managerial role had grown though she remained Hall's personal secretary and assistant. Then and in the federal court, her intuition and experience made his work more effective.[26]

Especially during the first two years after Hall became judge, he served the Beaumont court. On the way there one night his car broke down. Sue Jordan, the court coordinator and maybe another two persons were with him in the classic but well-kept 1960-model Chrysler Imperial sedan that had belonged to Sam Sr. The massive car was a familiar reminder of the elder Hall to the junior, and it overheated near San Augustine. It happened that Hall had left his bag with his judge's robe and his briefcase in Marshall, so Madeleine and Amanda brought them to San Augustine. About 11:00 that Sunday night, Hall called his friend and local resident Judge John Luther Smith from the local Dairy Queen saying he needed a car. Smith knew Hall's love for a good prank, but said, "Well, Sam, I can't think of a town that it would be harder to get you a car on Sunday night at eleven o'clock!" But Smith helped out, and Hall got a loan car from a dealer. At the weekend after Sam had returned from Beaumont, Madeleine put an end to any more trips out of town in the old Chrysler.[27]

Shortly thereafter, the news broke about how Judge Hall had referred to homosexual inmates in the Jefferson County Jail in Beaumont as "queers," which caused a brief but intense controversy. Smith declared that he had been happy to help Hall out with transportation to Beaumont, but that he "didn't help him get to Beaumont to make a fool of himself!" [28]

Hall's comments caused a stir after the Beaumont newspaper ran the story. He was in Beaumont, filling in for the vacationing Judge Joe Fisher. A convicted drug offender had been jailed, and his cellmates were engaging in homosexual activities, so he sued Jefferson County, Texas, for $100,000 plus damages. Questioning a county sheriff's lieutenant John Cascio, Judge Hall simply referred to the homosexual inmates as "a bunch of queers," which gave the opportunity for the controversy begun in the Beaumont newspaper. One of Hall's judicial law clerks, Julie Richardson, took the news reporter to task for taking comments completely out of context and writing a sensational and opportunistic story that asserted violations of the prisoners' civil rights. Hall had clear opinions and no reluctance to express them. Well, the homosexual prisoners had dyed their shirts pink, and he had no tolerance for that; how could this be allowed in the jail? The justice system should not allow such conduct; the comment was not directed against an individual so much as the situation [29]

Hall would not apologize, and Judge Charles Clark of the Fifth Circuit Court of Appeals dismissed a complaint against him. George S. Smith, the publisher of the *Marshall News Messenger*, characterized Hall's comment as a "slip" and reminded his readers about Hall's long record of caring for people and involvement in public service—things that were a truer indication of the man than certain comments which had caused the unintended controversy.[30]

The controversy belied Hall's basic good nature and desire to put people first, as revealed in the observations of Judge William Cornelius of Jefferson, who wrote,

> His service as our congressman and later as a federal judge taxed his deep concern for people almost to the breaking point. Yet, he never lost his faith in people, and he never lost his desire to help them in whatever capacity he was serving. His primary interest was not the philosophical or academic aspects of the law, but its human aspect. He looked on every problem as a human problem, and he applied the law in a way that, as far as he could make it, would benefit

> the human beings involved. He recognized that the legal issues that confronted him were not just academic and jurisprudential issues aloof from real life, but everyday issues that profoundly affected the lives of ordinary people and their families. This perspective gave him a keen insight into the problems of people, as well as a strong desire to help in any way he could.[31]

Judge Thomas M. Reavley, Senior United States Circuit Judge for the Fifth Circuit, identified the tension between Hall's role as a judge and his concern for people, speaking of it as a form of interference:

> When Socrates arrived for his dialogue with Gorgias, he first directed his companions to: "Ask him who he is." Too many of us in this hurrying, superficial culture never decide who we are. We never anchor, and never set a course. We are at the mercy of temptation and every passing storm. Not so Sam B. Hall, Jr. He knew who he was, what he stood for, and what his priorities were. He was decisive; he had the capacity to choose and decide when the time came. That faculty made him a natural judge. His gregarious nature, however, interfered with his life as a judge. He cared about people and their social and political affairs. His concerns drew him toward active participation in the lives of his friends. And his friends were many. One could join that company easily.[32]

Judge Hall readily overcame the interference to which Reavley referred in remarkable and memorable ways. His consideration for people actually helped him to fulfill his judicial role, Reavley thought. "When Hall became federal judge in Marshall, people, including longtime friends, asked what they should call him; what was the proper way to address him? 'Just call me Sam—that's my name—it'll be fine with me,' he replied. 'If I'm in the courtroom, of course you've got to honor the law, so say 'yes, sir' and 'no, sir'; but when you're in my office, my name is Sam.'" He carefully cultivated sociable relationships outside of the courtroom and a humane, affirming atmosphere in the courtroom.

Attorney Gilbert I. "Buddy" Low provided observations of Hall's gregarious nature:

> Judge Hall was a truly great man and a man of the people. Once he was in Beaumont, and we went out to a little restaurant about ten miles out of town. There were a number of people in the restaurant, and I sat down at a table. Judge Hall went around shaking hands with a few of the people he knew and introducing himself to others in his affable

> and sincere manner. When he sat down, I asked him, "You are not running for office, so what are you doing meeting all of these people?" He said, "How do you know I am not running?" He really never stopped "running for office," and he never lost touch with the people and his feeling for people.[33]

Even as a judge keeping distance between himself and the public, he still found ways to take delight in being with people, especially in the courtroom. Judge David Folsom remarked that Hall's interest in people translated into kindness and consideration in trials, both for the parties involved and their attorneys. Said Folsom, "He never lost contact with the people and had a strong sense of fairness in doing what he thought was right. You would often see his decisions and his findings tailored in that fashion; a fine combination of following the law, but occasionally blending that with a result that was justified under the facts and circumstances."[34]

Hall's sociability and enjoyment of people influenced his activities as a judge. Of course he was forced to restrain himself. Hall the congressman had relished the constant exchanges involved with service in Washington and the First District; no man ever enjoyed the social and relational aspects of congressional politics more than he did. Hall the federal judge could no longer speak about public policy or controversial legislation. He could discuss court cases only with members of the court, specifically his judicial law clerks. The confidentiality and objectivity expected in his position did not, however, exclude a kind of affirming and gracious familiarity.[35]

Yet Judge Hall's humanity never trivialized the court or his position in it. Where possible, he sought to meet people at their point of need and understanding. As a man with a happy wife and three daughters, healthy, strong relationships with his mother and a sister, Hall was comfortable with women, and they with him, and he knew how to treat girls. There was the day he donned his robe in the courtroom to interrogate the preteen daughter of attorney Don Bush. Hall warned her about lying in court, and asked, among other things, whether she had a boyfriend. She relished the whole line of questioning and the judge's interest in her.[36]

Bill Palmer's seven-year-old grandson, Trent, had asked to view the proceedings of a case being tried by a law firm for which his mother worked as a paralegal. Trent accompanied his grandfather to the federal courthouse. Judge Hall emerged from chambers, entered the reception room, greeted Trent with a handshake and told him he was happy to see him there. Judge Hall had the federal marshal bring Trent to the bench, where the boy swung the gavel to open court and remained throughout the day, holding the gavel and observing the proceedings. A certificate commemorated the court day as having been held in Trent's honor. This was unusual, but not so unusual in the court of Sam B. Hall Jr. Hall valued children but sought to honor distinguished elders. For example, Judge John Furrh who had suffered a stroke was a special guest at court, the day's proceedings dedicated to him.[37]

The "routine" situations were little different. An inmate trustee who had escaped from the federal corrections facility in Texarkana came before the judge. Possibly an illegal alien and with an American wife and children in Colorado, he simply left to visit his pregnant, ill wife because he knew she was in serious difficulties; in his mind that outweighed the added punishment he would probably get. Either the authorities found him or he returned to Texarkana on his own. His defense attorney had him request character references from friends, relatives and employers. In court, Judge Hall sat for twenty or thirty minutes reading the letters. After finishing, he asked everyone's attention. He spoke at length to the convict about the value of American citizenship and the importance of obeying the laws of the land, which included the laws about escape from prison.

The inmate had explained why he needed to see his wife. He also spoke fluent English, which impressed Hall, who asked why he simply could not wait eight more months. Actually, the situation fascinated him. He commented to the United States attorney and the probation officer that he believed the man, indeed, liked his curious sense of responsibility though his taking flight was wrong. Deciding on a minimum term of punishment, he ordered six months additional time and urged him to pursue American citizenship, promising to help him qualify. It helped that many people in Colorado had written on his behalf.

After an impassioned speech, Hall left the bench, shook hands with the man and chatted with him briefly before resuming the bench and finishing the day's court work. Speaking of the incident, attorney Stephen Arnold said that Hall looked beyond the obvious fact that the man was a lawbreaker to the potential he had as an American citizen.[38]

Hall characteristically guarded the interests of the powerless or helpless. A frail, elderly couple had married late in years. Armed with a power of attorney, the woman's daughter seized her mother's assets and moved her out of state, placing her in a nursing home. The elderly husband followed, got his wife, and they returned to East Texas. They filed suit and successfully reclaimed the woman's assets. With the judge's help the man made a good faith effort to assure that his wife's estate went into a proper guardianship. The decisive hearing involved a conversation between Judge Hall and the visibly angry and aggressive husband who had been beside himself with fear for his wife. Judge Hall promised that he personally would assure nobody took advantage of the wife or her assets and possessions. Visibly relaxing in response to Hall's words, the older man forgot his anger.[39]

Hall cared about the effect of sentencing on the individual and the circumstances behind criminal arrest. An elderly man was entrapped by federal investigators who monitored orders from pornographic video catalogs distributed to people known to buy regular videos by mail order. The defendant had no criminal record before his arrest by FBI agents at his home. Judge Hall considered it a clear case of entrapment, but federal law at the time allowed it, and the man got a minimum sentence of six months in the case after entering a guilty plea. Hall agonized over the unfairness of such a law. Granted, the man had ordered and received an "adult" videotape, but the consequences seemed unwarranted, and the procedures which led to the defendant's arrest, trial, conviction, and incarceration annoyed him. The Supreme Court later declared the relevant law unconstitutional. Hall discussed the situation afterwards with his law clerk Ed Hohn. He knew the punishment did not suit the situation. He habitually analyzed people who came into his court, watching to see how they presented themselves. He tried to discern whether a person had a depraved or a clear heart. Was the person's action clearly a mistake, something they did not understand they were doing at the time? In the case of the elderly man and the adult videotape, a bad law mandated punishment, so the judge complied with minimum sentencing, convinced, however, that justice was not served.[40]

Attorney Richard "Racehorse" Haynes recalled Hall's process of deciding on the "heart" of a court witness. His honesty being in doubt, evidence was presented that the man had urinated in a bulk shipment of wine, knowing others would drink it. Hall pondered what such an act revealed about the man's character and the condition of his conscience. He believed such testimony should compel jurors to think carefully about the veracity of such a witness.[41]

Hall could be very stern as in the case of a prominent businessman involved in a conspiracy that led to millions of dollars in losses among banks in East Texas. He scolded the man for his conscious manipulation of people and violation of the law.[42]

Justice knew no color, creed, or social distinctions in Hall's court. A young black man worked behind the counter in a convenience store. Federal agents observed him selling individual, unwrapped cigarettes, a violation of state tobacco tax laws. Interpreting the act as cause to search the establishment in the owner's absence, they found a handgun belonging to the owner, not the defendant whose probation was revoked, and he was brought to trial in federal court. The defense entered a motion to suppress the evidence, which Judge Hall read and denied, so the government could proceed with their case. He called the lawyers to his chambers in order to determine whether they would proceed to trial or the defense would enter a plea. The African-American civil rights lawyer was there with the United

States Attorney. Judge Hall asked his clerk, Ed Hohn, what the time of sentencing would be upon conviction. The current law emphasized jailing felons and keeping them there, and judges were strapped with mandatory minimum sentences and strict sentencing guidelines.

The U.S. Attorney said the man would receive a sentence of fifteen years on conviction. Attorney and formal judicial law clerk Ed Hohn recalled the judge's reaction:

> I will never forget the look on his face. I mean, he just exploded! Fifteen years! He didn't even say another word, wouldn't even entertain more discussion. He ordered everybody back in the courtroom, got on the bench, and granted the motion to suppress immediately. That gutted the government's case and actually made a statement to the U.S. Attorneys that their job was not just to seek convictions over and over again, to keep their numbers up for federal funding and all types of benefits that flow from high numbers of convictions, but actually to do justice in what they were doing. He took me back to chambers afterwards. He was still livid. He sat me down and said there is no reason why this man should do fifteen years for selling cigarettes without a package.[43]

Hall presided over a case involving a dozen or so Marines injured in the crash of a Sikorsky helicopter in Korea. They suffered burns from the fire fed by ruptured fuel lines. As a veteran and former member of the Veterans Affairs committee in Congress, Judge Hall was upset that these young men had permanent, disfiguring injuries. During the trial one of the defense contractor's lawyers posed questions to the effect that perhaps the men in certain helicopter seats could have evacuated faster and so reduced the number and extent of the burn injuries. The comments incensed the judge and set the courtroom on edge. Hall endured only briefly and said, "Now let me get this right, Mr. [the attorney]; you're telling this court and this jury that sitting in rows 13 and 14 should have made a difference in how fast they got out of there, compared to rows 10 through 12?" "Yes, judge, that's exactly my point." Hall replied, "Son, move on; you're wasting the court's time. Do you have anything else you would like to ask this witness?"

At recess, Hall said to Hohn, "Don't ever get into anything like that if you're on the defense side. Either the product is defective, or it's not. Don't start bugging people about where they're sitting, or where they're standing. It makes no difference to the case, and it makes the jury mad."[44]

The Sikorsky case gave Hall an opportunity to bring people together. As he frequently did after trials, he proceeded to the hallway of the federal court building to meet with the jurors and other visitors. Sue Jordan often quipped, "Oh, he thinks he's running for reelection again!" He wanted to know how the jurors were doing at the end of a trial. In the case involving the Marines and the helicopter crash, a settlement had been reached during the trial. The jurors felt the need to talk to the plaintiffs, to know more about some things, including how their families were doing. Michael Smith summarized what happened:

> Well, what ended up happening was very odd. The jurors, the plaintiffs and the lawyers from both sides all went and sat in the courtroom and had a little mixer for about an hour and a half. They looked at the videotapes, the computer recreations of the collision that had not yet been played. It was extraordinary because the jurors, the plaintiffs, and the defense lawyers were all standing around talking: "Yeah, this happened; no, it was like this ... Oh, I remember when this happened...." They had an interesting time talking about the case. Judge Hall came in and sat down. He just started having an informal visit with all the jurors where they got to ask questions about "why did you do this, why did you do that." He really enjoyed that because he never got to talk to them about that [why the trial proceeded as it did]. [45]

It was odd to have a jury stay around the courtroom after such a case, but they needed to deal with the powerful emotional nature of the plaintiff's claims in the trial proceedings.

A troubled young man hanged himself in jail and died. The man's mother sued, alleging violation of her son's civil rights. The case was dismissed for lack of evidence. But the mother's predicament bothered Judge Hall so much that he gave his undivided attention when she testified, and made certain she knew it. The case had no known legal merit or remedy, but Judge Hall forthrightly assured the mother, commenting that he could not express adequately the deep sorrow he felt about her son's death and the pain she had endured. He made sure the mother had every opportunity to express her anger, frustration and grief. The whole matter ended with the mother having said and done everything she could, the judge having respected her need for a forum, and a tearful hug between them both at the end of it all. People might ask whether it was proper for a federal judge to descend to such informality. But Hall's court could allow that because Hall was that kind of man. Who could question such a warm, personal act when something more essential than the law was served, and when the law itself was powerless to reassure and comfort in a tragic situation? Clearly, lawyers and judges could be a positive, healing influence simply by preserving human dignity and meeting a need, if not through application of the law, then by allowing the effects of personal compassion and respect to work through the crisis. United States Magistrate Earl S. Hines expressed the idea well, writing to Hall, "The temptation is great for judges to remain aloof in an effort to avoid the appearance of partiality. However, you somehow have been able to maintain personal intimacy with lawyers, litigants, jurors, friends, etc., without compromising your responsibility to preside without bias, prejudice or sympathy. That is a feature I will attempt to emulate for the rest of my career."[46]

During the years he was a federal judge Hall took advantage of his restored circumstances in Marshall to spend time with his former law partners—always valued friends. Just as he had done frequently while the Congress was in recess, he often went to his old law office to visit. He did not have to go far, only across the street. He was delighted when friends and acquaintances came by his office to visit. But he was dismayed that people treated him differently as a judge. Why did they not visit more often as they used to?

A friend visited at the courthouse, creating a security problem. In 1991, before the metal detectors were installed in the federal courthouse, the "Government Accounting Office, an entity Judge Hall said could not count to save their jobs," had put stickers prohibiting firearms on only the right side of the glass double doors to the courthouse. Hall's friend entered the building through the left side of the double doors. The U.S. Marshal searched him, found a firearm, and inquired with the judge. Asked what he had been thinking, the friend told Hall, "I thought it was OK if you walked in the side of the doors that did not have the gun sticker posted." Hall retorted, "Go back out to your truck, leave the gun, and walk back in on the right side of the doors!" One might bear a firearm in Sam Hall's presence, but not in the federal courthouse! Judge Hall knew this was no serious event, only a stupid oversight.[47]

Judge Sam B. Hall Sr. once told his son that "a district judge has all the power in the world, but a lot of times he doesn't have the right to use that power." Hall the federal district judge kept the approachability that had served him so well as Hall the civic leader and congressman. There was no hint of his having been changed by virtue of his new position; he surely had no exaggerated sense of his own importance. He also wanted to be accountable to valued friends. He confided with Joe Lovelace, his longtime friend from Linden, that he worried about abusing the power that he could wield as a judge. He asked Lovelace to "chew him out" if he ever saw him abusing his position or power. Lovelace quipped that he would never "come into the chambers of a federal judge and give him a lecture," but he might send in Don Dowd, his junior partner! [48]

Hall's experiences as an attorney contributed to his understanding of the judicial role, while his congressional experiences and patriotism assured that he put the constitution, nation, and flag foremost in the courtroom. Having discussed the bicentennial of the ratification of the U.S. Constitution with judicial law clerk Ernest Metzger, Hall suggested it would be appropriate to make a special presentation during a break in the current trial proceedings. New Hampshire ratified the Constitution on June 21, 1788; on that date, with nine states having ratified, the Constitution took effect. On the bicentennial date, Metzger opened the federal court at Marshall, giving a brief history that included the competition between Virginia and New Hampshire to be the ninth state to ratify. Judge Hall mused that people tend to consider that part of history insignificant, but at a time when the nation struggled for its "very existence, trying to forge this frontier into a nation, then you had some men who stood up and were counted" despite the risks. Metzger wrote, "I don't know how many billable hours were racked up during that time, but I got to talk to the jury for ten minutes about the Constitution. I thought it was an absolutely splendid thing to do, and the jury enjoyed it. . . . It was clearly a very congressional thing to do."[49]

The owner of an auto repair business between Marshall and Jefferson, Bobby Johnson was impressed with Hall's enthusiasm for public service and fidelity to country. He recalled the judge's emphasis on celebrating citizenship:

> As a federal judge, Sam called me one day and told me to be at the federal courthouse in Marshall on a certain date. Knowing Sam, I did not ask why. I just said, 'Yes, sir!' Sam then told me he was going to swear in new American citizens in Marshall, and that it was the first time he thought it had ever been done in Marshall, and he wanted the ceremony to be special. Sam went on to tell me that he was inviting me and some more of his veteran friends to sit in the jury box, and that I was going to be his Vietnam veteran. I told him I would be glad to be there and it was an honor. . . . In the jury box, I sat with former prisoners of war, veterans of each war, pilots and friends of Sam B. Hall. As the ceremony began, Sam introduced each one of us by giving everyone a brief history of our service to our country, praising us for our sacrifice, and telling the new citizens that it was because of veterans like us and many who did not survive the wars, that they were being given the privilege of becoming American citizens. Chills went up my arms as Sam spoke. What an honor he had just bestowed upon everyone in the

> jury box. There sat Sam in his black judge's robe that demanded respect, and he was praising us and thanking us for our service, and honoring us before new citizens. That day will stand out for the rest of my life in my memory. What a wonderful thing Judge Sam B. Hall did for those of us, his friends, his veterans. Sam never once faltered when it came to veterans or the United States of America. What you saw was what you got with Sam, and red, white and blue remind me of my friend Sam. [50]

Johnson also served as a district attorney's investigator and drug interdiction officer, often stopping people on the highway. He wrote, "Whenever I stop a military veteran or active duty soldier or sailor, I end our contact by telling the person, 'Thank you for serving your country!' A long time ago, Sam B. Hall, Jr., said that to me, and then as now, the veterans in our country don't hear it enough." Johnson urged other officers to follow his and Hall's example.[51]

Naturalization ceremonies were emotional, heartfelt events for Hall. He liked to involve as many people as possible in planning them, and the courtroom was to be full. At the first one he presided over, his daughter Becky and Dwight Mays from Marshall sang patriotic songs. It was the first naturalization ceremony ever conducted in Marshall, with eight or so immigrants taking the oath of allegiance to the United States of America.[52]

Naturalization ceremonies had to be made as special as possible in Hall's courtroom. His role was to officiate, surely, but citizens old and new were to have an unforgettable experience, and not just a lesson in civic virtues and the high value of American citizenship. He invited East Texans, introduced them and identified their roles. Military veterans and public servants, a military color guard, and representatives from the police and sheriff's office added to the spirit of the occasion. The new citizens were given the opportunity to identify with established citizens, and vice versa. For Sam Hall the judge, citizen and congressman, the United States could never have too many responsible, patriotic citizens. The entry to citizenship was important enough to be celebrated with an element of drama and dignity, soberly, yet with cheer. And so the naturalization ceremony conformed to the Judge's habit of celebration life itself. If Sam Hall could make a party in order to enjoy people, then life was at its sweetest. He liked people and valued citizens, wanted them to know how much he valued them, and why, even in the courtroom.[53]

Hall's religion and his patriotism were equally serious and a source of joy to him. His love of flag and country was legendary and absolutely unashamed, and as far as anyone knew his actions on behalf of country matched his words in praise of it. As a congressman dedicating a stretch of

Highway 155, the Gold Star Highway, in Northeast Texas, the American flag on display started to topple. A man grabbed it as Hall reached for it. He declared that he would take care of it, and did so with dramatic, spontaneous words and gesture, yet there was no "theater" to it, simply pure honesty. Many people there always remembered it, reminded that Hall's patriotism was one of the constants of life, something everyone could always count on.[54]

His zeal caught on with his grandchildren. Chase Palmer wrote, "Pop taught me patriotism. He genuinely loved this country and its freedoms. He understood the sacrifices others made so that we can enjoy our freedom today. He always seemed to be around flags, and you will be hard pressed to find him in many pictures while in Congress or on the Bench where there isn't a flag somewhere over his shoulder."[55]

Hall loved Veterans Day, Memorial Day and Fourth of July rallies, and spoke notably at rallies in Marshall and Hallsville. With absolute confidence he declared the blessings of American liberty and told stories to drive home the point with audiences. Having been with a congressional delegation to East Germany, he told about an East German who had found his lost passport. Returning it to Hall, the man tearfully begged the congressman to take him to the United States where he could be free. Hall wanted all Americans, especially the younger generations, to respect and emulate the founders' vision and examples of enduring freedom based in sacrifice and service. Not content to be the patriot, he wanted others to be patriots, too. He had absolute, forthright respect for the American flag, for military veterans, and for those in active service. He loved to salute flags and military personnel. Harrison County and First Congressional District residents always remembered his speeches given at special rallies, for example, when he spoke on Veterans Day at Marshall High School. In the presence of students and representatives of the American Legion and Veterans of Foreign Wars, Hall urged the students to take their citizenship and their roles as "defenders of freedom" seriously. Hall said, "Don't take for granted, as is so easy to do, the fact that your country is going to stand as it is today, without your help." [56]

In many of his speeches as a congressional representative, Hall used the diary of a schoolmate, Tom Austin, who had been a prisoner of war. Remarkably, as it was one of the few mementoes she had of her son, Austin's mother sent it, telling him to use it as long as he needed it. After Hall became a federal judge, he returned the diary. The diary itself inspired Hall. Austin's daily entries spoke of the privilege he felt to serve his country even as a prisoner of war.[57]

The law school graduate who becomes a federal judicial law clerk typically gains incomparable experience in the position, aside from the honor of serving. The law clerks are true partners in the judge's work in the court. Judge Hall's clerks hailed from a variety of law schools and they all considered their experiences with him irreplaceable. The clerkship shaped their professional and personal lives, and they regarded Judge Hall as the strongest factor in that process. It was an experience they cherished ever after.

Patrice Barron and John Crews were the first of Hall's judicial law clerks. Later a Houston attorney, in 1985 Barron asked for an interview with Hall before he actually became judge, visited him in Marshall and was offered a position. She later praised his "common sense and integrity" and noted the dignity and respect he accorded others. He put children first, always. "Judge Hall also had a fabulous sense of humor," Barron said. "We spent many a moment laughing so hard that tears came to our eyes." [59]

Crews, a law student at Southern Methodist University, read in *The Washington Post* that Hall was leaving the Congress to become a judge, and wrote asking whether he needed a law clerk. He was interviewed twice in Washington and once in Marshall. His father had worked with Wright Patman in Washington, so Crews thought it interesting he got to work with Hall, Patman's successor. After his two years with Hall, he served with the United States Attorney's office at Brownsville, Texas, almost ten years before taking a supervisory position with the U.S. Attorney's office for the District of New Mexico in 1997.[60]

After her graduation from the Baylor School of Law, Julie Richardson served from October, 1987, to March, 1989. After interviewing with Chevron, she came to interview with Hall. Immediately he offered her the job. She had expected to be told that he would get back to her, as Chevron had done. Richardson recalled, "I would never do this again—I guess I can blame it on being young or naive or stupid—I said, 'Well, let me think about it and I'll get back to you.' I look back now—I can't believe I said that to a federal judge."[61]

Serving with Judge Hall from August of 1987 to September of 1989, Ernest Metzger came to work convinced the judge disliked mulling over decisions because of the quick, decisive way he was hired. Metzger had failed to get a position with Judge William M. Steger at Tyler, but the three judges under whom he had worked at the U.S. Court of Appeals at Tyler recommended him, and Hall was happy to hire him at the conclusion of their first interview. Originally from Urbana, Illinois, Metzger took his law degree from Southern Methodist University in Dallas. He found that Hall took a bemused attitude toward clerks and lawyers when they were city people, especially if they were from northern states. They became subjects in the experiments in humor Hall relished. Hall inquired repeatedly as to whether Metzger had ever castrated a bull. He allowed of course he had not: "No, sir I haven't ever castrated a bull," to which Hall always said, "I need your help to castrate a bull. I want you to hold his hind legs." Hall was going to get him out to the farm, and teased him about it repeatedly, knowing Ernie was thoroughly unaccustomed with and fairly ignorant of what went on there. In a letter to the judge, Metzger later wrote, "I had to excuse myself at least three times after being asked to help you castrate a bull." If only he had known. Metzger made it to the farm perhaps twice, carrying papers for the judge to sign. Metzger once neglected to wear a proper jacket into the courtroom, and Judge Hall never let him forget it. Commenting on Hall's elaboration of the initial event, Metzger complained, "I wasn't too bothered that every lawyer in the county had to hear about it but somehow in the retelling of the story I kept losing articles of clothing and arriving in greater degrees of undress. If I had stayed much longer with you, the lawyers would have been told how I stepped out of the shower to dry myself on the flag." Evaluating his experience with Hall, Metzger continued, "I wouldn't have traded the experience for anything. I learned a special brand of law that I never saw before and I've never seen since. A lawyer was arguing before you [Hall] that persons in different professions could be disabled in different ways: 'An injured leg means something different to a man in the dairy business that it does to the kicker for the Cowboys.' You [Hall] ruled that 'the kicker for the Cowboys should be in the dairy business.' I assume this is now the law of the land."[62]

G. Hobart Miller served from July, 1989, to November, 1990, before taking a position with the tax division of the U.S. Justice Department. Having planned to interview with Judge Steger in Tyler but finding the position closed, Miller learned of an open position with Hall from his Baylor law professor Peeler Williams Jr. Miller enjoyed working with Judge Hall and appreciated how the judge affirmed his clerks' efforts on written opinions and in the preparation of pre-trial orders and briefs. He valued the lessons in courtroom conduct and professionalism.[63]

Ed Hohn clerked with Judge Hall from December, 1990, to August, 1992, interviewing with him in the spring of 1990:

> As I entered his office, Judge Hall sat behind his old-time war-horse of a desk, the walls covered with pictures of the likes of Tip O'Neill, President Jimmy Carter, President Ronald Reagan, and President George Bush. Strong, distinguished and charismatic, Judge Hall asked, "What do you expect to achieve through a federal clerkship with me?" My response was simple, showing my naiveté and complete lack of understanding of the greatness of the man I was dealing with: "I would like to get a little experience, learn how to try a lawsuit, and work on my writing skills."

Hohn was surprised when part of the interview involved going to the farm so that Judge Hall could show him around the property and check on his cattle, including a particularly scary Brahma-mix bull.[64]

Sharon Kacmarcik was also a clerk at the time, and Michael Smith followed Sharon after she left. Kay Lynn Vincent followed Ed Hohn in late 1992. Kacmarcik, a native of the Chicago area and an Emory Law School graduate, flew from Atlanta in 1991 for an interview, thinking it might be good to get experience in another part of the country and knowing Judge Hall had a good reputation. The city girl drove in from Shreveport, dressed appropriately in a suit and heels. The judge was in "jeans, cowboy boots and a cowboy hat." He invited her to the farm, and she accepted. In her recollections of Judge Hall, Kacmarcik said,

> He always drove this big, red, but kind of maroon truck. We drove out to the farm, and he showed me where his daughter had her shooting house. I guess she hunted deer. He drove me throughout the whole farm, and then we got back to the front where cows are fed. I guess it's a trough of some kind that you put the feed in. He got out of the truck and said, "Well, you could get out, or if you want to, you can stay in." I was just so confused. Why wouldn't I want to get out? I was in heels, but that wasn't a big deal. So, I got out of the truck and I'm standing there. He put the feed out, and all of a sudden, he clasped his hands together and starts making this, to me, more of a city girl, bizarre noise . . . these cows just start running towards us, these huge animals. Of course, now I realize why he asked me if I wanted to stay in the truck, because it's like a stampede of cows. I think it made him chuckle a bit to see me so dumbfounded by this. I tried to maintain composure and tried not to sprint back to the truck, but I did kind of cower behind him. The cows came running up to the trough, and went right by us. [65]

Kacmarcik returned to Emory Law School to direct the clerkship program there. Her story of the farm experience evolved to the point that her colleagues insisted she was offered the clerking position while standing with the judge in the middle of a herd of cows. She could never recover the story after it had strayed so far from the facts. [66]

Kay Lynn (Vincent) Brumbaugh first met Hall during a government class trip to Washington, D.C. The congressman hosted a luncheon where the teenagers were served burgers: "We all liked him as soon as we met him for he was responsible for the best meal of our trip—cheeseburgers, the gourmet meal of choice for teenagers." The seventeen-year-old Carthage, Texas, native could not have anticipated working for Hall seven years later, but she got an interview during her third year at the University of Virginia Law School. Brumbaugh recalled, "Although he was generally reluctant to hire law clerks from "those East Coast schools" where students have "different personalities" which do not always "fit in" in East Texas, Judge Hall was willing to take a chance on me since I was born and raised in Carthage. I served as one of his law clerks from August 1992 until December 1993. I am truly blessed that he offered me the opportunity of a lifetime, and I can honestly say that serving as Judge Hall's law clerk was the best job I have ever had." She claimed to be a better person and lawyer because she had worked with Hall. "He taught me to always look for the humor in life, to look for the good in my fellow man, to treat every person with respect and to have confidence in myself." [67]

Brumbaugh told what happened when she passed her bar examinations:

> Judge Hall's mischievous side revealed itself shortly after I received my bar examination scores in November 1992. For months prior to receiving my scores, I had moaned and groaned that I probably would not pass although I had never failed an exam in my life. Judge Hall good-naturedly teased me about my unnecessary worrying. Fortunately, I did in fact pass the exam and was honored to be sworn in as an attorney in the State of Texas by Judge Hall the very next day. Judge Hall, however, did not tell me that he planned to announce my bar exam scores from the bench in open court to a room full of lawyers before he swore me in to the bar. I almost crawled under the table. I learned a lesson in self-doubt that day: it is not productive and usually unwarranted.[68]

Jill Renfro Willis came as a judicial law clerk in August, 1993, and was the last to have any service time with Hall. After only a few more months Sue Jordan was shuttling paperwork between the office and the Hall home where Hall was recuperating from cancer surgery. Willis's last visit there with Hall was in early 1994. Jordan told him about "this boy" whom Jill had met—Greg, who became her husband. Willis recalled, "Judge Hall looked me straight in the eye and in his very serious, Southern drawl, said to me, "I have just one question for you—is he a Yankee or a Southerner?" Only because I knew him did I know he was teasing. Fortunately, Greg was Texas born and bred, so Judge Hall slyly smiled and nodded, saying, 'Good.'" Hall continued and told Jill about his grandfather, John Will Hall of Hallsville, who quizzed strangers passing through as to whether they fought for the North or for the South. If the man answered, "the North," then Hall would tell him to just keep moving. [69]

Willis focused on the personal benefits of serving with Judge Hall: "He had a profound impact on my life. He gave me a job although I was not in the top of my law school class. If he had not given me a job, I would not have met my husband, because one of the other law clerks, Kay Lynn Brumbaugh, introduced me to my husband." Serving with Hall facilitated her later position with a Dallas law firm. "I truly believe God used Judge Hall to guide and direct my life." [70]

Hired as a clerk in December, 1993, Katie Dukes grew up in Washington, D.C., the daughter of Mack Fleming, who was Chief Counsel and Staff Director for the Committee on Veterans' Affairs in the House. A graduate of Rice University and the University of Texas Law School, Dukes learned that Hall wanted clerks with lots of energy and drive, people who wanted to work hard, not necessarily those with the highest grades. He listened to his clerks' recommendations and mused that the only judgments he got overturned on appeal were in cases where he failed to follow his clerks' advice—and the clerks kept track of their recommendations in writing.[71]

No one served longer—almost three years—than Sally Socia. When Socia was about to complete her law degree, Hall's friend Frank "Bodie" Fuller passed her resume to him. The judge declared he had never seen such a full resume from a prospective clerk, as Socia also had a Ph.D. in Sociology with teaching and business experience. She proved to be an exceptional choice for the next three years. She recognized Hall's honest acceptance of her:

> You never felt uncomfortable in the slightest and to me that was one of the most—he admired you for your intellect, your interest in life, and that's it, I mean, you could be entirely comfortable with him. Of course he had three daughters and a marvelous wife, Madeleine, with whom he was desperately in love after I don't know how many years of marriage. So he certainly had a high regard for women, and also his mother was an enormous influence on his life.

Socia found him to be an affirming man, complimentary of her work, giving her the freedom to do her best work and appreciating it when it was done. [72]

The work of the judge's clerks in federal court involves reading briefs and researching case law, checking attorneys' citations for accuracy and preparing memorandums for review by the judge. The judge surveys all the background information, using the memorandum as a tool in formulating the decision. The clerks write orders describing the judge's decisions. They coordinate communication and scheduling between lawyers and the court. The judge may rely on the clerks' research to remain abreast of changes in the law, especially the technicalities. The clerks had responsibility for researching the laws, including the statements of fact pertinent to a case, and even writing out the options for interpretation. But the judge wrote directly on the parts of the opinion having to do with resolving the case. A clerk might do a great deal of the writing found in a published case, but the judge decided how to apply the law based on the facts of the case. Ultimately "the opinions went out over the signature of the guy with the presidential commission on the wall."[73]

Hall's published opinions were often relatively terse and concise. Judge Hall had two general criteria by which his clerks could gauge the suitability of a decision for publication: first, was the decision a particularly good, perhaps fresh, statement of the law, and, second, would the decision likely be any help to future court cases? Thus his published opinions clearly related to useful interpretations and were often cited in subsequent decisions. Hall was not concerned to have many case decisions published. Some judges seek to publish more, and they select clerks well suited to publishing long, scholarly decisions publishable in the major law review journals. Hall preferred to keep cases moving in the court docket, and so this discouraged much attention to writing long decisions to be published. Nevertheless, over fifty published decisions emerged from Hall's court. [74]

The more mundane features of the clerks' work included typing and filing any documents the judge's secretary was not responsible for. She took care of the formal opinions, the jury charge, verdict forms, findings of fact, conclusions of law, scheduling orders, notices of hearing, and special orders. The clerks took care of distributing the docket sheets to the proper parties, attaching pending motions for cases, and keeping the water pitchers in the courtroom filled with ice water. As members of the court, like the judge and court clerks, the law clerks were to obey rules of conduct governing speaking about cases with people other than the judge, having outside employment and being involved in politics. [75]

Hall employed his clerks at least as much as managers as researchers. Ed Hohn described the work, saying,

> You were running half the docket, you were making sure motions got ruled on, you were identifying problems early on, you were helping out the parties, the lawyers, if they had questions about how the court worked. You were expected to interact with the lawyers and to be the court's point person to help them get things resolved. You don't have to be a great lawyer to do that, and you don't have to be good at writing to do that. You just have to be good at trying to translate the judge's priorities into actual management of the caseload. Some judges won't let their

> clerks talk to the parties, because they are afraid the parties will take advantage of the clerks. Judge Hall expected you to work with the parties, and if they ever did try to take advantage of you, to let him know. You just didn't see a lot of that in his court.[76]

Hall's clerks benefited from his teaching and modeling role in the court. He brought strong intuitive gifts to the bench, seasoned, of course, with his own courtroom experience; for example, perhaps a witness was telling less than the whole truth. The judge was willing to ask pointed questions to reveal a lie or deception, to pose the most effective questions to clarify testimony. The clerks learned to watch his body language and the subtle changes in facial expression that would reveal whether he was perturbed or unconvinced or impatient with a line of testimony or an attorney's tactic. Judge Hall showed his clerks what kinds of things to watch for from a witness, the kinds of shading and masking of testimony that would arouse intuitive suspicion and were signals to watch out for further dishonesty. [77]

They might learn something about lawyers in the courtroom, too. Sharon Kacmarcik learned "not to assume that even though someone has a good reputation or tends to be a good lawyer all the time, that they are being a good lawyer or right this time." It was not a good idea to judge a lawyer's work on reputation rather than present performance, reputed expertise rather than the merits and uniqueness of the case at hand. Even an expert lawyer still had to prove the case on the facts. [78]

The clerks wanted to do all they could to enhance the judge's standing in the eyes of everyone who came to the court. Whatever augmented his reputation for fairness and impartiality, whatever enhanced the impression that the judge handed down fair rulings in an efficient and expeditious way, benefited everyone. But with Judge Hall, the clerks' policy was easy to implement because those things were foremost in his mind and constant objectives in his work. He hired competent clerks and entrusted them with great responsibility, but he made certain his own responsibility covered it all. Michael Smith recalled Hall's way of dealing with the clerks:

> I remember several times going back with him after a hearing or in the middle of a hearing. He would come off the bench, I would open the door, he would go into his chambers, I would walk in behind him, and close the door. He would spin around, look at me, and say what he thought about the hearing. He would tell me what he was thinking and ask what I thought because he wanted to make sure that he was doing the right thing. He was open to changing his rulings if he realized that he'd done something wrong. I remember one time I screwed up and said something in an order that

> I didn't realize at the time wasn't a correct statement of the law. One of the attorneys called me, not believing that the judge really intended to do that. I looked at it and realized that he was right. I went in to Judge Hall and told him I had made a mistake. I told him what I think we should have done. He didn't criticize me for the mistake. He didn't tell me, "You're embarrassing me because you're making it look like I don't know what I'm doing." He just was concerned that we got the result right. [79]

The judge took his clerks frequently to dinner at home or to local banquets and was always careful to introduce them to everyone. He enjoyed making them comfortable. This extended to the clerks' general experiences with judges, as clerking guaranteed—at least in Hall's case—a great deal of personal interaction with a judge. The frequent, personal contact humanized the judge and removed much of the clerks' awe or fear of federal judges in general. Sharon Kacmarcik remembered, "There were the days that I would be hesitant to interrupt him or bother him, and after I did I always wondered why I was at all hesitant. Never did he act as if I was bothering him. He always greeted me with a smile and wanted me to come in and talk."[80]

Ed Hohn summed up how Judge Hall influenced him, emphasizing that he learned to focus on the human factor first in the legal system—to put the people first. Those lessons and the values they taught surpassed all others. Hohn compared Hall to King Solomon: "Judge Hall the jurist constantly strove to achieve that which was just and right, rather than that which was popular or expected." Hohn gave his former boss high marks for Christian character: "His faith in Jesus Christ was the strongest that I have ever witnessed, and he truly practiced what he had been preached." A Church of Christ member, Hall overlooked the shortcoming of Hohn's being a Baptist in hopes he could be reformed. In Hall's last years the two made humorous comparisons of Baptist and Church of Christ members: The Church of Christ uses no instruments except to raise their voices to the Lord; the Baptists welcome instruments and any other noise-making devices to protect the Lord from their voices. Neither Baptists nor members of the Church of Christ should drink alcohol. Finally, a lifelong member of the Church of Christ could easily get his name attached to a professorship or chair at a Baptist university, but only if he went to the school and supported it throughout his life; a Baptist would have to settle for a stool at a Church of Christ university. Ed Hohn learned that Hall's love for East Texas Baptist University and his experiences there during the College of Marshall years left a strong mark on him. [81]

During Hohn's time of service with Hall, members of the Bureau of Alcohol, Tobacco, and Firearms interrupted trial proceedings to present an arrest, search and seizure warrant, which the judge read after Hohn handed it to him, sight unseen. Hall read through it and looked up with a shocked expression. He gave Hohn a look—their favorite barbeque restaurant was to be raided that afternoon on suspicion of connections with organized crime. This caused them extra concern because lunchtime was approaching and they had not decided where to go. When court adjourned at noon, Hohn declared he was going to beat the ATF to get his last shot at barbequed ribs, and Judge Hall recommended he not do that: "Don't go near the place, you'll be cooked too." Hohn went anyway and saw the person named in the writ, greeted him and placed his order. Recalling the scene, Hohn said, "He wrapped and weighed the ribs, looked up at me, and I found myself asking a strange question, "How's it going?" He quickly replied, "Hard all over, just hard!" I will never forget thinking to myself, "You have no idea about how hard the time is going to get in just a few minutes." I ate my last lunch from that barbeque smokehouse and enjoyed every bit of it." The judge never took Hohn back there.[82]

Hohn knew nothing about Freemasonry before he came to work with Hall. He had seen the symbols of Masonry from time to time and knew that historical figures, such as George Washington, Sam Houston, and Franklin D. Roosevelt had been Masons. He had never asked anyone about it, but, knowing that Hall wore a Masonic pin, one day in the office he asked, "Judge, what is this Masonry thing?" To his surprise, Hall ordered Sue Jordan to "get Brother Everett Young on the phone and get him over here right now, I need to talk with him about a young man!" Within the hour Hall had assembled a group of Masons who came to make sure his questions received satisfactory answers and to test his fitness as a prospective Mason. "A strange feeling that I had been drafted into the military came over me and I silently wondered what in the world was he getting me into," Hohn recalled. He soon became an active, committed, giving Mason, another feature of the powerful bond he developed with Sam Hall. At Hohn's entry into the lodge, Judge Hall was ill with cancer but refused to miss the opportunity to see Hohn raised to be a Mason. Present for the ceremony, he presented Hohn with one of his oldest, most cherished pins.[83]

Before he was elected to the Marshall City Commission, Michael C. Smith said that his uncle Harold Taylor, who was also one of Hall's lifelong friends, advised him to "do what's right, and don't do anything else," much as Sam Hall might have told him to do. Said Smith, "It didn't occur to me the test isn't to do what's right; the test is not to do anything but what's right. Your obligation is to conduct yourself in the correct manner all the time, not just some of the time, and I think Judge Hall was obviously very much like that."[84]

In mid-July, 1990, President George Bush was posed to make his first nomination to the Supreme Court. George S. Smith of the *Marshall News Messenger* touted Hall as qualified for nomination based on his reputation in Congress, independence of mind and acceptability to conservatives. "Mr. Middle America" became a federal judge because he was acceptable on those grounds, and aside from having been the "best congressman East Texas ever had." Evoking an image sure to raise eyebrows anywhere, Smith gushed that in the congressional approval phase, Hall would "fly through Congress like castor oil through a duck." Later the next year just prior to the Senate vote on the nomination of Clarence Thomas to the Court, the media spread Professor Anita Hill's allegations of indecent comments made to her by Thomas. Thus the Senate proceedings erupted in a controversy. Hall expressed his disgust, criticized the confirmation process, and said he considered the late-coming allegations to be suspicious. [85]

His service as a judge and career as a lawyer brought honor in 1991 when he was named Baylor Lawyer of the Year at the Baylor Law Day banquet. He fit the qualifications as one who brought legal ability and accomplishment, the admiration of his colleagues, his Christian character, civic accomplishments, and interest in the Baylor Law School. Hall was the first in his law class of 1948 to be so honored. A native Texan and Solicitor General of the United States, Kenneth W. Starr delivered the banquet address. [86]

Other honors came, among them one with a powerful symbolic connection between Sam B. Hall Jr., his late father and the three courthouses in which they served either as lawyers or judges on the square in Marshall. The Harrison County Bar Association and other members of the bar in East Texas hosted the presentation of Hall's portrait at the federal courthouse in Marshall on November 15, 1991. They had commissioned the artist Bradley Stevens of Arlington, Virginia, to portray Hall in his judicial robe seated facing away from his desk, the national flag behind him and the Harrison County courthouse in the background through a window. Everyone came for a celebration: twenty-two federal, state district, and county judges, and a portrait committee of colleagues in the law, including Sue Jordan. His law clerks and the various court officers were present: Libby Crawford, Nancy Williams, Ed Hohn, Sharon Kacmarcik, Julie Richardson, Peggy Anderson, Karla Doss, Patrice Barron, John G. Crews II, G. Hobart Miller, and Sally Cook Socia. Marshall Gary, the United States Marshal for the Eastern District, introduced the U.S. magistrates and state judges. And of course there were the family and friends from Marshall and Harrison County.

It was a festival of tall stories, jokes, and memorable experiences, presided over by Judge Robert Parker, whose family had counted the Halls as friends for over a century. Chief Judge Emeritus Joe Fisher introduced the federal judges. He noted how Hall had already accomplished the "enviable status" of being as well respected a judge, "reaching the judicial plateau of prestige" as he had in the Congress, something he had told Hall would come only after many years. "Your strength of judicial character is evident for all to see that."[87]

Congressman Ralph Hall set the tone with stories from Washington and praise for his friend. "And he's my best friend, but he is so just that if I ever appear before him, I hope I'm innocent." Houston attorney Richard "Racehorse" Haynes, former congressman Kent Hance, Marshall attorney Rosemary Snider, and Sue Jordan praised the honoree, after which he responded, returning the favor of stories—some true, some suspicious, some both—about the speakers and others in the audience. Hall was not many years past the conclusion of the Fredeman trial in Beaumont, where Haynes and numerous other lawyers, many nationally known, had been together with him in court for five or six months. He praised his fellow judges, most of them with years of experience beyond his, and a few who had been recently appointed as he had. Madeleine, his daughters, and Sue as his secretary and assistant, were all indispensable to him. He reflected on the blessings of friends, and made a subtle joke about having his picture hanging in the "post office" as a judge, not as one of the FBI's most wanted. Hall said, "A man's virtues can be extolled only so much; and I've never been blessed in any way that would surpass the love and affection I have received from those in the front row and the man whose picture is hanging outside. I never thought I would see our pictures hanging in the Post Office. Of course, this was the old Post Office, for the benefit of you that don't know it. But if Dad can hang out in front with Judge Fisher, I can hang in here alone." Judge Hall professed how proud he was of his portrait upon first seeing it that very day. He ended his remarks with a prayer first penned by William Barclay, the British Bible scholar, but adapted slightly for the occasion. He read,

> I give you thanks, oh, God, for those who mean so much to me, those to whom I can go at any time, those with whom I can talk and keep nothing back, knowing that they will not laugh at my dreams or my failures, those in whose presence it is easier to be good, those who by their warnings have held me back from mistakes I might have made. Above all, I thank you for Jesus Christ, Lord of my heart and saviour of my soul. [88]

In September 1992, Hall's friends, colleagues, family, and friends of East Texas Baptist University announced the establishment of an endowed history chair in his name. The money given, approximately $178,000, allowed the naming of a professorship. The Marshall attorney Franklin Jones Jr. chaired the committee. He explained that the endowment was a way to help ETBU and to give Hall "long overdue honor for his contributions to this community."[89]

A banquet and presentations at East Texas Baptist University inaugurated the professorship on September 24, 1992. Mr. Jay Orr, vice-president of development at ETBU, provided opening remarks, after which ETBU President Bob Riley welcomed the guests and offered a prayer. Academic Affairs Vice President Don Ellis delivered a challenge, declaring that everyone who took the opportunity to meet the challenge of endowing a professorship in Judge Hall's name had also passed the challenge on to ETBU. It was a challenge "to mold minds in a fashion that would produce yet another gentleman, scholar, and statesman along the model mirrored by the man that you have chosen to honor."[90]

Dr. Polly A. Davis, chair of the department of history and political science, presented the charge to Assistant Professor Summers, after which he delivered a response, focusing on the urgent need to "grasp the sense of history," and asserting that for the evening the group could do so by considering the "historical worth of a man." Judge Sam B. Hall Jr. was one of whom it could be said, "They have made a difference during their time, and they are properly regarded significant for all time."[91]

Franklin Jones Jr. introduced Judge Hall to the audience, after which Hall remarked about his love for history and the understanding it could give, making reference in one instance to the surrender at Appomattox as an illustration of the value of character to be found in historical figures. Various remarks followed from friends of the Judge, including Congressman Kent Hance. [92]

The professorship was accompanied by an annual lecture series, with Judge Hall presenting the inaugural lecture in 1993. Through 2004, subsequent lecturers were Dr. Jerry Summers, the Sam B. Hall Jr. Professor of History; Mr. Joe Lovelace of Linden, an attorney, close friend and fellow graduate with Hall of the College of Marshall; Dr. Ronald A. Wells, Professor of History at Calvin College in Grand Rapids, Michigan; Judge William Cornelius of Jefferson; Dr. Inez Jenkins, Professor Emerita in Religion and Philosophy, Wiley College, Marshall; D. Glenn Elliott, Texas Ranger, retired; Chase Palmer, a Marshall attorney and grandson of Judge Hall; Don Adams, an Austin attorney, trustee of East Texas Baptist University and a former Texas representative and senator; Edward Hohn, an attorney and former federal court clerk, of Daingerfield, Texas; Texas State Representative Bryan

Hughes; and, in 2004, Dr. Don Newbury, the former president and chancellor of Howard Payne University and an internationally known humorist and speaker. Intended as an annual memorial to Judge Hall's contributions, the lecture series promoted the ideals of integrity and service that he honored in his own life.

Sam Sr. and Sam Jr. in the Jeep.

13

The Final Years: Family and the Country Refuge

"No man in his time better exemplified the virtues of an East Texas gentleman—a kind and devoted husband, a wise, indulgent, and adoring father, a devout and righteous church leader, and a just, honest, and upright person to all of those whom he encountered. The judges of the Eastern District, in their joint pursuit of justice, were greatly honored to be associated with such a man."—U. S. District Judge William Wayne Justice, retired.[1]

"He was a good man, with no vices that I knew of. He never drank or smoked or cussed. Senator Phil Gramm said if he had a son he would like for him to grow up like Sam Hall Jr. What else can I say?" —Fred C. Hall Jr., cousin [2]

"Sam Hall was a straight shooter. You knew where you stood with Sam. If he had any fault, it may be laid to his candor and forthrightness, and never to hypocrisy." —U. S. District Judge Howell Cobb[3]

"I don't know that I have ever known such a complete man as Sam Hall."

"I think about him all the time."—Dwight Hartley, Texas cattleman [4]

"Daddy's life was a seminar on how to deal with people." —Becky Hall Palmer [5]

"Judge was a walking intellectual hug." –Sally Cook Socia [6]

The Hall family farm west of Marshall was Hall's retreat for decades before and after his parents' deaths. He and his sons-in-law kept cattle on the land that amounted to 300-plus acres of meadow, native hardwoods and pines, and pines cultivated from seedlings for pulpwood, in accordance with common practice in East Texas. Among other cash and feed crops, cotton and corn had been the farm's main crops until the 1960s. Hall took refuge on the land, especially during his years as a judge. There he took guests, good friends, associates, and his judicial law clerks, often simply to ride around in the old Willys Jeep or a pickup truck, or to sit on the cabin porch. Conversation was optional.

Judge Hall often brought an attorney or two who, even if they were at first amused that a federal judge would show them around the old home place as he did, were delighted about it when they saw how special it was to him. He enjoyed the clean air and the break from office and court responsibilities, and the cattle needed feeding anyway. Ed Merritt of Longview represented clients from Chicago in a work injury suit. Gil Gilliam with the Baldwin firm in Marshall represented the plaintiff. During the jury recess, Merritt and the clients accompanied the judge to the farm. On the drive there Hall turned to Merritt and told him he thought he was one of the best young lawyers in East Texas and that he recognized how difficult a trial this was for him. He said he was doing a fine job on the case; of course the clients in the back seat of the car overheard. Merritt's clients won the suit. After the trial, Hall confessed how nervous he had been about the case, and Merritt disclosed his curiosity about Hall's comments. Judge Hall responded that he thought clients sometimes failed to recognize when an attorney was doing an exceptional job for them. He wanted Merritt's clients to recognize that fact, regardless of how the case was resolved. Merritt's Chicago clients asked him whether Texas judges took people out to feed the cattle all the time. Merritt responded, "No, guys, that was kinda unique."[7]

His activities on the farm were a revelation to amazed visitors. Ed Hohn marveled at how Hall called the cattle with a great "whoop-whoop" at feeding time: "Here he was, this six-foot-three or four guy with almost a presidential air about him; he commanded authority by his mere presence. You'd see this six-foot-four-almost-a-statesman type guy out there going 'whoo, whoo, whoo!' you know, whooping up those cows to come to the truck so he could feed them. The first time you see it, you're just kind of going, 'There's something wrong with this picture!'"[8]

Marguerite Ratcliff convulsed with laughter when she remembered the day she met Hall at the farm to gather cow chips to use as fertilizer in her flowerbeds and around her banana plants. She took sacks to the farm on a Saturday morning. The two of them collected the dried cow chips, most a foot or so across, and the thought hit her that most people would not imagine a United States district judge at such work. She exclaimed, "I wish the Congress and Senators in Washington could see you at this point!"

Working, Hall kept silent. [9]

Hall's connection with the land allowed him complete seclusion, with no telephones, though the family persuaded him to get a mobile phone after a tractor accident. His small white cabin originally had been a house for farm workers. It sat facing east about a hundred paces back of the house on Highway 80 where Sam Sr. and Valerie Hall had moved in the mid 1940s. Sandra Bodenhamer believed her dad always considered himself to be in "hog heaven" when he was at the family home place. Inside the cabin Hall kept only those things he cared about and needed. It was crude: there were a small television and radio above a small book case, which held a few history books; numerous "gimme" caps from feed stores, oil companies and other businesses and organizations hung on the walls; changes of clothes for those days when the work was particularly dirty; a worn-out, Naugahyde-covered recliner; a Dearborn space heater; a simple kitchen with a microwave; half-empty shell boxes for the shotgun and a .38 caliber handgun; several stray partial manicure kits; and a basic bathroom with a tub that would serve well if he was too filthy to get into the car or pickup, not to mention through the door at home. The cabin decorations also included a walking stick that Hall Sr. had used. Hall's son-in-law Tom Wynn had mounted it, framed it and hung it on the wall. Hall never hunted regularly, and then only when he was younger, but had hunting trophies, such as the head from a mule deer he had shot in Brown County, Texas, in 1964; such trophies were in the cabin if only because they would never be permitted at home. In his later years he preferred to hunt deer with binoculars. He did not spend nights in the cabin, though during the 1990 Gulf War he and Ed Hohn fell asleep in the old recliners while watching the evening news. After leaving the Congress, Hall spent time every day on the land while he was home, tending and feeding the cattle or finding physical work to do. The hard physical work was a welcome relief from the inactivity of office and courtroom.

From the cabin's front porch swing, Hall could survey the pasture and tree line to the east. Just to the south stood a cattle pen and a storage shed for cattle feed and supplies. A low chain-link fence enclosed a front yard, probably twenty by thirty paces in size, so that the cattle could not graze or drop their leavings close to the cabin. To the northeast was the pond, perhaps 200 yards long, stocked with fish, and formed by a dam on Potter's Creek. There was a small flock of domesticated geese, and migrating birds came and went in season. Silhouetted against the tree line to the east, deer often crossed the pasture to drink from the pond. Close by the north side of the cabin ran a primary high-voltage line that broke the landscape in its cross-country run west and east. Never matter that, and the scene was peaceful enough despite the faint sounds of highway traffic to the south.

The birdsongs, occasional cattle calls and the honking of geese punctuated a soundscape dominated by the background of wind in the trees. Behind the cabin to the west lay a meadow used for haying and grazing in season.

On days he did not sit in court, Hall often sat on the porch, visiting with a guest brought from town or a friend who had dropped by hoping to find him there. Madeleine brought sandwiches and conversation. Or they took a walk. Marshall attorney and Hall relative Richard Anderson reminisced about working cattle—probably when he came with his father Paul, the veterinarian—as on the day he and Hall simultaneously lassoed both ends of a cow that was intent on jumping the corral fence. Otherwise, conversation varied as to subject but was always optional. Sam enjoyed being alone or in the company of a friend or loved one, away from the public eye and official duties, but at the heart of personal and family life; it was at least as important as being anywhere else. Nonetheless, Son-in-law Pinkie Palmer jested, but with some seriousness, that after Hall left Congress his cabin was a new White House. He was indisputably in charge there.[10]

The ceremony of sitting the porch included many friends. Wendy Klennert came mostly for fishing but enjoyed sitting. One Fourth of July, while family and friends had a barbeque picnic by the pond, Klennert pulled a nine-pound catfish from the water, creating excitement and a round of snapshots of the great catch. What was he going to do with the fish? Well, put it back. Casting out a newly baited line, Klennert presently landed a twelve-pounder. What was he going to do with this fish? Hall yelled, "If you put that one back in there, I'm going to put you in there!" Klennert took the twelve-pounder home, cleaned and filleted it.[11]

On other occasions, Arthur O. Wesley joined Hall on the porch or rode in the passenger seat of Hall's pickup while they distributed feed to the cattle. Wesley was a Harleton native and 1949 graduate of Bishop college, the historic black Baptist college in Marshall, a veteran First Sergeant of the Normandy invasion and Bastogne during the Battle of the Bulge, and retired after forty-two years as a principal in the Marion County and Jefferson "colored" schools. Their conversations ranged through world affairs; they agreed it would be best for people to work together in harmony. Both agreed a man could do no better than to live the life of service: "The life of service is really what counts." Hall opened his heart to Wesley, and left the door to the ranch cabin open, too, giving him a key, "because you just might want to come out by yourself." Going to and coming from the federal court in Texarkana, the judge frequently stopped in Jefferson to visit his friend, just as he had when as a congressman he had come at Wesley's invitation to speak in the Jefferson schools.[12]

In this habit and method of relaxing and "getting away from it all," Hall emulated the lifelong habit of Sam Hall Sr., who sat by the hour on the front porch of the brick house that faced the highway. The rear of that house was in view of the cabin, about seventy or so yards distant. Usually with his Bible close by, Hall Sr. had a succession of friends who stopped to sit and chat a while before moving on toward Marshall or Hallsville. After Sam and Madeleine moved their young family to town, the State Trooper and later Texas Ranger Glenn Elliott and his family rented the white frame house they vacated next door. Elliott often shared a seat on Hall Sr.'s porch. On Sunday evenings after returning from church where their families worshiped together, they sat, observed the highway traffic, waved to passers by, and visited by the hour. Long after he moved his family to Longview, Elliott stopped for a few minutes if the Senior Halls were at home. Thus Sam Jr.'s front porch ritual was a restorative continuation of the family art and relaxing recreation to boot.[13]

Houston attorney Richard "Racehorse" Haynes observed that going to his land and cabin was a kind of "communion" for Hall, something more than just recreation and relaxation. It was a spiritual experience, which Haynes asserted was the essence of life for Hall. [14]

Peace and quiet were important, too. Family members perhaps never fully understood why Hall loved the simple pleasure of sitting on the porch of a small cabin watching the pond, the cattle and geese, listening to the wind in the trees, watching the seasons come and go. Becky Palmer told her mother, "Well, we lived out there first of all for all those years. Then he had all those experiences with Grandaddy out there. And Grandaddy loved it so out there; it was a solace for both of them. They just had such a good time doing things together out there."[15]

Apart from the Hall home in town, the cabin and the land focused his "at-home feelings." He had spent so many good times on the land with his father and family. He and Madeleine left the garage apartment, which was attached to his parents' home, to occupy the white frame house next door for about thirteen years. That house, which was moved from town, and where Hall was born, was their home during the years when Sam and Madeleine established their family and Sam established his law practice. Hall was uncomfortable being separated for long from the land and its numerous associations with family. Not just a recreational refuge, it was a haven where he could return to those values that firmly anchored his life.

One day as deer season approached in the fall, Hall drove his tractor to the back of the farm property and returned to the front. A thunderstorm had built to the point of wind and lightning. Many yards away, a lightning bolt struck a pine tree, killing the tractor engine and frightening Hall so that he lost his composure.[16]

Hall habitually pushed his farm equipment to see what it would do, perhaps just to see how much he could get away with. Overconfident, perhaps reckless with it, he sometimes overdrove his machinery, riding the tractor with the bush hog, a large rotary mower, all over the property, cutting down underbrush and tree sprouts where they were unwanted. The bush hog destroyed hats and in one instance his billfold. He repeatedly got the tractor or Jeep or truck stuck in boggy ground, and kept Elgin Poole, a tow truck operator in Hallsville, so busy the family said he ought to put him on retainer. The Chevron dealer in Hallsville said Hall was his best towing customer. He frequently needed tractor repairs, and the dealer at East Texas Tractor joked that if it weren't for Hall, he could not stay in business. Ed Hohn recalled, "I was nervous every time I went out there with him because he was going to get that truck stuck. And I can't remember if it was a two-wheel drive or a four-wheel drive, but it didn't matter. If he had a four-wheel drive, he would still get it stuck." Operating the machinery was a type of challenge, and usually amounted to nothing more than the equipment winning out over nature. The worst exception was an accident that almost killed and absolutely unnerved Hall. It involved the tractor and bush hog, not long before he was diagnosed with cancer. He ran over a stump that was too large for the bush hog to cut. The tractor and bush hog jack-knifed and twisted with a great lurch, so that he was leaning back on the tilted tractor, with the bush hog blades rotating just inches from his head. The fear that shot through him so weakened him that he thought he would lose his grip, fall from the seat and be mangled to death. Somehow, even Hall could not say how, he killed the tractor engine and so escaped serious injury. He was very sore, though, and after calming himself, walked back to the cabin, called for help with the tractor, and went home, still weak and trembling when he arrived.[17]

After the accident, Hall carried a cellular telephone with him on the property in case of an emergency. The accident left him leery of the tractor, but soon thereafter the diagnosis of cancer reduced his activities, and he did not use the tractor much, though he did drive the pickup truck around the property. The accident reinforced the general perception of family and friends that he handled machinery poorly; Hall was never, and never chose to be, a home handy man or repairman. He probably never had a mature respect for potentially dangerous heavy machinery until it almost killed him.[18]

Such accidents thus came honestly because Hall made them happen. But he was not alone. His son-in-law, Tom Wynn, had a new four-wheel-drive Chevrolet Blazer that he had not fully tested until he got the vehicle completely stuck in a mud hole on the back property. Dressed in his business suit, he walked to the front of the property, about half a mile, to get the tractor, emerging from the woods into the pasture where Hall happened to be tossing feed cubes to the cattle from the Jeep. Startled to see anyone in a suit and tie walking from the back pasture, Hall later said, "I thought you were one of those Mormons, trying to get me to go to church with him."[19]

Bobby Johnson, an auto body repairman, was among the men whom Hall won over and whose loyalty and esteem never wavered. Johnson reminisced about unusual jobs Hall brought to him:

> Sam brought us a unique repair one time on a Cadillac. The hood had strange cuts out in the middle of the hood over a two-foot area. I asked Sam what caused the damage, and he laughed and grinned and said one of his horses bit the hood. Sam was out at the farm, and one of the horses decided to take a bite out of the shiny new car hood. We worked on that hood several times before we were able to get paint to adhere to the metal. Sam told me he would park farther away from the horses in the future. On another occasion, he had his Jeep delivered to our shop. Sam's Jeep was a real World War II Jeep, over forty years old with a few bent panels. Actually, there was not a straight panel anywhere on it. Sam wanted the Jeep painted bright red. We have a rule at our business—Sam or his family will always get whatever they want, so Sam got a very bright red Jeep. When Sam came by the shop to inspect his Jeep, he smiled and told me the red was exactly what he wanted. I repaired several other cars and trucks for Sam, but none gave me more pleasure than repairing his white Chrysler Imperial. The Imperial was Sam's father's car. He kept the car in storage and drove it on occasion. I took one look at the Imperial when Sam drove into my driveway, and he smiled. The car was in original condition except for a fresh scrape down the side. Sam reassured me that I could fix anything. I asked him what happened to the car, and he said a curb or something got too close to it.[20]

Sam and Madeleine Hall were able to resume their longtime social routines after he left the Congress to be a federal judge. They were glad to be back with their friends in the supper club and other organizations. The richness of older relationships enhanced the joy of being home with family and provided regular fun and relaxation. Hall as a federal judge also found other, less direct ways to influence the community welfare than he was accustomed to, without crossing any improper lines. For example, the former mayor of Marshall, Audrey Kariel, told how Hall helped as a district judge simply by shaping the conditions to discuss the preservation and restoration of the historic Texas & Pacific Railroad depot. Judge Hall invited Mayor Kariel to meet with a Union Pacific attorney at the Federal Court Building in order to discuss the issues involved in the depot preservation and restoration. Thus Hall spurred the city and railroad to seek a common solution to the problem by facilitating the meeting. Kariel wrote, "I feel that this meeting was one of the turning points that saved the depot for our city. Sam watched our project, usually teasing me into telling him what was happening. He joked that no matter what subject we discussed, I always managed to bring up the depot!" [21]

Judge Hall was always just Sam Hall, whose greatest burden was his inability to leave a need unmet if he could do anything about it, a tendency that only intensified as he matured. Marshall attorney Ned Dennis provided a striking example of Hall's generosity on a hot summer afternoon around five o'clock. The judge in shirt and tie was mowing a yard in the sweltering heat: "He was mowing a little, gray-haired lady's back yard. He had seen her out there mowing her yard, stopped, got out, and mowed that yard for her." Hall could not stand the thought of that widow having to mow her grass in such heat.[22]

There were chances to help out, but also familiar comforts and delights, signs of appreciation and affection from long time friends and former clients. Florine Miller of Marshall made a wonderful Millionaire Pie, a rich cooked concoction of bananas, Eagle Brand milk, and whipped cream, which was one of Hall's favorites; she made him one every chance she got.[23]

The sons-in-law, Tom Wynn and Pinkie Palmer, got a first-hand view of the Hall charm at work on a summer day when they went with him to dump trash at the Hallsville dumping station. The younger men emptied the trailer while Hall sat in the shade with a cool drink. On the trip home a trailer tire went flat, and Tom and Pinkie proceeded to change it. There was no mistaking his priorities. Some acquaintances pulled up, and Hall "sat in the truck and talked to those people just like it was absolutely necessary for him to carry on a conversation." When the flat had been changed, he said, "Come on boys, let's go."[24]

Hall and, from year to year one or more of his daughters, regularly attended and participated in a comic-melodramatic, continually evolving play presented in Jefferson. Hall's law-school classmate, Bill Cornelius of Jefferson, presented his observations of Hall and his role in the play, writing,

> Sam's wit was legendary. I realized its full potential when he played the role of the prosecuting attorney in the famous "Diamond Bessie Murder Trial," which has been presented by the Jessie Allen Wise Garden Club for more than forty years at the annual Historical Pilgrimage in Jefferson. Sam played the prosecutor for seven years while I played opposite him as the defense attorney.

> The play is about the trial of Abe Rothschild for the murder of Diamond Bessie, a famous beauty who was murdered while visiting in Jefferson in its heyday in the late 1870s. Both the murder and Rothschild's trial occurred in Jefferson. The trial was one of the most famous in Texas history, and several years after Jefferson's historical pilgrimage began, the Garden Club decided to get the local citizens to re-enact the last stages of the trial as an added tourist attraction for the pilgrimage. Through the years the local citizens of Jefferson have presented the play, always to packed houses. There are six performances of the play each year. The play was originally written to be a kind of morality play, but through the years so many funny lines and bits of testimony have crept into the script ad lib, the play ultimately developed into a hilarious comedy. The actors have enthusiastically embraced this development, and they delight in making the play as funny as it can be.
>
> A great many of the witticisms and comedic exchanges that are still used in the play were originated by Sam ad lib during many of his performances. As Sam and I made our speeches to the jury, we tried to outdo the other by flinging insults and surprising new arguments at each other, and we also constantly tried to trick the witnesses with surprise questions we hoped they could not easily answer. These humorous exchanges and gaffes that are still a part of the play constantly remind me and all who knew Sam, of his quick wit and his delightful playfulness. [25]

Hall loved the holidays, especially Christmas. He spent hours on the telephone on Christmas Eve and Christmas morning, calling family and friends from an extensive and ever-growing Christmas phone list. He did that for many years. His Christmas ritual was a way of making as much personal contact as possible; even if it was only a voice contact, it was better than a greeting card, and he was not fond of writing, anyway. The note of emotion in familiar voices met his need to renew old bonds of relationship, besides being immediate and fulfilling. Judge Hall called his friend Bill Bradford, the radio broadcaster in Sulphur Springs, Texas, on Christmas day when he knew he might be at the station, which could not cease operations for a holiday. Hall declared that Bradford should be home at Christmas if he wanted to get a call from a real federal judge.

The Hall's eldest grandchild was Chase Palmer who by the year 2000 had entered into law practice in Marshall, settled down with his bride, Sarah Caccioppo, and commenced a career. He could be expected to draw from the family legacy of his father, W. F. "Pinkie" Palmer, his grandfather Sam B. Hall Jr., his great-grandfather Sam Sr., and his great uncle Reuben Hall. Palmer's experiences in the family ran in typical lines as he was growing up; he pursued many high school activities, including football, and his grandparents enthusiastically affirmed him in those good pursuits. They were at the least proud grandparents, and their support was unfailing, even if for Sam Hall it meant not missing a football game even though he was ill with cancer.

Chase Palmer shared with his granddad, "Pop," the experience of having grown up in a close family where parents, grandparents, even great-grandparents, were close by every day of life. Palmer wrote, "I grew up with Pop sitting at the end of the pew every Sunday. I grew up in the passenger seat of an old, red army jeep on Pop's farm feeding Mandy and looking for the cows. Both Meme and Pop played a big part in my upbringing and they were excellent teachers." He learned patriotism, a love for history, a love for his hometown of Marshall, "the best place in the world to live and grow up," and the importance of family, a lesson learned well by each member of the extended clan. Like the other grandchildren, the arrival of his grandparents meant excitement. Palmer recalled, "I used to wait anxiously for him and Meme to come home on the weekends from Washington, D.C., because I knew that he would have a book for me. They always brought these Random House books entitled *Meet the Presidents*, for example. I would be finished with them by that night. I still have every one of those books."[27]

Rebecca Palmer had a granddaughter's awe of a big man who she knew loved her absolutely, if not always gently. There were the harder than intended love pats, the large but gentle hands, the trademark cowboy hat, the numerous forays into the woods and pastures of the Hall place in the red World War II vintage Willys Jeep, the visits to Washington, D.C. and the wonder of being the granddaughter of a congressman—a very patient congressman who did not get unduly upset when his granddaughter spilled Dr. Pepper on the office carpet with the Seal of the United States Congress. "Pop" came unannounced to a high school pep rally to watch Rebecca lead cheers for the first time ever, and his congratulations were never forgotten.[28]

The younger grandchildren, the Bodenhamers, revered their grandfather no less. Darren was a high school junior when his grandfather died, and was so moved by the loss he recognized he must do all he could to be the kind of good person his grandfather was. Hall was a "regal man" but also a typical grandfather, Darren wrote, "A lot like the Santa Claus figure to me, always giving and asking nothing in return." The winter deer hunting season was a special time, when Hall awakened Darren with a loud "Hey, boy! There isn't much good hunting in this bed!" And Hall was not as much interested in the hunt as he was in his grandson's experience of it—he delighted in each of Darren's accomplishments.[29]

Born on Hall's birthday in 1986, Madelyn Bodenhamer loved staying many days with Sam and Madeleine in Marshall, waking to loving grandparents, smelling her grandfather's strong cologne, and going with him to court to observe proceedings. The best part came later in the day and on weekends, after court hours, when the grandchildren went to the farm. Madelyn recalled how "I always loved being with him there. He was such an easy man to get along with (if you were in the family)." After the illness took its toll in the last months of Hall's life, it was hard for the younger children to understand what was happening, but they knew how he declined though their parents shielded them from the worst of it. For young Madelyn the memory of a last gift, a teddy bear with balloons, made it a cherished memento of Hall's final weeks and months. But his death never took away the good memories they had made together, simple things Madelyn and her younger sister Meredith remembered, such as feeding the geese while Pop fed the cattle, riding his horse Butterfinger, simply being with him in the one place he probably loved best among all places. Having the grandchildren with him surely sweetened the experience of being at home.[30]

Chase Palmer remembered the painful day when he first learned about the extent of his grandfather's cancer and the expectation that in all too short a time he would be gone. Palmer well remembered Hall's plea: "'Please don't forget me' are the four words that ring in my ears everyday." His grandfather's words stunned him on the day the family was told Hall would not live to see Christmas: "I understood that death was imminent and something that was now unavoidable. But I got lost in the statement. How in the world could we forget someone who has touched so many lives?"[31]

Ray Lawson counted Sam B. Hall Jr. as one of the best friends he ever had, one whom he saw often, and who often asked to go with him to the farm. After the cancer settled in, Hall had Lawson install a picture window in his cabin so that he could sit inside and look out at the scene he normally would have viewed from the porch swing. The window was Lawson's Christmas present to Hall—the last he would be able to give him.[32]

Florine Miller shared how Hall told her about the cancer; he confessed to her, "You will never know what it is like for a doctor to look you in the eye and tell you that you've got cancer. That absolutely killed me. I just almost gave up then."[33]

Hall's good friend and colleague from the Congress, Ron Mazzoli of Kentucky, was struck by the effect his illness had on others:

> I remember vividly and with sadness a time when I was conversing with one of the House floor clerks—an African-American man whose name was George but whose last name I cannot recall—a man of very different station in life than Sam, but a man who had formed a very close and lasting bond of friendship with Sam. George told me with tears in his eyes that "Mr. Sam" was very ill back home in Texas. I, and I am sure many others, wrote letters and made phone calls to Texas to inquire after Sam's health.[34]

After Hall learned the diagnosis, he talked to his Army friend Bob Wainscott on the phone, sobbing, and Wainscott agreed to come to Marshall after the surgery. In Marshall Hall could drive himself around town. He took Wainscott to see a collection of antique cars that a friend was going to auction away. Wainscott wanted to bid on a beautiful Model-A Ford, but could not be at the auction, so Hall said he would have someone bring him to bid for him. Wainscott might bid up to $7,000. The next evening after the auction, Hall called his friend and raked him over the coals for being such a cheap so-and-so—he had stayed all day to bid on the car, and the bidding had started at twelve thousand dollars![35]

Friends remembered the last visits before Hall's death, as in the case of Bobby and Judi Johnson:

> When Sam's health began to give him problems, he surprised Judi and me one day by stopping by my office and just visiting. He came in and put his feet up, drank a soda and told Judi he was hiding from everyone that day. We talked about life, about work, about our country. Sam made me aware that he had some health problems, and I listened to my friend Sam's concerns that day. In the following weeks, I stopped by his home and visited with him, and he invited me in and teased me about a black eye I had from Tae Kwon Do. We both laughed, and I told him that I could never be happy doing anything "normal." He laughed so loud that day, and we had a good visit. Sam held my hand when it was time to leave, and I promised him that I would always take care of Madeleine's car or anything else she ever needed, and he said, "I know you will." I did not know at the time that I would never see my friend again. I gave Madeleine a hug without words at Sam's funeral. She understood! In April of 1997 when I lost my daughter Amanda, Madeleine gave me a hug. I understood![36]

Mike Chapman had grown up close to the Hall family. In late

winter 1994 Chapman, a railroad executive, arranged for a Union Pacific dining car to be brought to Marshall and parked in the old rail yards. He hired the car and the services of a chef to host the Halls for a meal to show his gratitude. Everyone enjoyed a fine meal and sat for hours visiting, reminiscing, and enjoying each other. Chapman's was a gesture grand enough to convey his deep respect and admiration for Hall. The gesture also created quite a stir in the neighborhood near the rail yard. Retired railroad employees and most individuals who crossed the viaduct over the rail yard tried to find out why there was a dining car in the otherwise mostly empty expanse. They called the newspaper office and a reporter was dispatched to inquire what the Union Pacific railroad was up to.[37]

As the illness took its final toll, and in the days after Hall's death, friends, colleagues and family sent expressions of prayer and appreciation. There was a note from a proud godson, Michael Shappell, and a letter from O. Ivan White, whose admiration for Hall extended to keeping his portrait on his office wall. The Halls' granddaughter, Rebecca Palmer, urged "Pop" to fight the cancer and remember "You have an incredibly strong wife." Carolyn and Bob Richardson, the parents of Hall's judicial clerk, Julie Richardson, expressed their appreciation for his positive influence on their daughter. The judges of the Eastern District sent notes of encouragement, and, afterwards, of condolence.[38]

Libby Crawford worked for many years as a court reporter, and took the suggestion from her pastor during a "Journey of Love" week to write an encouraging letter to Sam and Madeleine Hall. She wrote about what it was like for her to be in Hall's court: "I always felt good when people were tried in your court because they were always judged fairly."[39]

Many friends called on the phone or visited in the last weeks and days. Hall impressed Joe Waggonner with his courage and strength—already traits Waggonner admired and expected. Hall confessed he was confident his family would "do fine" after he was gone.[40]

Chase Palmer came home from Baylor University on the weekend his grandfather died. He changed from his habit of visiting his grandparents as soon as he arrived home, delaying until Sunday just before he returned to Waco. Only on that Sunday afternoon did he realize how close to death his granddad had come. Palmer wrote, "When I got down to kiss him goodbye, I knew that he had been waiting on me. I told him that I loved him and I knew this would be the last time I would see him. Two hours later he died."

The Palmers called Chase only after he had arrived in Waco to let him know, but he had sensed the time of his grandfather's passing during his drive:

> I was only about two miles outside Corsicana. The entire trip was cloudy and the sun hadn't been out all day. All of a

> sudden, the clouds opened and the sun fell down on the road in front of me. It was there only for about a minute, then the clouds swallowed up the hole. It remained cloudy for the rest of the day. I immediately looked at my clock when that happened because I knew he had died. I cried all the way back to Waco.[41]

Amanda Wynn went to the funeral home one last time the morning before her father's funeral. There in the viewing room, she turned to see a little black lady whom she did not recognize. The lady declared, "Oh, I had to come just one more time. I just have one more thing to talk to him about." The family knew that though he was theirs, he belonged as much to the people he had served, and they wondered how his death would affect many of them. In a way nobody could explain fully, he was widely respected because he had been available to help so many when they needed him—"black, white, rich or poor. It didn't matter." Verta Williams, an employee at the Marshall hospital and a long-time family friend, exclaimed to Tom Wynn, "When I die, I'll go to heaven. I'm going to bring him back. We need him back."[42]

O. Ivan White Jr. came from a family that had been involved in education in Marshall, serving with the schools. Sam B. Hall Jr. had been their lawyer and friend and a mentor to Ivan Jr. A newly-appointed regional director of the Federal Bureau of Prisons when Judge Hall died in 1994, White lamented missing Hall's funeral because of his new responsibilities:

> I recall how vividly ironic it seemed that my achieving a goal Judge Hall had inspired me to strive for was preventing me from attending his funeral. I thought of how, accompanied by his charming wife, Madeleine, while speaking at Wiley College, Judge Hall had heard a song sung by Roosevelt Washington that touched him so deeply, he requested it be sung at his funeral. Whether this came to be or not, I am not certain. However, I fondly recollect many fund-raising events at which Judge Hall would specially request that "Ro'" share his inspiring singing talents.[43]

Sam B. Hall Jr. died on Sunday, April 10, 1994. His passing provoked many recollections of his significance to people in Marshall and East Texas, and his colleagues in the Congress and the judiciary.

The *Marshall News Messenger* offered reactions to Hall's death from prominent figures. The former U.S. Representative Barbara Jordan of Houston remembered what a "very good friend" Hall was to her, though they seldom agreed on issues. "He was a conservative with a humane face," Jordan wrote. "He would fiercely defend his point of view, but without cruelty. People never could understand that we were really good friends, that we never voted together but we always sat together." Senator Phil Gramm expressed his sadness and how privileged he had been to recommend Hall for the judiciary. "Sam was a figure straight out of Texas history: honest, courageous and tough. His passing leaves a deep void, both on the federal bench in Texas and in the hearts of the thousands of people who loved and admired him." Judge Ben Z. Grant of the Texas Sixth District Court of Appeals noted Hall's prominence as like that of his father Sam Sr. and uncle Reuben, but emphasized his greater importance as a friend to him and to the people of Marshall and East Texas. He simply stated, "Sam's leadership and his vibrant personality will be greatly missed."[44]

Houston attorney and former Hall judicial law clerk Patrice Barron praised Hall as an unparalleled role model she would miss.[45]

Speaking before the U.S. Senate on the day of the funeral, Senator Phil Gramm reminisced on Hall's three careers devoted to "practicing, making and applying the law with remarkable ability and compassionate concern." Delivering high praise he said,

> Sam was an archetypal Texan: honest, courageous, and tough. It is no exaggeration to say that without Sam Hall, much of the good we accomplished in Washington would not have happened. He was a man who placed principle above party, and service to God, country, and family above all else.[46]

The funeral service at the Eastern Hills Church of Christ in Marshall saw a throng of people that included county, state and federal judges, congressmen, senators, and numerous other friends and family. The church building could not hold everyone. Before he died, Sam had given Madeleine "a worn piece of yellow paper that he had carried in his wallet regarding his funeral." In accord with his wishes, Joe Lovelace of Linden, Texas, delivered the eulogy at the funeral service, speaking about Hall and their College of Marshall days, and characterized his attitude and accomplishments as a public servant in the Congress and as a Federal judge. He summed up Hall's fundamental beliefs about what the United States needed: ideals, goals, heroes, greatness, honesty, hard work, and productivity. In expressing how Hall fulfilled those virtues, he said, "Life has been good to Hall. He was blessed materially, received the accolades of the voters and his peers. He was a giver and not a taker. He has left the world better for his efforts."[47]

Hall's minister at the Eastern Hills Church of Christ delivered a sermon reflecting on his friend's service and attitude. Perhaps his most striking statement was, *"Whatever you knew about Sam Hall you learned from somebody else."*[48]

The New Grover cemetery sits on the west side of a farm-to-market road south of U.S. Highway 80, near Marshall and Hallsville, but even closer to the Hall farm, and in the middle of lands that in the 1840s comprised that plantation holdings of the extended Hall family. Behind Hall's great marble headstone Wendy Klennert placed an aluminum-pipe flagpole for the Stars and Stripes. Klennert installed the flagpole extension and flag on a windless day. He had just finished the task when the wind came to snap the flag out, fully unfurled. The experience moved him deeply. There was no one to see it with him.[49]

In the House of Representatives on May 25, the Members reminisced. Jack B. Brooks of Texas emphasized Hall's "compassion and understanding" as a legislator and the "high standard of excellence" as a Federal judge. Romano L. "Ron" Mazzoli knew Hall quite well, having sat with him on the House Judiciary Committee and on a memorable eighteen-hour flight home from Bangkok, Thailand. Duncan Hunter of California knew Hall evoked strong memories because he had provoked strong friendships; he had a sense of humor "in spades." Robert K. Dornan of California recalled how only months previous—it seemed like only weeks—Hall had waited "in ambush in the center aisle for friends from both sides of the aisle, and he grabbed me as I was walking out and said, "Young fella," which was pretty nice when you're 60 years of age. He said: I want you to know that sometimes after a hard day on the Federal bench I'll watch the House during special orders to see all of my friends on both sides of the aisle. I'm keeping track of all you guys." Dornan exclaimed, "I do not know what it is about you Texans, you just keep producing these heroes that remind me of everybody I read about at the Alamo. He is certainly a proud American and son of Texas that our country is much the less for his passing."[50]

Greg Laughlin of Texas was elected to the House of Representatives after Hall became a judge, and became acquainted with him whenever he visited Washington. He eulogized Hall for his earnest commitment to support assistance for teenaged children regardless of the time it took to make a difference. [51]

Earl Hutto of Florida, Floyd Spence of South Carolina, Mike Synar of Oklahoma, E. De La Garza of Texas, and Ralph Hall of Texas, offered further tributes in Hall's memory.

Congressman Jim Chapman, Hall's successor in the Texas First District, had introduced a bill on February 10, 1994, proposing the renaming of the federal building and courthouse in Marshall after Judge Hall. Sponsored by Chapman, co-sponsored by the entire Texas delegation to Congress and a number of other representatives, the bill was passed in the House of Representatives on May 23. Various Members of the House of Representatives urged passage of the bill to rename the courthouse: James A. Traficant Jr. of Ohio, Thomas E. Petri of Wisconsin, Jim Chapman of

Texas, Romano L. Mazzoli of Kentucky, G. V. Montgomery of Mississippi, and Norman Y. Mineta of California, spoke in praise of Judge Hall and in support of the bill to rename the courthouse. The Senate bill with Senators Phil Gramm and Kay Bailey Hutchison as co-sponsors was passed by the Senate on July 15, and signed by President William J. Clinton on August 1. [52]

The ceremony to name the courthouse in Hall's honor was held in the early afternoon of May 29, 1995, with an audience of hundreds from East Texas and beyond. They assembled on the courthouse square, where a grandstand stood with the federal building to the rear. John C. Pouland, the Regional Administrator for the General Services Administration, hosted the event along with Congressman Jim Chapman, who delivered the keynote address. Marshall attorney Franklin Jones Jr. served as Master of Ceremonies; Judges Robert M. Parker, Richard A. Schell Jr. and Joe J. Fisher offered remarks, as did Congressman Ralph M. Hall of the Texas Fourth District and members of the Hall family, Becky Palmer, Amanda Wynn, and Sandra Bodenhamer. Judge Hall's grandson, Chase Palmer, led the assembly in the Pledge of Allegiance, and Dwight Mays, whom Hall loved to hear sing, closed the program with his rendition of "God Bless America." [53]

Becky Palmer, speaking proudly for her father, reminded the assembly how honored he was to have the building named after him, explaining that he would have loved being there for the ceremony. "He loved a crowd. He loved people everywhere. He would have loved this day. This is a bittersweet day for us, bitter because daddy is not here with us to enjoy it, but sweet because you are." Madeleine Hall and her three daughters released the bunting covering the new building name: "Sam B. Hall Jr. Federal Building and United States Courthouse."[54]

The witness is consistent and strong: Hall possessed a reputation for fairness and integrity that overcame any animus people might have for his convictions and policies. Those who knew him repeatedly emphasized that he might have had many people who considered him too narrow or conservative or who disagreed with his political stances. But never was there any question of his personal character being inadequate. His intentions and integrity could not be impugned. Ronald Reagan was said by some to be the "Teflon president" because scandal would not attach to his name. It would be fair to say that Sam B. Hall Jr. was like that in his very character; there was no scandal to attach to his name.[55]

Hall was most noted for his sociability and love of people. Social situations were pure joy for him. He was not satisfied with quick exchanges of greetings, but would rather stay with someone a few minutes, at least to catch up on the news about the family or business. That tendency explains his frequent tardiness, though not for work or important meetings, more like football games when he would be late getting to his place. Frank Fuller noted that his concern for people was fully sincere. No one has more strongly stated Hall's character as a perfect politician, in so many ways a "perfect" person whom people could not imagine wanting to improve. Hall was the kind of person who drew unqualified highest praise. Such a person of course might draw unjust criticism; however, because so many people had no thought of holding back praise suggests Hall had their complete confidence. Here was a man who impressed people as being genuinely interested in them and committed to treating them as they truly wanted to be treated. Dr. Orin Littlejohn of Marshall expressed a common opinion: "He was just a really fine guy. He liked everybody, and again, whether you were black or white, rich or poor, or whatever. It didn't make any difference to Sam. He was always friendly towards everyone."[56]

Dwight Hartley wrote to Madeleine Hall after Hall's death to reminisce about this accomplished, "tremendously strong" man who was gentle and cared about others. Hartley never forgot being with Hall at the Fort Worth stock show and trying to get him to leave the exhibits barn to attend the rodeo performance. "Sam stopped to visit every vendor in the place, regardless of age or position in life." On another occasion Hartley and Hall stopped at a country store near Hartley's ranch for "just a minute" so that Hall could get something to drink. Hartley recalled that "Forty-five minutes passed while he visited with everyone there and in the feed store next door, swapping stories about common acquaintances." It took "close to an hour to buy a soft drink and a Baby Ruth candy bar!" Hartley marveled at Hall's comfort with total strangers. "They sure didn't remain strangers long."[57]

Hartley visited with the Hall family and shared a meal with them. He admired the closeness and love of the extended family. He returned home to Austin resolved to strengthen the bonds with his own family.[58]

Hall never endeared himself better to anyone than his wife and daughters, but Sue Jordan came close. For Sue, Hall was not just the boss as lawyer, congressional representative, or judge; he was much like a father:

> I knew Sam the man, this six foot, four inch, 200-plus pound man who would wipe tears from his eyes, when he told of the boat people from Vietnam who begged him to take them to the United States. When he heard "White Christmas" because it was one of his Dad's favorite songs, when he spoke of freedom and what it meant to him; this man who never failed to place his hand over his heart when the national anthem was played or the United States flag was presented, who wept when he related the adversities he

> had heard and seen at congressional hearings regarding his fellow man, when he saw the airing of the starving children who were orphaned in Rwanda, when he called a young man or woman to tell them of their appointment to one of the military academies; this man who got so frustrated with the bureaucratic system when a social security or veterans claim was denied for one of his constituents, who returned to his court chambers devastated because he had sentenced a father and son to prison, or because he had heard testimony regarding the death of a boy who fell from a tractor while riding with his grandfather, or in hearing the testimony of a mother telling the death of her little boy killed by a falling garage door, or the testimony of a daughter that her daddy was dying of asbestosis. This was the man I knew. I have seen him after he saw a young man standing on the street with a sign asking for food and clothing for his family, turn the car around, go to a store, buy diapers and food, go back and give to the man. He was the man who sent a note to me from the courtroom asking that I go to the farm and check on the calf born in freezing weather and abandoned by its mother—he bottle-fed this calf. He spent hours on a hot August day to save a pine tree bent by the wind. He called me from the floor of the U.S. House of Representatives or sent a note from the courtroom asking that I call the hospital to check on a friend. He flew from Washington to Marshall in a storm to see his newborn granddaughter. He would not let me schedule anything that would conflict with a special family event. He lived in Washington, D.C., but never let his staff refer to Washington as his home, was never too busy to take a call from his family, dined with presidents, heads of state, but his most enjoyable meals were at Neely's, or Joe's, or some other place in the First Congressional District of Texas. This was the man I knew.[59]

B. B. Boon of Linden reminisced about Hall's consistency and honesty, saying, "One thing about Sam whether he was a federal judge or a congressman, no matter where he met you, he was still the same man. I've seen him on the other side. Sam didn't ever walk out the front without coming around and saying hello. He was that kind of a guy."[60]

Last in the recollections is that of the one person who knew him better than any other, and whose support served him so well. Madeleine Hall reviewed their lives together. The Hall daughters were curious many times in the years they were growing up, and after, asking how Madeleine knew Sam Hall Jr. was the right one for her. Of course, there was no clear answer, she said,

> You just know. I told them that I loved quite a few boys in my day, my young life. But I was *only in love* with one. That's the difference. But really, like I say, it happened early. It didn't really falter. Well, we may have broken up twice in the four years, but it didn't last over a week or two.[61]
>
> I look back and realize that I was married to four different men. He was a student, a lawyer, a congressman, and he was a judge. What a full life! And I tried to keep up. But he never felt that I couldn't. He always would say, "I couldn't do this without you." He probably could have, but I wouldn't have wanted him to.

As to whether she had any premonition or vision about what might come of her husband's contributions and desire to be useful, Madeleine Hall confessed her vision was limited; it never occurred to her to look too far ahead.

> I don't guess I saw too far. I was just madly in love with him. He was just the knight on a white horse to me. I saw all of his good qualities. But as Barbara Bush once said about George—she said she looked up and she saw this gorgeous thing coming toward her. I guess I just saw that gorgeous thing coming toward me.[62]

Sam and Madeleine: Vacationing at Destin, Florida

L-R: Sam Jr. and Madeleine, Valerie and Sam Sr., John and Kathleen McLendon

At the Hall home in Marshall, Texas, about 1983. L-R: Amanda and Tom Wynn, Sandra Bodenhamer, Sam and Madeleine, and grandchildren Chase and Rebecca Palmer, Pinkie and Becky Palmer.

Thanksgiving 1983. L-R, standing: Tom and Amanda Wynn, Becky and Pinkie Palmer, Sam and Madeleine with granddaughters Meredith and Madelyn Bodenhamer, Don and Sandra Bodenhamer, Rebecca Palmer; L-R, front: Chase Palmer, Darren Bodenhamer.

Sam B. Hall Jr. watches his granddaughters Meredith and Madelyn as they ride Butterfinger.

Sam with Meredith and Madelyn in the Jeep.

Porchsitting: Amanda Wynn and Sam Hall Jr.

A public servant's retreat – the "Western White House"?

Conclusion

People will always remember Sam B. Hall Jr. primarily as a local figure, best known in and identified with Marshall and Harrison County, Texas, though remembered as a popular representative for the Texas First Congressional District and a respected federal judge. The statewide and national memory of him cannot match the renown of Texans Wright Patman or House Speaker Sam Rayburn, both of whom served longer in the Congress and had greater seniority and legislative accomplishments. His death at age 70 curtailed a successful judicial career that under ideal circumstances might have lasted another five years or so before he chose retirement. Otherwise vigorous apart from the disease that killed him, Judge Hall could meet the demands of whatever tasks he chose, and would have enjoyed finishing his duties in normal fashion during some golden years with his wife, family and friends. Nevertheless, death only shortened the time span of his life achievements and relationships; it could not diminish them.

Americans in the twenty-first century change residences and careers frequently, and some just as often change spouses. The concepts of community, civic service, integrity, faith, and character, though sometimes they seem lost or antiquated to us, are present with us in leaders who serve unselfishly, keep their commitments, build communities, and by their words and example encourage others to do the same. This author disagrees with a historical view that glorifies an idealized past in which people truly knew how to live, love, and contribute unselfishly. In its details, history reveals just as much confusion, disappointment and disgrace in circumstances and in people as are present today. History also reveals the kinder side of every era and its institutions and society. In every generation, one's private, interior life counts, but only actions over time allow evidence leading to a reliable, valid judgment. This biography has tried to show that Sam B. Hall Jr. was the kind of man people wanted as an advocate, a representative, a model, and a friend. Its author hopes the biography, as a witness gathered from among many witnesses, proves true over time.

Sam's life evokes images of stability and consistency, whether in regard to his home and family life, or to the virtues of hard work and meaningful accomplishment. These virtues arose from his family background in a county settled by frontiersmen during an unstable period of history, during the transition late in the brief life of the Republic of Texas, shortly before the United States annexed Texas. His own experiences, apart from the minor dislocation produced by the Second World War, were much different from those of his earliest Texan ancestors, but the Halls as a settled family gave him a stable base in his community for confident growth, a law career, and many opportunities to serve, including as a U.S. Representative.

It is inconceivable, or perhaps simply rare, that significant leadership emerges apart from that sort of stability. Civic leaders cannot serve apart from extensive webs of relationship. The life of a civic organization and the functions of politics require intensive interpersonal cooperation. In short, Sam Hall Jr. was prepared to participate and serve because he belonged to Marshall, Texas, and there he had developed his capacity to serve, making of it a high virtue.

Sam belonged also to a loving family, being born to mature parents already well established in the community, a couple whose personalities guaranteed a secure home infused with energy and humor, not surprisingly two hallmarks of Sam Jr.'s personality. From Sam Sr. and Valerie both, Sam Jr. learned to hold family tightly but to season the spirit of home with generous measures of humor and fun. It was that very quality that had tempered his mother's occasional gruffness and his father's august position in Harrison County. The Hall family's religious life began and ended with their home, centering in their firm belief there should be personal accountability before God. They expressed and strengthened that belief through lifelong commitment to their Church of Christ congregation in Marshall. Hall family members did not marry and accompany a spouse elsewhere; through four generations the Halls brought willing husbands and wives into the Church of Christ. Thus, the Hall family was grounded not just in marriages, but in the traditional foundations of God and the church.

Sam B. Hall Jr. thus grew up and lived in a familiar social system that included family and friends, church and community, a system that nurtured him, so that he thrived in it. The community continued to provide life-shaping opportunities when he studied at the College of Marshall in the early 1940s, and it received him and his bride of two years when they returned to Marshall after he completed law school. His community benefited from his sanguine, gregarious personality and his assumption that he should be a civic servant. Already a master in its society, his responsibility was to prove himself an able professional, civic leader, and civic servant. Neither he nor anyone else could have conceived his refusing those roles; after all, he was Judge Sam's son—capable, bright, and popular as ever, and motivated to be both in the center of society and in leadership, as his actions proved. He served in order to see people, organizations, his community, and his nation transformed.

Sam emerged as a true leader from early in his professional and civic life. Pushed always to the presidency or chairmanship of organizations and boards, he delivered on expectations, though later, as a school board member and president dealing with desegregation issues, not adequately for some expectations. That point of contention reflected individually the broader, historical contention present in Marshall and East Texas society, a contention always much more obvious on the black side of the color line. Consequently, despite the contributions to positive change by Sam Hall Jr. and others, the fact they did not accomplish more in the 1970s simply emphasized how the Jim Crow racist past hung on tenaciously among many whites. However, it is also a reminder that African-Americans, the descendants of slaves, belonged to the society that Sam Jr. loved. Though school integration in Marshall, Texas, came with relatively minimal difficulty, no board, under any compulsion of public law, could change hardened attitudes.

Hall's experience with that political and social tightrope in his hometown was just a hint of the challenge of national politics that he entered first in 1962 in a failed primary election race, and again in 1976 when he won election to Congress. Going toe to toe with the seasoned veteran Wright Patman and his equally seasoned campaign team, the thirty-eight-year-old Hall brought a winsome personality, a clean image and an obvious mix of principles, youthful idealism and naiveté to the campaign. None could question Hall's urgent concern for his country and the dangers he sensed arrayed against Americans during that phase of the Cold War. Moreover, none could doubt his sincere, unabashed patriotism. The disappointments he experienced surprised none of his older, more experienced supporters, and he gained useful experience and many personal contacts from which he could benefit later. In that resounding 1962 defeat, Hall's performance nonetheless matched what any other strong contender would have achieved against the venerable Representative Patman.

The 1976 campaigns for the First Congressional District required considerable tenacity and energy not normally required of candidates. The incumbent's death early in the year necessitated a special election to fill his vacated seat. A runoff election, the primary, and the November election brought the total number of elections to four. Though one might argue Hall had sewn up his bid for a full term by the primary election, only the November results would make it certain, but by then he had the advantage as an incumbent. At fifty-two years of age, Sam Hall entered the House of Representatives having made many promises to honor the desires of his home district, and armed with the personal, administrative and legal skills to commence laudable work immediately. It helped that he brought his administrative assistant, Sue Jordan, to assure stability in his personal scheduling and organization, and it helped greatly, too, that the congressional office staff of Wright Patman remained to assure continuity in legislative and constituent matters, as well as the operations of the larger office. Baron Shacklette, Dorothy Councill and others kept the Washington office going without missing a beat. His lack of previous experience in elected public office, except for his membership with the Board of Education, appeared not to limit his effectiveness or his ability to adjust to new demands. Indeed, he considered himself and his constituents just as well off that he had no other experience, for example, if he had been a state legislator.

Part of Hall's community leadership involved his efforts to lead his community to forsake its negative, painful legacy of Jim Crow segregation.

Sam and others in leadership could not help but displease people on both the white and black sides, at least, by integrating the Marshall schools, by doing it at first in a tentative, and then in a negotiated fashion, thus avoiding the dramatic change that would incense segregationists, but in the process frustrating integrationists and the black leadership. Often repeated, the question was why Sam did not step up more forcefully, using his considerable personal influence to set a firm, progressive standard that for once fully recognized the equality of Marshall's black citizens and school children, achieving integration more quickly. Two observations apply here: the first, that Sam Jr. as a high-profile representative of the white leadership in Marshall and Harrison County could not and did not operate as free of his society's own background and tradition of Jim Crow as he and others would have liked. Wanting to shed the stigma of tradition, and despite his identification and genuine friendship with many members of the black community, Sam nonetheless moved no more quickly for integration than could be done in an orderly, timely, perhaps even patient, fashion. It was just so with the broader white community, whose will to forsake the ideology and practice of Jim Crow segregation changed slowly, and, at the last, reluctantly, especially for the more resistant whites. Many who straddled the fence on the issue found relief from the tension, however, many citizens never relinquished their deeper attitudes. The fact of generalized social and economic segregation in Marshall, Texas, remained evidence enough of that. Thus, in his role as a change-agent, Sam B. Hall Jr. stood with others in his generation who were, simply, transitional figures whose specific actions contributed to a broader, but still incomplete, transformation of attitudes and practices. Yet, Sam's openheartedness and capacity to nurture friendship and cooperation across color lines still provides a respected model.

The favored son of a leading family and community might serve because of a sense of *noblesse oblige*, as the old explanation goes. Sam Jr., however, took his motivation as much out of the injunction that to whom much is given, much is required, thus he respected and lived out those basic values and virtues one finds in the maxims about social leadership and personal responsibility to God, community, and country. Consequently, as with a first-class meal, we might find ourselves wanting more from Sam Hall yet still feel largely satisfied with the results of his influence and memory of his presence. No person can do much better; even the best humans have left even some good things aside in order to fulfill the calling that came to them at a crucial point, or points, in their lives. One can be grateful that one such as Sam Hall chose carefully and unselfishly to respond to his calling, and because he served in order to make a positive, enduring difference.

Notes

Texas newspapers are cited, unless otherwise noted.

Abbreviations:
BCPM/HP—Baylor University Collections of Political Materials, Waco, Texas, Sam B. Hall Jr. Papers

Chapter 1

1. George Hall, "W. W. Hall—Shropshire Families," n.d., vertical file, Harrison County Historical Museum and Research Library (HCHMRL); Jim Caldwell, "The Shropshire Family," 1985, vertical file, HCHMRL; W.W. Vawter, "Shropshire-Hall and Allied Families," n.d., vertical file, HCHMRL; Scotty Hall, "James Stuart Blalock," n.d., vertical file, HCHMRL. Edgemont remains the property of a descendant, Marshall attorney, former county judge and state legislator Richard Anderson.

2. *Harrison County Texas Deed Record*, Vol. G, 126, 167-8.

3. *Ibid.*, Vol. O, 634-635; Vol. P, 599-600; Vol. Q, 617-618. C. M. Hall's 1857 purchases included 586 acres in Upshur County.

4. *Texas 1850 Slave Schedule, Harrison County*, 19, 21; *Texas 1860 Slave Schedule, Harrison County*, 53, 59.

5. *Harrison County, Texas, Probate Minutes*, Vols. A-J, 1002.

6. Patsy and Jimmy Oliphant, comp. *Confederate Soldiers that Served in Units Formed in Harrison County, Texas* (Marshall, Tex.: Harrison County Genealogical Society, n.d.; *The War of the Rebellion: A Compilation of the Official Records of the Union and Confederate Armies,* Series I, Vol. XIII (Washington, D.C.: Government Printing Office, 1885), 33, 43; Anne J. Bailey, "The Texas Cavalry's Race to Reinforce Arkansas Post, Jan. 1863," *East Texas Historical Journal* 23:1 (Spring 1990), 53; Dan Hall, telephone interview with author, Jan. 11, 2001; Office of the Commissioners for Marking Graves of Confederate Dead, War Department, comp., *Confederate P.O.W.'s: Soldiers and Sailors who Died in Federal Prisons and Military Hospitals in the North* (reprint: Frances Ingmire and Carolyn Ericson, Nacogdoches, Tex.: Ericson Books, 1994).

7. Nell Hall, interview with author, tape recording, Marshall, Tex., Mar.15, 1999; Dan Hall, interview.

8. Nell Hall, interview; *Hospitality with the Halls*, Olathe, Kan.: Cookbook Publishers, n.d.), ii-iii; *Harrison County, Texas, Probate Minutes*, Vols. A-J, 1002; Nancy Blakeley Ruff, *Harrison County, Texas, Caucasian Residents in 1880* (Baltimore: Gateway Press, 1987), entries 407, 432; Nancy Blakeley Ruff, "The Blakeleys," HCHMRL, notebook.

9. *Harrison County, Texas, Estate Record*, Vol. K, 237.

10. *Harrison County, Texas, Estate Record*, Vol. K, 507-508.

11. Nell Hall, interview; Dan Hall, interview.

12. Nell Hall, interview; Julia Anderson Hall, "Reuben Adair Hall," in vertical file "Charles Maclin Hall Family," HCHMRL.

13. *Marshall News Messenger*, Nov. 3, 1968.

14. Nell Hall, interview.

15 - 16. *Ibid.*

17. Dan Hall, interview.

18. *Marshall News Messenger*, Dec. 15, 1934.

19. Nell Hall, interview.

20. *Marshall News Messenger*, Jan.14, 15, & 18, 1924.

21. Madeleine Hall, telephone conversation with author, Jan. 27, 2001. In 1991 at the time of Judge Hall's portrait presentation, his former judicial law clerk, Ernest Metzger, wrote, "It was tactless to mention after my clerkship was over that my new judge, fifty years before, had gotten first prize in a baby judging contest." Ernest Metzger, letter to Judge Sam B. Hall Jr., Oct. 29, 1991.

22. Nell Hall, interview.

23. *Ibid.*

24. Kathleen Hall McLendon and John McLendon, and Madeleine Hall, interview by author, tape recording, Marshall, Tex., Nov. 17, 1998.

25. Nell Hall, interview.

26. Becky and Pinkie Palmer, interview by author, tape recording, Marshall, Tex., June 14, 1999.

27. Kathleen Hall McLendon and John McLendon, and Madeleine Hall, interview.

28. Charlene Carrington, Dorothy McKay, and Ballard A Dinwiddie III, interview by author, tape recording, Marshall, Tex., July 28,1998.

Chapter 2

1. Kathleen Hall McLendon, John McLendon, and Madeleine Hall, interview by author, tape recording, Marshall, Tex., Nov. 17, 1998.

2. *Ibid.*

3. *Ibid.* On the morning of Jan. 22, 1927, the bus carrying the basketball team, coaches, student team manager, and a student along for the ride to Austin, was struck by the "Sunshine Special." Ten students died then or soon after, and most of the rest were injured. The ten are remembered among the Baylor University family as the "Immortal Ten." Sam B. Hall Jr.'s grandson, Chase Palmer, initiated the drive to construct a statue memorializing the "Immortal Ten" in 1996 after a discussion of the importance of the tradition of the Texas A&M University "Twelfth Man." *Baylor Line* 64:1 (Winter 2002): 42-53.

4. McLendon, McLendon, and Madeleine Hall, interview.

5 - 11. *Ibid.*

12. McLendon, McLendon, and Madeleine Hall, interview.

13. *Ibid.*; Madeleine Hall, letter to author, June 29, 1998; Sam B. Hall Jr., letter to Madeleine Segal, Sept. 22, 1942, Madeleine Hall personal files.

14. Madeleine Hall, interview by author, tape recording, Marshall, Tex., Aug. 20, 2002, letter to author, June 29, 1998.

15. Madeleine Hall, letter to author, June 29, 1998.

16. Madeleine Hall, interview.

17. College of Marshall, *The Martian* (college yearbook), 1942, 1943.

18. Carl Norris, telephone interview by author, tape recording, Nov. 28, 2000; Madeleine Hall, interview, Aug. 20, 2002; Lon Bates, letter to author, Sept. 24, 2002; Helen Williamson, letter to author, Mar. 30, 1998; recital program, East Texas Baptist University, Jarrett Library, vertical file "COM 1942."

19. Bill Taylor, telephone conversation with author, May 5, 1999.

20. Sam Hall, inscription, May 12, 1942, Harold Taylor copy of *The Martian*, COM yearbook for 1941-1942.

21. Madeleine Hall, interview.

22. Sam and Madeleine Hall, interview by Sandy Toussaint, East Texas Baptist University, COM Reunion videotape recording, 1994; Joe Berry Pyle, conversation with author, Oct. 26, 1998.

23. *The Compass* (COM student newspaper), Nov. 24, 1941.

24. Madeleine Hall, interview.

25. Marion G. Holt, telephone interview by author, tape recording, Apr. 5, 1999; Rex Narramore, telephone conversation with author, June 24, 1999; Joe W. Lovelace, letter to author, Mar. 3, 1998; Jack Ritchie, telephone interview by author, tape recording, Feb. 7, 2000.

26. Sam B. Hall Jr., letter to Madeleine Segal, June 8, 1942.

27. Sam B. Hall Jr., letters to Madeleine Segal, Sept.18 and 22, 1942.

28. Sam B. Hall Jr., letters to Mr. and Mrs. Sam B. Hall and Daughter, Sept.15, 1942, Mr. and Mrs. Sam B. Hall, Sept. 20 and 23, 1942. Jack Baldwin was the older brother of F. Scott and Phillip Baldwin of Marshall.

29. Madeleine Hall, interview by author, tape recording, Marshall, Tex., Aug. 29, 2000.

30. Sam B. Hall Jr., letter to Mr. and Mrs. Sam B. Hall and gal, Oct. 5, 1942.

31. Madeleine Hall, interview, Aug. 29, 2000.

32. Ralph Watson, interview by author, tape recording, Marshall, Tex., Jan.15, 1999.

33. Sam B. Hall Jr., letter to Madeleine Segal, Apr.16, 1943.

34. Don Luna, telephone conversation with author, June 22, 2001; Madeleine Hall,

conversation with author, June 4, 1999.

35. Sam B. Hall Jr., letter to Madeleine Segal, Dec.10, 1943.

36. Sam B. Hall, Jr., letter to Sam and Valerie Hall, no date.

37. Sam B. Hall Jr., letter to Kathleen Hall, June 7, 1943; Kathleen Hall McClendon and Madeleine Hall, interview by author, tape recording, Marshall, Tex., Nov. 24, 1998.

38. Sam B. Hall Jr., letter to Madeleine Segal, Apr.18, 1943.

39. Sam B. Hall Jr., letters to Madeleine Segal, Dec.10, 1943, Feb.12 and 13, 1944.

40. Fred Hudson, telephone conversation with author, Jan. 3, 1999.

41. Sam B. Hall Jr., letter to Madeleine Segal, Aug. 30, 1945.

42. Sam B. Hall Jr., Western Union telegram to Madeleine Segal, July 27, 1945; Madeleine Hall, interview by author, tape recording, Marshall, Tex., Aug. 29, 2000; Madeleine Hall, letter to author, June 29, 1998.

43. Cloyd Taylor, letter to author, Apr. 8, 1998; Judge William J. Cornelius, letter to author, Feb. 16, 1998; *Marshall News Messenger*, Oct. 3, 1993.

44. Kathleen Hall McLendon and Madeleine Hall, interview, Nov. 24, 1998; Robert Wainscott, telephone interview by author, tape recording, Jan. 20, 1999.

45. Sam B. Hall Jr., letter to Madeleine Segal, Dec.7, 1945.

46. Sam B. Hall Jr., letter to Madeleine Segal, Dec.13, 1945.

47. Madeleine Hall and family, conversation with author, Marshall, Tex., July 20, 1998.

48. McLendon, McLendon, and Madeleine Hall, interview.

49. Madeleine Hall, interview by author, tape recording, Marshall, Tex., June 29, 1998.

50 - 51. *Ibid.*

52. *Baylor Law: A Rich and Proud Tradition* (Baylor School of Law, Waco, Tex., Accessed July 30, 2002); available from http://law.baylor.edu/History/Time_Periods/growth.htm; Internet.

53. *Ibid.*, Madeleine Hall, interview, Aug. 29, 2000; letter to author, June 28, 1998; interview, July 29, 1998.

54. Judge John Luther Smith, telephone interview by author, tape recording, Feb. 16, 1999.

55. Judge William J. Cornelius, letter. Cornelius was Chief Justice, Court of Appeals, State of Texas, Sixth District, at Texarkana.

56. Joe Lovelace, letter to author, Mar. 3, 1998.

57. *Ibid.*

58. Judge Vernon L. Smith, interview by author, tape recording, Apr. 5, 1999. Madeleine Hall, interview, Aug. 29, 2000.

59. Madeleine Hall, interview, Aug. 29, 2000.

Chapter 3

1. Franklin Jones Jr., interview by author, tape recording, Marshall, Tex., Jan. 20, 1999.

2. William Huffman, interview by author, tape recording, Marshall, Tex., Sept. 23, 1998; Don Rives, interview by author, tape recording, Austin, Tex., Feb. 11, 2000.

3. The last cotton gin in Harrison County closed in the 1970s; by some accounts L. Aaron Rives, the father of Don Rives, produced the last bale ginned in the county. Rives, interview.

4. Madeleine Hall, interview by author, tape recording, Marshall, Tex., Aug. 29, 2000.

5. Huffman, interview; William M. Huffman, letter to author, Aug. 27, 1998.

6. Huffman, interview.

7. Jerry Beane, letter to author, Dec. 16, 1998.

8. Judge Rodney Gilstrap, interview by author, tape recording, Marshall, Tex, Oct. 2, 1998.

9. Beverly Hines Harris, interview by author, tape recording, Marshall, Tex., Apr. 20, 1999.

10. *Ibid.*

11. Memorandum, Apr. 6, 1966, Secretaries to Ernest F. Smith, Sam B. Hall, Jr., and William M. Huffman, photocopy given by Beverly Hines Harris, Apr. 20, 1999; Gladys Kornrumpf, Beverly Hines, Blanche Turlington vs. Ernest F. Smith, Sam B. Hall, Jr., and William M. Huffman: "Original Answer," photocopy given to author by Beverly Hines Harris, Apr. 20, 1999.

12. Harris, interview.

13. Jones, interview.

14. Ronald Ned Dennis, interview by author, tape recording, Marshall, Tex., Feb. 17, 1999.

15. Harris, interview.

16. Dennis, interview; Rives, interview.

17. F. Scott Baldwin Sr., interview by author, tape recording, Marshall, Tex., Feb. 10, 1999.

18. Annie Mae Hall, interview by author, tape recording, Marshall, Tex., Sept. 14, 1998.

19. Jewell (Mrs. U. S.) Gray, interview by author, tape recording, Marshall, Tex., June 28, 1999.

20. Sue Jordan, interview by author, tape recording, Marshall, Tex., June 21, 1999.

21. Mrs. Charles Wilson, interview by author, tape recording, Marshall, Tex., Oct. 26, 1998.

22. Becky Hall Palmer and Pinkie Palmer, interview by author, tape recording, Marshall, Tex., June 14, 1999.

23. Amanda Hall Wynn and Tom Wynn, interview by author, tape recording, Marshall, Texas, July 15, 1999.

24. Verta Williams, interview by author, tape recording, Marshall, Tex., July 15, 1999.

25. *Ibid.*

26. Judge William M. Steger, letter to author, Sept. 17, 1998.

27. Bill Palmer, interview by author, tape recording, Marshall, Tex., Oct. 20, 1998.

28. F. Scott Baldwin Sr., interview; *Marshall News Messenger*, Nov. 3, 1968. Texas State District judges could cite a string of U.S. Supreme Court decisions reversing state court rulings on petitions to overturn convictions based on violation of 14th Amendment rights and the absence of blacks in the venire—the jury selection pool—or grand juries or petit juries, in such cases as *Patton* v. *State of Mississippi*, 332 U.S. 463 (1948), and *Cassell* v. *Texas*, 339 U.S. 282 (1950).

29. Rodney Gilstrap, interview; William M. Huffman, interview; Judge Robert M. Parker, interview by author, tape recording, Tyler, Tex., Jan. 18, 2001.

30. Huffman, interview.

31. Frank Finn, letter to author, Sept. 15 , 1997.

32. Jones, interview.

33. Rives, interview. In 1976 as a new congressman, Sam Hall Jr. reminisced in a letter about his father as a marrying judge: "I remember one time in the dead of summer that Dad married a couple in the back yard. He was chewing tobacco and was wearing a straw hat. The groom was dressed in a black wool double-breasted suit and was wearing white spats. The temperature was about 102. If I could have recorded the "jury speech" that Dad made to them, I could have placed in on tape and put Justin Wilson [a Louisiana Cajun humorist] in the shade. I never have known whether it was a valid marriage or not, but that couple damn well knew something had happened to them when they left him. I hope you will make a good jury speech on the 19th of Aug. [a reference to his addressee's performing a wedding on that date]." Sam B. Hall Jr., letter to Honorable C. L. Ray Jr., Court of Civil Appeals, Sixth Supreme Judicial District (Tex.), Aug. 17, 1976. Concerning Hall Sr. and the *Post-Dispatch*: Kathleen Hall McLendon, John McLendon, and Madeleine Hall, interview by author, tape recording, Marshall, Tex., Nov. 17, 1998.

34. Glenn Link, interview by author, tape recording, Marshall, Tex., Sept. 26, 2000.

35. Jones, interview.

36. *Marshall News Messenger*, Nov. 7, 1968; Judge Sam B. Hall Jr., interview by Michael C. Smith, typed notes, Fall, 1993, "Sam B. Hall Jr." vertical file, HCHMRL, Marshall, Tex.

37. Phillip B. Baldwin, interview by author, tape recording, Marshall, Tex., Feb. 2, 1999.

38. *Ibid.*

39. Rives, interview.

40. Phillip B. Baldwin, interview.

41. Sue Jordan, letter to author, May 12, 1998.

42. *Ibid.*; Rives, interview; Sue Jordan, interview by author, tape recording, Marshall, Tex., Apr. 20, 1999.

43. Jordan, interview, Apr. 20, 1999.

44. *Ibid.*

Chapter 4

1. Kathleen Hall McLendon, John McLendon, and Madeleine Hall, interview by author, tape recording, Marshall, Tex., Nov. 17, 1998; John McLendon, letter to author, Mar. 18, 1998.

2. Madeleine Hall and family, conversation with author; McLendon, McLendon, and Hall, interview; John McLendon, letter to editor, *Marshall News Messenger*, Apr. 26, 1994.

3. Becky Hall Palmer and Madeleine Hall, conversation with author, June 27, 2002.

4. Amanda Hall Wynn and Tom Wynn, interview by author, tape recording, Marshall,

Tex., July 15, 1999.

5 - 6. *Ibid.*

7. Sandra Hall Bodenhamer, letter to author, May 2, 1998.

8. Becky Hall Palmer and Madeleine Hall, conversation.

9. Becky Hall Palmer and Pinkie Palmer, interview by author, tape recording, Marshall, Tex., June 14, 1999.

10. Beverly (Hines) Harris, interview by author, tape recording, Marshall, Tex., June 20, 1999.

11. Amanda Hall Wynn and Madeleine Hall, conversation with author, June 24, 2002.

12. *Ibid.*

13. Becky Hall Palmer and Madeleine Hall, conversation.

15. Amanda Hall Wynn and Madeleine Hall, conversation.

15. Madeleine Hall, interview by author, tape recording, Marshall, Tex., Aug. 29, 2000.

16. *Ibid.*

17. Dorothy Runnels, letter to author, Sept. 30, 1998.

18. *Marshall News Messenger*, Feb. 28, 1977.

19. Madeleine Hall and family, interview, Marshall, Texas, July 20, 1998.

20. Madeleine Hall, interview by author, tape recording, Marshall, Texas, July 29, 1998.

21. Becky Hall Palmer and Pinkie Palmer, interview.

22. Madeleine Hall and family, interview.

23. Becky Hall Palmer, letter to author, no date.

24. Brent Fox, telephone conversation with author, Apr. 12, 1999; Dennis Watson, letter to author, Aug. 28, 1998.

25. Amanda Hall Wynn and Tom Wynn, interview.

26. Kathleen Hall McLendon and Madeleine Hall, interview by author, tape recording, Marshall, Tex., Nov. 24, 1998.

27. Sandra Hall Bodenhamer, letter to author, May 2, 1998.

28. Erin Rienstra, telephone interview by author, tape recording, July 6, 2001.

29. Madeleine Hall, interview, Aug. 29, 2000.

30. *Ibid.*

31. Kathleen Hall McLendon and Madeleine Hall, interview by author, tape recording, Marshall, Texas, Nov. 17, 1998.

32. Sandra Bodenhamer, letter to author, no date.

33. Madeleine Hall, interview; letter to author, June 29, 1998.

34. Emmett Baker, telephone interview by author, tape recording, Feb. 25, 1999; Robert F. Wagner, letter to author, Dec. 13, 1997.

35. Richard Anderson, interview by author, tape recording, Marshall, Texas, Nov. 17, 1998.

36. Becky and Pinkie Palmer, interview with author, tape recording, Marshall, Texas, June 14, 1999.

37. Ned Dennis, interview by author, tape recording, Marshall, Tex., Feb. 18, 1999; Frank Fuller, interview by author, tape recording, Marshall, Tex., Jan. 18, 1999.

38. William M. Huffman, interview by author, tape recording, Marshall, Tex., Sept. 23, 1998; Fuller, interview.

39. Phyllis B. Hirsch, letter to author, Aug. 20, 1998.

40. Ruby (Mrs. George)Yates, interview by author, tape recording, Marshall, Tex., July 6, 1999.

41. Ralph Watson, interview by author, tape recording, Marshall, Texas, Jan. 15, 1999.

42. W. G. "Buck" Buchanan, conversation with author, no date.

43. Ernest Marshall and Mark Marshall, interview by author, tape recording, Marshall, Tex., July 15, 1999; Mark Marshall, letter to author, Sept. 9, 1998.

44. "Don Ratcliff Ends Highway Career," *Marshall News Messenger*, Jan. 20, 1978; Sam B. Hall Jr. MC, telegram to State Dept. of Highways and Public Transportation, Atlanta, TX, Jan. 11, 1978. Hall wrote, "It is a well-known fact that we have counted on the friendship and support of the Ratcliffs – Don and Marguerite – over a long period of time. They are tremendous people, loyal, hard-working and dedicated, as well as being courageous and constructive Americans. Their devotion to civic improvement and to the well-being of their neighbors should be common knowledge."

45. Watson, interview.

46. *Marshall News Messenger*, Jan. 15, 1971. Hall's civic awards and honors also included: service three times as emcee, annual banquet honoring Young Texans, Texas Junior Chamber of Commerce; award for outstanding achievement and leadership in human relations, Bethesda Baptist Church, Marshall; Richard Blaylock Award for Outstanding Young Citizen of Marshall; guest speaker, Abilene Christian College Annual Speaker's Forum on preservation of American heritage.

47. *Marshall News Messenger*, Dec. 17, 1970, Feb. 28, 1971, Sept. 14, 1972, Jan. 15, 1989, June 17, 1992, Nov. 28, 1991, Nov. 19, 1992, Oct. 17, 1983 (Hall quote), Jan. 27, 1977 (resigned as chair of hospital board upon going to Congress); Becky Hall Palmer & Pinkie Palmer, interview.

48. Patsy Smith-Gasperson, letter to author, Nov. 16, 1997.

49. Franklin Jones Jr., interview by author, tape recording, Marshall, Tex., Jan. 20, 1999.

50. *Ibid.*

Chapter 5

1. Kenneth C. Martis, *The Historical Atlas of United States Congressional Districts 1784-1983* (New York: The Free Press, 1982), 270, 273.

2. Nancy Beck Young, *Wright Patman: Populism, Liberalism, and the American Dream* (Dallas: Southern Methodist University Press, 2000), 11, 32-33, 302; Bill Bradford, letter to author, July 26, 1999; Bill Bradford, interview with Representative Wright Patman, tape recording of KSST radio broadcast, Sulphur Springs, Tex., no month and day, 1962.

3. *Ibid.*, 128-9. Young's book is the definitive political biography of Congressman Wright Patman. His numerous contributions to the economy and society of East Texas are carefully recounted; moreover, Patman must be counted, along with Lyndon B. Johnson, Sam Rayburn, and Jim Wright, as among the most influential Texans in American national life and politics (303).

4. B. B. Boon, telephone interview by author, tape recording, July 14, 1999.

5. *Ibid.*, Young, *Wright Patman*, 300. Speaker of the House Carl Albert used the anecdote in eulogizing Patman.

6. Don Rives, interview by author, tape recording, Austin, Tex., Feb. 11, 2000; Michael Smith, interview by author, tape recording, Marshall, Tex., Mar. 3, 1999.

7. Smith, interview; Marion G. Holt, letter to author, Mar. 20, 1998.

8. Joe W. Lovelace, letter to author, Mar. 3, 1998.

9. Lovelace, letter; Thomas F. Lanier Sr., telephone interview by author, tape recording, Jan. 11, 2001; Rives, interview.

10. *Marshall News Messenger*, Apr. 1, 1962. The Patman ad cited two federal cases that invoked the 1954 Communist Control Act: *United States* v. *Silverman*, 132 F. Supp. 820, (2d. Cir. 1957), and *United States* v. *Flynn*, 216 F. 2d 354 (2d. Cir. 1954).

11. *Marshall News Messenger*, Apr. 6, 1962.

12. *Ibid.*, Apr. 15, 1962.

13. *Ibid.*, Apr. 13, 1962.

14. *Ibid.*, Apr. 15 and 19, 1962.

15. *Ibid.*, Feb. 20, 1962.

16. *Ibid.*, Apr. 22 and 29, May 1, 1962.

17. "Sam B. Hall Jr.," vertical file, Harrison County Historical Museum and Library, Marshall, Tex.

18. *Marshall News Messenger*, Apr. 24, 1962.

19. Bill Bradford/KSST radio, Sulphur Springs, Tex., tape recording, telephone transmission broadcast of Marshall, Tex., *Political Rally for Sam B. Hall, Jr.*, Apr. 24, 1962.

20 - 22. *Ibid.*

23. *Marshall News Messenger*, Apr. 8, 11, 12, and 15, 1962. Bailey Moseley of Marshall chaired the Youth for Sam Committee. Hall wanted to speak specifically to young people about his views, even if they were not yet voters.

24. Bradford, *Political Rally.*

25. *Ibid.*

26. Bill Bradford/KSST radio, interview with Rep. Wright Patman, 1962.

27. *Ibid.*

28. *Ibid*; 88th Congress, 1st sess., *Congressional Directory* (Washington, D.C.: U.S. Government Printing Office, 1963), 300.

29. Bill Bradford/KSST radio, interview with Sam B. Hall Jr., tape recording, no day and month, 1962.

30. *Marshall News Messenger*, May 3, 1962.

31. Jerry Beane, letter to author, Dec. 16, 1998.

32. *Marshall News Messenger*, May 3 and 4, 1962.

33. *Ibid.*, May 4, 1962.

34. "A New Bill . . . And A Letter," Ibid.

35 - 37. *Ibid.*

38. "Eleventh-Hour SMEAR," *Ibid. The Texas Observer* noted the alleged incident on May 2, 1962: "An altercation in which Hall was reported involved has not helped his candidacy, but stories continue to appear in the Dallas *News* in which he is chipping away at Patman." (p.8).

39. William M. Huffman, interview by author, tape recording, Marshall, Tex., Sept. 23, 1998; Charles Thompson, interview by author, tape recording, Atlanta, Tex., Sept. 30, 1998.

40. Gerald Smith, telephone interview by author, tape recording, June 24, 1999.

41. Madeleine Hall, interview by author, tape recording, Marshall, Tex., July 29, 1998.

42. Thompson, interview; Bill Palmer, interview by author, tape recording, Marshall, Tex., Oct. 20, 1998.

43. Huffman, interview.

44. "Hall Concedes House Race to Patman," *Marshall News Messenger*, May 6, 1962; Becky Hall Palmer and Pinkie Palmer, interview by author, tape recording, Marshall, Texas, June 14, 1999; Becky Hall Palmer and Madeleine Hall, conversation with author, July 2, 2002.

45. Huffman, interview; *Politics in America*, (Washington, D.C.: Congressional Quarterly, Inc., 1984), 1445.

46. U.S. Rep. Max Sandlin, interview by author, tape recording, Marshall, Tex., Feb. 20, 2001.

47. Huffman, interview.

48. *Ibid.*

49. Charlene Carrington, Dorothy McKay, and Ballard A. Dinwiddie III, interview by author, Marshall, Tex., July 28, 1998; Bill Palmer, interview.

Chapter 6

1. Charlene Beane, letter to author, no date, July, 1998; Max Lale, interview by author, tape recording, Marshall, Tex., Sept. 20, 1999.

2. Minutes, Marshall Board of Education, May 26, 1958; Minutes of Joint Meeting of Marshall Board of Education and Marshall City Commission, June 8, 1961.

3. *Marshall News Messenger*, Aug. 22, 1968; J. Stanley Pottinger, Director, Office of Civil Rights, Department of Health, Education and Welfare, letter to Truitt Ingram, Superintendent, Marshall Public Schools, Aug. 18, 1970 (Board of Education Minutes 1970); *Marshall News Messenger*, Aug. 4, 1970.

4. *Marshall News Messenger*, Aug. 27, 1970, June 23, 1971, Apr. 24, 1973, Aug. 11, 1981.

5. Author's conclusions, Franklin Jones Jr., interview by author, tape recording, Marshall, Tex., Jan. 20, 1999.

6. Franklin Jones, Jr., interview, my interpretation.

7. Mrs. Charles Wilson, interview by author, tape recording, Marshall, Tex., Oct 26, 1998.

8. Ora Asa Johnson, interview by author, tape recording, Marshall, Tex., Feb. 4, 1999.

9. Arthur O. Wesley, telephone interview by author, tape recording, Dec. 29, 2000.

10. Bill Palmer, interview by author, tape recording, Marshall, Tex., Oct. 20, 1998; Wilson, interview.

11. Jones, interview.

12. Isadore J. Lamothe, interview by author, tape recording, Marshall, Tex., Jan. 22, 1999.

13. Jewell (Mrs. U. S.) Gray, interview by author, tape recording, Marshall, Tex., June 28, 1999.

14. Anna Bell Hall, interview by author, tape recording, Marshall, Tex., Sept. 14, 1998; Gray, interview.

15. Gray, interview.

16. Phillip B. Baldwin, interview by author, tape recording, Marshall, Tex., Feb. 2, 1999.

17. *Longview Daily News*, Sept. 8, 1980.

18. O. Ivan White Jr., letter to author, Feb. 19, 1998.

Chapter 7

1. Editorial, "Hall Choice," *The Atlanta Times*, Mar. 25, 1976; Editorial, "We Endorse Sam B. Hall Jr.," *Marshall News Messenger*, Apr. 4, 1976. One week after Wright Patman's Administrative Assistant Baron Shacklette announced he could not work with Glen Jones if he were elected, but would work with Hall, the *Texarkana Gazette* endorsed Jones: *Texarkana Gazette,* May 23, 1976.

2. *Marshall News Messenger*, May 23 and 28, 1976; *The Atlanta Times*, May 23, 1976.

3. Ray Lawson, interview by author, tape recording, Marshall, Tex., Oct. 7, 1998.

4. "Harrison County," *The New Handbook of Texas*, Vol. 3 (Austin: Texas State Historical Association), 488. Concerning the "iron collar," "Conservative Hall has no iron collar," *The Houston Post*, July 5, 1976.

5. Kenneth C. Martis, ed., *The Historical Atlas of the United States Congressional Districts, 1789-1983* (New York: The Free Press, 1982), 270, 273. Considerations about East Texas and Little Dixie are drawn partly from a telephone conversation with Fred Hudson, Feb. 2, 1999; "Fannin County," *The New Handbook of Texas*, Vol. 2 (Austin: Texas State Historical Assn., 1996), 945-947.

6. Nancy Beck Young, *Wright Patman: Populism, Liberalism, and the American Dream* (Dallas: Southern Methodist University Press, 2000), 293-300.

7. Madeleine Hall, interview by author, tape recording, Marshall, Tex., Aug. 29, 2001.

8. Ray Lawson, letter to author, Mar. 19, 1998.

9. George Christian, letter to author, Aug. 18, 1998.

10. *Ibid.*

11. Lon Bates, letter to author, Sept. 24, 1997.

12. Bishop B. Curry Jr., letter to author, Mar. 19, 1997.

13. Arthur O. Wesley, telephone interview by author, tape recording, Dec. 29, 2000.

14. Dr. R. D. Douglas, campaign support letter, Hall family records, no date.

15. Richard Morehead, "Secret weapon for candidate's race," *Dallas Morning News*, Feb. 29, 1976; "Sam Hall, Jr., Honored At Chili Supper," *Hallsville Herald*, Feb. 19, 1976.

16. Becky and Pinkie Palmer, interview by author, tape recording, Marshall, Tex., June 14, 1999.

17. Florine Lundy Miller, interview by author, tape recording, Marshall, Tex., Jan 28, 1999; Lawson, interview.

18. Mimeographed song sheet, Hall family records, no date.

19. Judge John Luther Smith, telephone interview by author, tape recording, Feb. 16, 1999.

20. Audio tape, Hall family files.

21. *Marshall News Messenger,* May 2, 1976.

22. Fred Hudson, telephone conversation with author, Feb. 12, 1999; *Texarkana Gazette*, June 13, 1976.

23. *Ibid.; Atlanta Times*, June 3, 1976.

24. *The Odessa American*, June 20, 1976; *Atlanta Times*, June 24, 1976.

25. Madeleine Hall, interview.

26. Jean (Mrs. Sam) Birmingham, conversation with author, July 28, 1998.

27. *Atlanta Times*, July 1, 1976.

28. *Cong. Rec.*, 122, no. 17, daily ed. (June 28, 1976): H20979-20980.

29. Becky Hall Palmer and Pinkie Palmer, interview by author, tape recording, Marshall, Tex., June 14, 1999.

30. *Ibid.*

31. William M. Huffman, letter to author, Aug. 27, 1998.

32. Emmett C. Baker, telephone interview by author, tape recording, Feb. 25, 1999; Palmer and Palmer, interview.

33. Bill Palmer, interview by author, tape recording, Marshall, Tex., Oct. 20, 1998.

34. *Citizens Journal* (Atlanta), Oct. 17, 1976.

35. *Citizens Journal* (Atlanta), May 23, 1976; Harlan and Flovice Craig, telephone interview by author, tape recording, June 25, 1999.

36. Mary Maddox, telephone conversation with author, Sept. 14, 1999.

37. Bonnie Spellings, telephone conversation with author, June 28, 1999.

38. Charlie and Louise Ayers Walters, telephone interview by author, tape recording,

June 28, 1999.

39. Bobby Johnson, letter to author, Aug. 20, 1998.

40. "Hall Logging Road Miles," *Texarkana Gazette*, Apr. 18, 1976; Sue Jordan, interview by author, tape recording, Marshall, Tex., Apr. 20, 1999; Sue Jordan and Madeleine Hall, conversation with author, Marshall, Tex., June 21, 1999.

Chapter 8

1. U. S. District Judge William Wayne Justice, letter to author, Aug. 11, 1998.

2. Richard F. Fenno Jr., *Home Style: House Members in Their Districts* (Boston: Little, Brown, 1978), 1-29, 31-40, 54-6, 144; *Guide to U. S. Elections*, 3d ed. (Washington, D. C.: Congressional Quarterly, Inc., 1994), 1282, 1287, 1292, 1297, 1302.

3. *Paris News* (Texas), June 17, 1980, BCPM, Box 744, File 4.

4. Richard Anderson, interview by author, tape recording, Marshall, Tex., Nov. 17, 1998; Harrison County Judge Bonnie Leggatt, telephone conversation with author, Oct. 14, 1998.

5. Judge Lanny Ramsay, letter to author, Oct. 27, 1998.

6. Jewell (Mrs. U. S.) Gray, interview by author, tape recording, Marshall, Tex., Sept. 21, 1998.

7. *Guide to U. S. Elections*, 1282; B. H., editorial, *Henderson Daily News* (Tex.), Feb. 15, 1977.

8. *Shreveport Times*, June 29, 1976.

9. *Ibid.*; *Citizens Journal* (Atlanta), Oct. 28, 1976; *The Midland Reporter-Telegram*, Feb. 18, 1977.

10. *Marshall News Messenger*, June 15, 1980.

11. *Reports from Washington,* Aug. 30, 1976, BCPM, Box 746 File 1.

12. *Marshall News Messenger*, Apr. 7, July 21, and Aug. 30, 1977.

13. Don Womack, letter to author, Mar. 18, 1998.

14. Rep. Ralph M. Hall, letter to author, Nov. 9, 1998.

15. Susan Brenna, "Hall pleases East Texans by riding high in conservative saddle," *Dallas Times Herald*, June 26, 1984; BCPM, Box 744, File 5; Madeleine Hall, personal journal notes, no date.

16. BCPM, Boxes 529, 531.

17. Madeleine Hall, interview by author, tape recording, Marshall, Tex., July 29, 1998.

18. *Marshall News Messenger*, Mar. 7, 1983. The Youngs were longtime black educators before and after school desegregation; Price T. served as a principal in the Marshall schools.

19. Ralph Watson, interview by author, tape recording, Marshall, Tex., Jan. 15, 1999; Madeleine Hall, interview.

20. *Ibid.*

21. Madeleine Hall, interview.

22. Wayne Elizabeth Emery, letter to author, Mar. 31, 1998.

23. *Ibid.*

24. Sandra Hall Bodenhamer, letter to author, Mar. 2, 1998.

25. *Ibid.*

26. Sandra Hall Bodenhamer, letter to author, July 11, 1998.

27. Madeleine Hall, interview.

28. Amanda Hall Wynn, letter to author, no date, 1998.

29. Nancy Beck Young, *Wright Patman: Populism, Liberalism, and the American Dream* (Dallas: Southern Methodist University Press, 2000), 299; "Patman, John William Wright, 1893-1976," Biographical Directory of the United States Congress, 1774-present [directory on-line], accessed July 2, 2003; available from http://bioguide.congress.gov/biosearch/biosearch.asp; Internet.

30. *1976 Official Congressional Directory*, 94th Cong., 2d sess. (Washington, DC: Government Printing Office, 1976), 361; *Dallas Times Herald*, June 26, 1984.

31. *Atlanta Times* (Texas), Mar. 10, 1985; BCPM, Box 745, File 18; "Teague, Olin Earl," *The New Handbook of Texas,* Vol. 6 (Austin: Texas State Historical Association, 1996), 230-1.

32. BCPM, 418-423 boxes.

33. Ray Lawson, interview by author, tape recording, Marshall, Tex., Oct. 7, 1998.

34. *Ibid.*; Frank Stover, telephone interview by author, tape recording, July 21, 1999. Stover was Deputy Chief Counsel for the Veterans Affairs committee.

35. BCPM/HP, Box 360, Files 1-3. Hall's files on the Criminal Code run to several boxes: 360-380; on Special Prosecutor Legislation (H.R. 4292, S. 555, 1977), Box 360, Files 8, 9; Box 361, Files 1, 2.

36. Editorial, "He fits in perfectly," *Midland Reporter Telegram*, Feb. 18, 1977; BCPM/HP, Box 744, File 2.

37. 95th Cong., 1st sess., *Cong. Rec.*, 123, No. 1 (Jan. 11, 1977): H909.

38. *Ibid.*

39. U.S. Congress, House, *Resolution insisting upon retention of undiluted U.S. Sovereignty over the Canal Zone and the Panama Canal*, 95th Cong., 1st sess., H.RES 186, *Cong. Rec.*, 123, No. 2, daily ed. (Jan. 26, 1977): H2396; *Concurrent Resolution expressing the sense of the Congress regarding the sovereign rights of the United States in the Canal Zone*, 95th Cong., 1st sess., H.CON.RES 403, *Cong. Rec.*, 123, No. 28, daily ed. (Nov. 3, 1977): H37036; *A concurrent resolution requesting that the President withdraw the instruments of ratification of the Panama Canal treaties*, 96th Cong., 1st sess., H.CON.RES. 75, *Cong. Rec.*, 125, No. 4, daily ed. (Mar. 15, 1979): H5368; *A Bill to amend the Canal Zone Code in order to establish procedures with respect to the disposition of land in the Canal Zone*, 95th Cong., 1st sess., H.R. 9186, *Cong. Rec.*, 123, No. 73, daily ed. (Sep 19, 1977): H29875.

40. BCPM/HP, Box 744, File 2.

41. *Longview Daily News*, May 10, 1980; *Atlanta (Tex.) Times*, May 15, 1980; BCPM/HP, Box 744, File 13.

42. Editorial, *Marshall News Messenger*, May 13, 1980; BCPM/HP, Box 744, File 2.

43. In March, 1977, the Presidential Commission on Americans Missing and Unaccounted for in Southeast Asia sent a delegation to Vietnam and Laos. Mr. Leonard Woodcock, the President of the United Auto Workers union, led the group. Accompanying him were former Senator Mike Mansfield, a Montana Democrat, former Ambassador Charles W. Yost, Congressman. G. V. Montgomery, a Mississippi Democrat, and Mrs. Marian Wright Edelman who directed the Children's Defense Fund. The Vietnamese wanted to talk and were gracious to the Commission, though the delegation report noted the "element of reserve" based on the former adversarial relationship. Twelve airmens' remains were offered to the commission. The Vietnamese declared there were no more prisoners of war; they would work to locate other remains, which would be returned to the American authorities as soon as they were discovered.

The Hanoi government also asserted that the United States should in turn provide help to reconstruct Vietnam. The commission's work also involved Laos and Cambodia, but the Khmer Rouge-induced chaos in Cambodia prohibited travel to Phnom Penh; besides, the Cambodian Foreign Ministry had denied entry. The Cambodians wanted no more to do with the "U.S. imperialists" as they had from 1970 to 1975. See the White House press release, Mar. 23, 1977, BCPM/HP, Box 566.

44. Congress, House, 95th Cong., 1st sess., H. Con. Res. 331, *Cong. Rec.*, 123, no. 22, daily ed. (Aug 5, 1977): H27286.

45. *Report of the Special Committee on Southeast Asia*, 95th Cong., 2d sess., *Cong. Rec.*, 124, no. 22, daily ed. (Sept. 20, 1978): H30484-H30487; Trips: Special Committee on Southeast Asia, BCPM/HP, Box 566, files 5-7, Box 567, files 1-3.

46. *Marshall News Messenger*, Aug. 28, 1978; *Terrell* (Tex.) *Tribune*, Aug. 26, 1978.

47. United Press International wire report, BCPM/HP, Box 566, File 4; Trips: Special Committee on Southeast Asia, BCPM/HP, Box 566, Files 5-7, Box 567, Files 1-3.

48. *Marshall News Messenger*, Sept. 3, 1978.

49. First quote, Ike Skelton, letter to author, Aug. 6, 1998; Groward's inscription: the actual bag is in the trip file, BCPM/HP, Box 567.

50. BCPM/HP, Box 566, File 4.

51. *The Washington Star*, Aug. 2, 1978.

52. *Report of the Special Committee on Southeast Asia*, 95th Cong., 2d sess., *Cong. Rec.*, 124, no. 22, daily ed. (Sept. 20, 1978): H30484-H30487; BCPM/HP, Box 566, File 7.

53. *Marshall News Messenger*, Sept. 3, 1978.

54. *The Washington Star*, Aug. 24, 1978; *The Times* (Shreveport, La.), Aug. 25, 1978.

55. Hall later participated in a twenty-five member Congressional delegation to view interment of the remains in the Tomb of the Unknowns at Arlington National Cemetery on Memorial Day 1984. The day was overcast and occasionally rainy. President Ronald Reagan offered a eulogy for that fallen veteran of the war about which there were "no parades, no flags and so little

thanks." POW/MIA families had opposed the interment because they thought it would harm the continuing search for MIAs, but a 1973 law mandated it. Reflecting on the day Hall said, "One of the greatest honors I have ever received was to be appointed to represent my colleagues at the ceremonies honoring the unknown from the Vietnam War." Ironic also for the day was that the service member's remains were the only unidentified remains the military had after many years, a stark contrast to the technological and forensic inability of the specialists of former wars to identify all remains. Doubly ironic in retrospect is that those remains ultimately were identified in the summer of 1998 as those of a 24-year-old aviator whose aircraft was shot down in Vietnam in May, 1972. On July 11, 1998, the family of Lieutenant Michael Blassie buried his remains at the Jefferson Barracks National Cemetery in Saint Louis, Missouri. *Marshall News Messenger*, May 28, 1984; *Longview Daily News*, May 29, 1984; *Atlanta* (Tex.) *Times*, May 27, 1984; *The New York Times*, June 30, 1998; *Dallas Morning News*, July 12, 1998.

56. Joe D. Waggonner Jr., letter to author, Feb. 26, 1998

57. BCPM/HP, Box 747, File 6.

58. *Dallas Times Herald*, Aug. 30, 1978.

59. *The Washington Star*, Sept. 4, 1978; *The Longview* (Tex.) *Daily News*, Sept. 13, 1978.

Chapter 9

1. "Congressman Hall is representing his district," Editorial, *Paris News*, Apr. 30, 1978; *Henderson Daily News*, May 23, 1978; BCPM/HP, Box 744, File 2.

2. *Sherman Democrat*, Mar. 11, 1980; BCPM/HP, Box 744, File 11; Congress, Senate, *Veterans' Judicial Review Act* and *Veterans' Benefits Improvement Act of 1988*, 100th Cong., 2d sess., 1988, S.11. During Hall's tenure: Judicial review file, 1980, BCPM/HP, Box 429, Files 1, 2. A veterans' appeals court separate from the federal judiciary would serve veterans' claims more efficiently. Yet the Veterans Administration could not evaluate or police its own actions; judicial review of administrative decisions followed constitutional principle. Developing the court required cooperation with the House Judiciary Committee, and, concerned about the possible consequences, veterans' organizations opposed the change. Mack Fleming, telephone interview by author, July 21, 1999. Fleming was staff director of the Veterans Affairs Committee during Hall's tenure.

3. Editorial: "Sam Hall Jr.: A Big Plum For An E-Texan," *Longview Morning Journal*, Jan. 18, 1979, BCPM/HP, Box 744, File 2.

4. Alan Ehrenhalt and Robert E. Healy, eds., Politics in America: Members Of Congress In Washington And At Home (Congressional Quarterly Press, 1981), 1153; *Atlanta Times*, BCPM/HP, Box 744, File 2.

5. *Texarkana Gazette*, Jan. 20, 1980; *Longview Daily News*, Jan. 20, 1980.

6. Fred Pool, letter to Sam B. Hall Jr., Nov. 20, 1979, BCPM/HP, Box 744, File 3.

7. *Henderson Daily News*, Feb. 9, 1979.

8. Sam B. Hall Jr., interview by Bill Bradford (KSST radio, Sulphur Springs, Tex.), tape recording, Jan., 1979; "Afghanistan: Four Years Later," Rep. Sam B. Hall Jr., congressional office media tape, Mar. 4, 1984, Madeleine Hall personal files.

9. Sam B. Hall Jr., interview.

10. About the budget, Hall said, "In real dollars (dollars before inflation) we have whacked and hacked the defense budget pretty hard in recent years. Weapons systems have [been] especially hurt due to an increase in defense spending for personnel needs such as salaries, housing, etc. This year's defense budget will increase somewhat, but when you consider inflation the increase is very slight. In the meantime, look for the anti-defense establishment in Congress to cut it more, in favor of spending for domestic social programs. I will vote against any cuts in our defense budget." *Henderson Daily News*, Feb. 9, 1979; BCPM/HP, Box 744, File 1.

11. *News Telegram* (Sulphur Springs), Dec. 10, 1979; BCPM/HP, Box 744, File 7.

12. "Hall predicts entailment for U.S. in Iran-Iraq," *Texarkana Gazette*, Oct. 12, 1980; *Kilgore News Herald*, Sept. 24,1980; BCPM/HP, Box 744, File 15.

13. Prisoners and disability: 96th Cong., 1st sess., H.R. 5610, *Cong. Rec.*, 125, no. 22, daily ed. (Oct. 16, 1979): H28520; Social Security earnings test: 96th Cong., 1st sess., H.R. 5295, *Cong. Rec.*, 125, no. 19, daily ed. (Sept. 14, 1979): H24565; made Public Law 96-473 on Oct. 19, 1980.

14. Congress, House, *Hospital Cost Containment and Reporting Act of 1979*, 96th Cong., 1st. sess., H.R. 5635, *Cong. Rec.*, 125, no. 25, daily ed. (Nov. 15, 1979): H32673-H32753. Draw-

ing from his experience on the Marshall hospital board, Hall conferred frequently with hospital administrators about the bill, which was intended to reduce the costs of excessive regulatory paperwork, encourage voluntary cost-containment programs in the states and philanthropic giving to hospitals, decrease federal and state laws that limited hospital revenues, and allow Medicaid and Medicare payments for extended care. The bill did not go to Senate; *Jacksonville Daily Progress*, Dec. 4, 1979; BCPM/HP, Box 744, File 7; *Kilgore News Herald*, July 6, 1980; BCPM/HP, Box 744, File 9; *Wood County Democrat* (Quitman), Feb. 10, 1980. The Chrysler loan of 3.5 billion dollars passed the House, 241-124, and passed the Senate. It included a wage freeze agreement with the United Auto Workers.

15. *Bonham Daily Favorite*, Jan. 20, 1980; BCPM/HP, Box 744, File 3.

16. Editorial: "Hall is acclaimed by Texas Business," *Longview Daily News*, Jan. 30, 1980; BCPM/HP, Box 744, File 2; *Atlanta Times*, Oct.16, 1980. Hall consistently supported pro-small business legislation, with a 93 per cent favorable voting record.

17. *Marshall News Messenger*, Apr. 25, 1980; BCPM/HP, Box 744, File 12.

18. *Pittsburg Gazette*, Jan. 10, 1980; BCPM/HP, Box 744, File 10.

19. Hall received 137,665 votes in November. *Guide to U. S. Elections*, 3d ed. (Washington, D.C.: Congressional Quarterly, Incorporated, 1994), 1292; *Henderson Daily News*, Nov. 7, 1980; BCPM/HP, Box 744, File 17.

20. *Reports from Washington*, Feb. 11, 1977.

21. *Henderson Daily News*, Dec. 18, 1983; BCPM/HP, Box 744, File 6; *The Shreveport Times* (Louisiana), May 14, 1977.

22. *Kilgore News Herald*, Dec. 5, 1982; BCPM/HP, Box 744, File 17.

23. In terms reminiscent of Alexander Hamilton and Calvin Coolidge, the Reagan Administration supported a theory of "supply-side economics" intended to provide more money for Americans to invest for economic growth. This accompanied the president's emphasis on tighter control of the federal budget. President Carter had worked to change tax rates and to reduce the budget, but had nothing like what came to be called "Reaganomics," a program political opponents ridiculed and criticized, its "supply-side" ideology often referred to as the "trickle down" theory of economics. *Longview Daily News*, Jan. 30, 1980, BCPM/HP, Box 744, File 2.

24. President Ronald Reagan, letters to Sam B. Hall Jr., June 25 and 27, 1981, July 30, 1981; Hall family files; Congress, House, *A joint resolution proposing an amendment to the Constitution altering Federal budget procedures*, 97th Cong., 1st sess., H.J.Res. 350, *Cong. Rec.*, 127, no. 20, daily ed. (Oct. 29, 1981): H 26106; Congress, House, *A resolution providing for the consideration of the resolution [H.J.Res. 350]*, 97th Cong., 2d sess., H.Res. 450 (discharge petition), *Cong. Rec.*, 128, no. 7, daily ed. (May 4, 1982): H8659. The resolution lay tied up in the House Rules Committee until forced out by a discharge petition in May, 1982, and failed, being tabled by a voice vote of the House in Oct., 1982.

25. Congress, House, *Omnibus Budget Reconciliation Act of 1981*, 97th Cong., 1st sess., H.R. 3982, *Cong. Rec.*, 127, no. 15, daily ed. (Aug. 13, 1981): H20598; Public Law 97-35: *Statutes at Large*, 95, sec. 498 (1981); Public Law 97-34: [STATUTES AT LARGE] The Economic Recovery Tax Act included a 25 per cent reduction in income taxes, with the maximum rate reduced from 70 to 50 per cent.

26. Rep. Charles W. Stenholm, letter to author, Oct. 6, 1998.

27. BCPM/HP, Box 646, File 5, Box 744, Files 2-4.

28. *Henderson Daily News*, Oct. 22, 1982.

29. Congress, Senate. *Cong. Rec.*, Jan. 5, 2001, S34.

30. Michael J. Sandlin, telephone interview by author, tape recording, Feb. 19, 1999.

31. Buster Hale, "'Boll weevils' stir up wrath of fellow Democrats," *Henderson Daily News*, Oct. 22, 1981; BCPM/HP, Box 744, File 4. Hale, the *Daily News* managing editor, reminded readers that Hall had been consistent in voting for years and went with the wishes of his district.

32. *Atlanta Times*, Jan. 29, 1981; BCPM/HP, Box 744, File 8; Becky Hall Palmer and Pinkie Palmer, interview by author, tape recording, Marshall, Texas, June 14, 1999.

33. *Atlanta Times*, Sept. 3, 1981; BCPM/HP, Box 568, File 9.

34. Hall commented, "The Hmong tribesmen helped us during the war in Vietnam. They live in Laos and they come down out of those hills. They have no language, they just have a guttural sound. Some of those people over there are trying to get those people into this country and there is absolutely no place for them. They won't fit into our society." *The Longview Daily News*,

Aug. 25, 1981; BCPM/HP, Box 568, File 9.

35. *International Herald Tribune*, Aug. 15-16, 1981; BCPM/HP, Box 568, File 9.

36. *Longview Daily News*, May 24, 1982; BCPM/HP, Box 745, File 4; President Ronald Reagan, letters to Sam B. Hall Jr., Nov. 2, 1981, Aug. 9, 1982; Congress, House, *A concurrent resolution to express the sense of the Congress that the foreign policy of the United States should reflect a national strategy of peace through strength*, 97th Cong., 1st sess., H.Con.Res. 163, *Cong. Rec.*, 127, no. 13, daily ed. (July 28, 1981): H17774.

37. *Cong. Rec.*, 127, no. 17, daily ed. (Oct. 1, 1981): H22799-H22800.

38. *Ibid.*

39. Washington newsletter, Jan., 1981, BCPM/HP, Box 744, File 8.

40. Ralph M. Hall, in "Presentation of the Portrait of the Honorable Sam B. Hall, Jr.", Nov. 15, 1991, *Federal Supplement*, Vol. 781 (St. Paul, Minn.: West Publishing, 1992), lxx-lxxi.

41. Sue Hanna, letter to *Citizens Tribune* (DeKalb), Apr. 11, 1982; BCPM/HP, Box 745, File 3; *Kilgore News Herald*, Apr. 12, 1982; BCPM/HP, Box 745, File 3.

42. "VA life insurance," BCPM/HP, Box 426, Files 1, 2.

43. BCPM/HP, Boxes 380-385; Box 385, Files 1, 2, 8, 9; *Congressional Quarterly's Politics in America* (Washington, D.C.: CQ Press, 1984), 1444; Temporary workers program, employer sanctions: Congress, House, *A Bill to Amend the Immigration and Nationality Act*, 97th Cong., 1st sess., H.R. 944, *Cong. Rec.*, 127, no. 1, daily ed. (Jan. 19, 1981): H413; BCPM/HP, Box 406, Files 9, 10; *A Bill to Amend the Voting Rights Act of 1965*, 97th cong. 1st sess., H.R. 3112, *Cong. Rec.*, 127, no. 5, daily ed. (Apr. 7, 1981): H6565; BCPM/HP, Box 354, Files 2, 3; *A Bill to Abolish the Legal Services Corporation*, 97th Cong., 1st sess., H. R. 1911, *Cong. Rec.*, 127, no. 2, (Feb. 18, 1981): H2380; BCPM/HP, Box 351, Files 8-10, Box 352, Files 1-3; *Congressional Quarterly's Politics in America* (Washington, D.C.: CQ Press, 1984), 1444.

44. *Pittsburg Gazette*, June 24, 1982; BCPM/HP, Box 745, File 4; Congress, House, *Debt Collection Act of 1981*, 97th Cong., 1st sess., H. R. 749, *Cong. Rec.*, 127, no. 1, daily ed. (Jan. 6, 1981): H228; BCPM/HP, Box 382, Files 1-4. The legislation became public law during the next Congress: Congress, Senate, *A Bill to Amend the Debt Collection Act of 1982*, 98th Cong., 1st sess., S. 376, *Cong. Rec.*, 129, no. 2, daily ed. (Feb. 2, 1983): S1394; *Statutes at Large* 97, sec. 1104 (1983); BCPM/HP, Box 387, File 4; *The Champion* (Shelby County), May 19, 1982, BCPM/HP, Box 745, File 4; *Jacksonville Daily Progress*, June 14, 1983; *Henderson Daily News*, June 16, 1983, BCPM/HP, Box 744, File 18; "Chairman Hall Takes on Regulatory Reform," *Regulatory Eye*, 4 (May 1982): no page, BCPM/HP, Box 744, File 9.

45. *The Shreveport Times* (Louisiana), Aug. 29, 1976.

46. Leighton Cornett, letter to the Honorable William Wayne Justice, Jan. 26, 1982, BCPM/HP, Box 287, File 1.

47. In the Subcommittee hearing, Hall reported the $1.5 million request for land acquisition and construction in 1982 and urged its appropriation. He also explained the proposal to study construction of a multi-purpose reservoir on the Little Cypress Creek, so that greater water supply could be acquired for the Longview and Marshall area. That, and a proposal to maintain support and funding of the Big Pine Dam in Red River County, Hall presented as necessary for water supply and employment opportunities in the region. "Cooper opponents hit with $22 million suit," *The News-Telegram* (Sulphur Springs), Feb. 7, 1982; "Statement by Representative Sam B. Hall, Jr., Before Subcommittee on Water Resources, House Public Works and Transportation Committee, July 21, 1982," BCPM/HP, Box 287, File 1; *Marshall News Messenger*, May 28, 1985; "Original Tape of the Hair-Lipped [sic]Dog," KSST-Bill Bradford, Aug. 23, 1984, BCPM/HP, Box 757, Cassette 70.

48. *Marshall News Messenger*, July 18, 1982. The Newhouse wire service, apart from misidentifying Hall as a former lieutenant governor of Texas, had carried the story as an "expose."

49. Sue Jordan and Madeleine Hall, interview by author, tape recording, Marshall, Tex., June 21, 1999.

50. Charles B. Brownson, *1977 Congressional Staff Directory* (Mount Vernon, Va.: Congressional Staff Directory, 1977), 286.

51. David Lawson, telephone interview by author, tape recording, Feb. 12, 1999.

52. *Ibid.*

53. Walt Sears, telephone interview by author, tape recording, Oct. 30, 1998.

54. Sue Jordan, interview by author, tape recording, Marshall, Tex., Apr. 20, 1999.

55. *Ibid.*

56. Walt Sears, telephone interview by author, tape recording, Oct. 30, 1998; Mike Coker, telephone conversation with author, Apr. 4, 1998.

57. *Ibid.*

58. David Lawson, telephone interview by author, tape recording, Feb. 12, 1999.

59. Michael J. Sandlin, telephone interview by author, tape recording, Feb. 19, 1999; Charles Thompson, interview by author, tape recording, Atlanta, Tex., Sept. 30, 1998.

60. Judge Robert M. Parker, interview by author, tape recording, Tyler, Tex., Jan. 18, 2001.

Chapter 10

1. Chase Palmer, letter to author, undated.

2. *Congressional Quarterly's Politics in America* (Washington, D. C.: CQ Press, 1984), 1446; *Panola County Post*, Jan. 2, 1983; BCPM/HP, Box 745, File 8; President Ronald Reagan to Sam B. Hall Jr., May 25, 1983, Oct. 1, 1983, Mar. 27, 1985; Hall family files. He was among the bipartisan supporters of H. Con. Res. 113, part of a process of legislation to achieve "deployment of 100 Peacekeeper missiles beginning in 1986 and development of a new, small and mobile single-warhead ICBM." On Wright-Perkins Amendment: President Ronald Reagan to Sam B. Hall Jr., Nov. 16, 1983; Hall family files; H.AMDT. 520, in H.J.RES 403, inserted in H.J.RES 413 on Nov. 10, 1983: Congress, House, *A joint resolution making further continuing appropriations for the fiscal year 1984*, 98th Cong., 1st sess., Public Law 98-151 (Nov. 14, 1983), *Cong. Rec.*, 129, no. 22, daily ed. (Nov. 9 & 10, 1983): H31846-H32114, *passim.*

3. *Cedar Creek Pilot* (Seven Points), Oct. 28,1984; BCPM/HP, Box 745, File 17; *Henderson Daily News*, Dec. 18, 1983; BCPM/HP, Box 745, File 2.

4. *Panola County Post,* Mar. 9, 1983, BCPM/HP, Box 745, File 9.

5. *The Dallas Morning News*, Mar. 26, 1983; BCPM/HP, Box 745, File 10.

6. *Marshall News Messenger*, Sept. 21, 1983, BCPM/HP, Box 744, File 18; *The Roxton Progress*, June 16, 1983; *Cong. Rec.*, 129, no. 2, daily ed. (Mar. 24, 1983): E1288-E1289; H.R. 5110, Public Law 103-465, passed House, Nov. 29, 1994; passed Senate, Dec. 1, 1994, *Cong. Rec.*, H11536, S15379.

7. *Dallas Times Herald*, June 26, 1984; Congress, House, *An amendment providing for the exemption of small employers from employer sanctions* (H.AMDT 851, agreed to by House June 20, 1984), and *An amendment to establish a telephone verification system* (H.AMDT.852, Passed in Committee of the Whole by Recorded Vote: 242-155, Record Vote No.230, June 12, 1984); BCPM/HP, Box 415, Files 7-10; Small employers exemption: Box 413, File 6, Box 416, File 6. The first amendment to exempt employers of three or fewer employees from civil and criminal charges in the law was referred to by some as the "Beverly Hills" amendment because of the stereotype of illegal immigrants serving as house servants to the rich. The amendment passed on a voice vote. The second amendment, for which Hall asked a recorded vote, was to require telephone verification of employees being legal residents of the United States. Hall's concern for amnesty provision: see editorial, *Texarkana Gazette*, Aug. 6, 1983; BCPM/HP, Box 744, File 18.

8. *Texarkana Gazette*, Jan. 5 & 6, 1983; BCPM/HP, Box 745, File 8.

9. *Henderson Daily News,* Sept. 21, 1983; *Honey-Grove Signal Citizen*, Sept. 23, 1983; BCPM/HP, Box 744, File 18.

10. Dewey W. Grantham, *Recent America: The United States Since 1945* (Arlington Heights, Illinois: 1987), 411.

11. 98th Cong., 1st sess., *Cong. Rec.*, 129, no. 17, daily ed. (Sept. 13, 1983): H6731.

12. *Marshall News Messenger*, Sept. 16, 1983; BCPM/HP, Box 744, File 18.

13. *Jacksonville Daily Progress*, Sept. 21, 1983; BCPM/HP, Box 744, File 18; *San Augustine Tribune,* Apr. 19, 1984; BCPM/HP, Box 745, File 15.

14. "Congressman Hall Reports On Mission To Germany and Lebanon," *Jefferson Jimplecute*, Nov. 24, 1983; BCPM/HP, Box 744, File 18; *Cong. Rec.*, 129, daily ed. (Oct. 24, 1983): H8539-H8540; *Marshall News Messenger*, Nov. 1, 1983.

15. Susan Brenna, "Hall pleases East Texans by riding high in conservative saddle," *Dallas Times Herald*, June 26, 1984; BCPM/HP, Box 744, File 5.

16. On returning Cubans incarcerated in the U.S.: 98th Cong., 1st sess., H. Con. Res. 215, *Cong. Rec.*, 129, no. 24, daily ed. (Nov. 10, 1983): H32202; "Cuban Drug Connection," congressional office media tape, May 24, 1983, BCPM/HP, Box 757, tape 65 cassette and reel-to-

reel, tape and typescript, Madeleine Hall personal files; "Castro's Criminals," congressional office media tape and typescript, Dec. 20, 1983, Madeleine Hall personal files; "Drug Connection," congressional office media tape, Aug. 27, 1984, BCPM/HP, Box 757, tape 71, cassette and reel-to-reel, also Madeleine Hall files; "Drug War," congressional office media tape and typescript, 10 Apr. 1984, Madeleine Hall files; "Future of El Salvador," media tape and typescript, June 19, 1984, Madeleine Hall files.

17. On proposed constitutional amendment, and in an extended series of resolutions and amendments: 98th Cong., 1st sess., H. J. Res. 100, *Cong. Rec.*, 129, no. 1, daily ed. (Jan. 26, 1983): H381. Hall joined as co-sponsor in Aug., 1983.

18. "Prayer Amendment," congressional office media tape, Mar. 6, 1984, Madeleine Hall files.

19. *Engle* v. *Vitale*, 370 U.S. 41 (1962). The Supreme Court reversed a decision of the New York State Court of Appeals on the issue of a daily prayer delivered in a New York school, with approval of the State Board of Regents, as in violation of the Establishment Clause of the First Amendment. *Dallas Morning News*, Mar. 11, 1984; BCPM/HP, Box 745, File 14; *Cong. Rec.*, 130, no. 4, daily ed. (Mar. 5, 1984): H1182-H1183.

20. *Cong. Rec.*, 130, no. 4, daily ed. (Mar. 5, 1984): H4445-H4446; extended debates, H4379-H4522.

21. "Future of Prayer Amendment," congressional office media tape, Mar. 6, 1984, Madeleine Hall personal files. Hall closed his remarks in the House with a reference to his upbringing in the Marshall community: "I cannot help recalling, Mr. Speaker, that when I grew up in a small town in Marshall, Texas, that we had a school principal named C. J. Collier, who every morning prior to going into the classes had all of that group of young people come into a long and large room where he read one chapter from the New Testament. Now he did that for a period of 10 or 15 years. And I dare say that no person who has grown to maturity and who is objective has ever said for one moment that the chapters of the Bible that they heard Mr. Collier read to us did anything but help them in their future lives. And I would like to say with all sincerity that it is time that we had more C. J. Colliers in the schoolrooms of the Nation in order that young people, not being coerced, not being told what they must do or must not do, but I think that it is time once again that those young people have an opportunity, if they so desire, to pledge allegiance not only to their country, but to pledge allegiance to the Almighty." *Cong. Rec.*, 130, no. 4, daily ed. (Mar. 5, 1984): H4445-H4446.

22. *Cherokee County Banner*, Aug. 9, 1984; BCPM/HP, Box 744, File 5.

23. *Greenville Herald Banner*, Jan. 8, 1984; BCPM/HP, Box 745, File 12; Public Law 98-176 (Nov. 29, 1983), Public law 98-269 (Apr. 18, 1984), Public law 98-564 (Oct. 30, 1984), Public Law 98-184 (Nov. 30, 1983), H.R. 2717, amending Ethics in Government Act of 1978, tabled in House, S. 461 passed instead (Sept. 19, 1983), Public Law 98-359 on the Postal Savings System (July 13, 1984), Public Law 98-587 to update authorities of the US Secret Service (Oct. 30, 1984). In the 98th Congress of 1983 and 1984, Hall served on the Committee on the Judiciary, and chaired the Subcommittee on Administrative Law and Governmental Relations. Among deliberations in Mar., 1983, was consideration of the "Appropriation Authorization of Office of Government Ethics" (H.R. 2717, instead passed as S. 461, becoming Public Law 98-150 on Nov., 11 1980); *Cong. Rec.*, 129, (Nov. 11, 1983): S34684, H30017. Hall introduced a bill on Mar. 20, 1984, which became Public Law 98-587 on Oct. 30, having passed the House unaltered on Sept. 17 and Senate on Oct. 11: Congress, Senate, *A bill to amend section 3056 of title 18, United States Code, to update the authorities of the United States Secret Service, and for other purposes.* 98th Cong., 2d sess., H.R. 5189, *Cong. Rec.*, 130, no. 23, daily ed. (Oct. 11, 1984): H32348.

24. *Tyler Morning Telegraph*, Nov. 23, 1984; and editorial, *Tyler Morning Telegraph*, Nov. 28, 1984; *Jacksonville Daily Progress*, Nov. 27, 1984; BCPM/HP, Box 745, File 17.

25. *Athens Daily Review,* Sept. 10, 1984; BCPM/HP, Box 745, File 17.

26. *The Dallas Morning News,* Feb. 7, 1985; BCPM/HP, Box 745, File 17.

27. *Commerce Journal,* Nov. 21, 1984.

28. Comments regarding debate on the *Anti-Crime Act of 1984*, 98th Cong., 2d sess., H.R. 5690, *Cong. Rec.*, 130, no. 128, daily ed. (Oct. 2, 1984): H10818. Brackets indicate some of the variations from the official record, taken from the Hall family videotape.

29. *Atlanta Times*, Mar. 10, 1985; BCPM/HP, Box 745, File 18; *Henderson Daily News*, May 26, 1985; BCPM/HP, Box 745, File 18. Hall received other awards during his time in Con-

gress: an honorary life membership in the Texas Congress of Parents and Teachers, Apr. 1979; named a Paul Harris Fellow by Rotary International, 1982; with wife Madeleine, first recipient, annual J. Wesley Smith Award for outstanding achievement, East Texas Baptist University, 1977; Baylor University Distinguished Alumnus Award, 1984; Boss of the Year, Paris, Texas, chapter of Business and Professional Women, 1984; United Daughters of the Confederacy Jefferson Davis Award, 1985.

30. *Marshall News Messenger*, May 8, 1985.

31. Joe D. Waggonner Jr., letter to author, Feb. 26, 1998.

32. Hall quote, *Presentation of the Portrait of the Honorable Sam B. Hall, Jr.*, in Federal Supplement, Vol. 781 (St. Paul, Minn.: West Publishing Co., 1992), lxxxiv; Waggonner, letter.

33. Charles E. "Buddy" Roemer, telephone interview by author, tape recording, Feb. 20, 1999.

34 - 36. *Ibid.*

37. G. V. "Sonny" Montgomery, letter to author, Sept. 11, 1997; J. J. "Jake" Pickle, letter to author, Aug. 6, 1998.

38. Kent Hance, letter to author, Apr. 14, 1998.

39. *Presentation of Portrait*, lxxxiii-lxxxiv.

40. Charles W. Stenholm, letter to author, Oct. 6, 1998.

41. Arthur O. Wesley, telephone interview by author, tape recording, Dec. 29, 2000.

42. Robert Krueger, letter to author, Sept. 30, 1998.

43. Romano L. Mazzoli, letter to author, Dec. 15, 1998.

44. Pickle, letter.

45. Jack Hightower, telephone interview by author, tape recording, July 23, 1999; Ralph M. Hall, letter to author, Nov. 9, 1998.

46. Pickle, letter.

47. Hightower, interview.

48. Ike Skelton, letter to author, Aug. 6, 1998.

49. Harold S. Sawyer, letter to author, Sept. 12, 1997.

50. Dorothy Runnels, letter to author, Sept. 30, 1998.

51. Judge Thomas M. Reavley, letter to author, Sept. 15, 1997.

52. Roemer, telephone interview.

53. Daryl J. Arey, letter to author, Jan. 11, 1999.

54. Harlan and Flovice Craig, telephone interview by author, tape recording, June 28, 1999; Don Edwards, interview by author, tape recording, July 26, 1999.

55. Roemer, interview.

56. George W. Christian, letter to author, Aug. 18, 1998.

57. Judge Phillip B. Baldwin (U. S. Court of Customs and Patent Appeals, U. S. Court of Appeals, Federal Circuit, retired), interview by author, tape recording, Marshall, Tex., Feb. 2, 1999.

Chapter 11

1. Judge Howell Cobb, letter to author, Dec. 2, 1998.

2. W. R. "Bob" Poage, letter to Hon. Billy Wilson, Chairman, Planning Committee, Sam Hall Appreciation Dinner, Marshall, Texas, Mar. 18, 1986.

3. *Henderson Daily News*, May 26, 1985; BCPM/HP, Box 745, File 18; Ernest Metzger, letter to author, Aug. 26, 1999.

4. Judge Paul Brown, letter to author, Sept. 1, 1998; *Dallas Times Herald*, Apr. 17, 1985, BCPM/HP, Box 745, File 18; Gramm quotes: *The Paris News*, Mar. 3, 1985.

5. Sheldon Goldman, *Picking Federal Judges: Lower Court Selection from Roosevelt through Reagan* (New Haven, Conn., & London: Yale University Press, 1997), 298, 300; *Congressional Quarterly Weekly Report* 38 (July 19, 1980): 2046, quoted in Goldman, 297.

6. Goldman, 316-17.

7. Quote: Marshall News Messenger, May 28, 1985; my conclusions suggested by Charles Thompson, interview by author, tape recording, Atlanta, Tex., Sept. 30, 1998.

8. Rep. Barbara Jordan, letter to The Honorable Sam B. Hall Jr., June 11, 1985, Hall family files.

9. Robert Krueger, letter to author, Sept. 30, 1998.

10. Ray Lawson, interview by author, tape recording, Marshall, Tex., Oct. 7, 1998; Ray Lawson, letter to author, Mar. 3, 1998; Franklin Jones. Jr., interview by author, tape recording,

Marshall, Tex., Jan. 20, 1999.

11. William M. Huffman, interview by author, tape recording, Marshall, Tex., Sept. 23, 1998.

12. Judge William L. Peek Jr., telephone interview by author, tape recording, July 25, 2000; Becky Hall Palmer and Pinkie Palmer, interview by author, tape recording, Marshall, Tex., June 14, 1999; Amanda Hall Wynn and Tom Wynn, interview by author, tape recording, Marshall, Tex., July 15, 1999; Madeleine Hall, interview by author, tape recording, Marshall, Tex., Aug. 29, 2000.

13. Sam R. Moseley Jr., letter to editor, *Marshall News Messenger*, Apr. 17, 1994.

14. Joe W. Lovelace, letter to author, Mar. 3, 1998; Goldman, 294.

15. "Hall sails through judgeship hearing," *The Times* (Shreveport, La.), June 5, 1985. Budget deliberations hindered a Senate quorum and thus the vote. *Atlanta Times,* May 28, 1985, BCPM/HP, Box 745, File 18.

16. Editorial, "Sam B. Hall getting what he deserves," and second quote from another article, *Marshall News Messenger*, May 28, 1985.

17. Representative G. V. Montgomery, letter to author, Sept. 11, 1997; Rep. Charles B. Rangel, letter to Sam B. Hall Jr. (Appreciation Dinner, Greater Marshall Chamber of Commerce), Mar. 27, 1986, Hall family files; Carl Albert, letter to The Honorable Sam B. Hall Jr., Apr. 1, 1986, Hall family files; *The Atlanta Times*, May 30, 1985; *Dallas Morning News*, June 2, 1985.

18. Amanda Hall Wynn and Tom Wynn, interview by author, tape recording, Marshall, Tex., July 15, 1999.

19 - 20. *Ibid.*

21. Judge Robert M. Parker (United States Court of Appeals, Fifth Circuit), interview by author, tape recording, Tyler, Tex., Jan. 18, 2001.

22. Judge Richard A. Schell, letter to author, Dec. 29, 1998.

23. *Ibid.*

24. "In the United States District Court for the Eastern District of Texas, Marshall Division, *Presentation of the Portrait of the Honorable Sam B. Hall, Jr.*, to the United States District Court, Eastern District of Texas, by the Harrison County Bar Association and Attorneys in and for the Eastern District of Texas," Nov. 15, 1991, in West's *Federal Supplement,* Vol. 781 (St. Paul, Minn.: West Publishing, 1992), lvix-lxxxvi.

25. Judge Thomas M. Reavley, letter to author, Sept. 15, 1997.

26. Judge Phillip B. Baldwin, interview by author, tape recording, Marshall, Tex., Feb. 2, 1999.

27. Romano L. Mazzoli, letter to author, Dec. 15, 1998.

26. J. J. "Jake" Pickle, letter to author, Aug. 6, 1998.

29. Franklin Jones Jr., interview by author, tape recording, Marshall, Tex., Jan. 20, 1999.

30. Jack Brooks, letter to author, Aug. 29, 1998.

31. *Presentation of the Portrait of the Honorable Sam B. Hall, Jr.*, lxx.

Chapter 12

1. Ernest P. Metzger, letter to author, Aug. 26, 1999.

2. John G. Crews II, telephone interview by author, tape recording, July 22, 1999.

3. Ed Hohn, letter to author, Nov. 16, 1998.

4. Crews, interview; John McLendon, letter to editor, *Marshall News Messenger,* Apr. 26, 1994.

5. William M. Huffman, interview by author, tape recording, Marshall, Tex., Sept. 23, 1998.

6. "Sam Hall Sr., 94, Texas' oldest judge dies," *Marshall News Messenger*, Oct. 18, 1982; Crews, interview; Marcus F. Vascocu, letter to author, Sept. 14, 1998.

7. Gilbert T. Adams, Jr., telephone conversation with author, June 21, 2001; Judge Henry A. Politz, telephone interview by author, tape recording, Jan. 12, 2001.

8. John G. Crews III, letter to Madeleine Hall, Feb. 1, 1994, Madeleine Hall personal files. The trial was *United States of America* v. *Henry F. Fredeman, II, Et Al.*

9. Judge Gilbert I. Low, letter to author, July 30, 1998.

10. Ernest P. Metzger, telephone interview by author, tape recording, July 9, 1999.

11. Judge Henry A. Politz, telephone interview by author, tape recording, Jan. 12, 2001.

12. Ed Merritt, telephone interview by author, tape recording, Apr. 5, 1999.

13 - 14. *Ibid.*

15. Crews, interview; Sheldon Goldman, *Picking Federal Judges: Lower Court Selection from Roosevelt through Reagan* (New Haven, Conn., & London: Yale University Press, 1997), 336-42.

16. Metzger, letter.

17. Ronald Ned Dennis, interview by author, tape recording, Marshall, Tex., Feb.18, 1999.

18. Dennis, interview; Michael C. Smith, interview by author, tape recording, Marshall, Tex., Mar. 3, 1999; Gail K. Beil, "Legal Legends," *Marshall News Messenger*, Jun. 25, 2000, and a "Primetime" article on Franklin Jones Sr., *Marshall News Messenger*, Mar. 1993. Beil and Joe Goulden paired comments on Franklin Jones Sr., Goulden citing Jones's being hated and reviled as a "damned nigger lover" by segregationists in the 1940s and beyond, but praising him because he "gave our town a conscience." *Marshall News Messenger*, May 7, 1996.

19. Smith, interview. The courthouse project was underway well before the election.

20. *Ibid.*; F. Scott Baldwin Sr., interview by author, tape recording, Marshall, Tex., Feb. 10, 1999; Huffman, interview.

21. Crews, interview.

22. Ed Hohn, interview by author, tape recording, Mar. 9, 1999.

23. Smith, interview.

24. Dennis, interview.

25. Smith, interview; Judge William L. Peek Jr., telephone conversation with author, July 25, 2000.

26. Crews, interview.

27. Fred Hudson, telephone interview by author, tape recording, Jan. 3, 1999; Madeleine Hall, interview by author, tape recording, Marshall, Tex., June 28, 2001; Judge John Luther Smith, telephone interview by author, tape recording, Feb. 16, 1999.

28. Hudson, interview; Madeleine Hall, interview; John Luther Smith, interview.

29. *Marshall News Messenger*, Aug. 20, 1991; Julie Richardson, telephone interview by author, tape recording, May 3, 1999.

30. *Marshall News Messenger*, Aug. 20 & July 15, 1991.

31. Judge William J. Cornelius, letter to author, Dec. 21, 1997.

32. Judge Thomas M. Reavley, letter to author, Sept. 15, 1997.

33. Judge Gilbert I. "Buddy" Low, letter to author, July 3, 1998.

34. Judge David Folsom, telephone interview by author, tape recording, Dec. 5, 2000.

35. Smith, interview.

36. Don D. Bush, e-mail to author, June 22, 2001.

37. Bill Palmer, interview by author, tape recording, Marshall, Tex., Oct. 20, 1998.

38. Stephen Arnold, telephone interview by author, tape recording, Feb. 13, 1999.

39. *Ibid.*

40. Hohn, interview.

41. Richard Haynes, telephone conversation with author, July 9, 2001.

42. "Judge Hall scolds ex-banker at trial," *Marshall News Messenger*, Aug. 30, 1992.

43. Hohn, interview.

44. *Ibid.*

45. Smith, interview.

46. Hohn, interview; U. S. Magistrate Earl S. Hines, letter to Honorable Sam B. Hall Jr., Nov. 15, 1991, Hall family files.

47. Ed Hohn, letter to author, Nov. 16, 1998.

48. Madeleine Hall, interview; Joe W. Lovelace, letter to author, Mar. 3, 1998.

49. Ernest Philip Metzger, *Ratification of the Constitution*, Heard in the United States District Court for the Eastern District of Texas, Marshall Division, Before the Honorable Sam B. Hall, Jr., United States District Judge, and a jury, June 28, 1988, personal copy given to author; Metzger, interview.

50. Bobby Johnson, letter to author, Aug. 20, 1998.

51. *Ibid.*

52. "New Americans take oaths of citizenship," *Marshall News Messenger*, June 30, 1992.

53. Palmer, interview.

54. Thomas F. Lanier Sr., telephone interview by author, tape recording, Jan. 11, 2001.

55. Chase Palmer, letter to author, undated.

56. "Hall says freedom not a gift," *Marshall News Messenger*, Nov. 12, 1991.

57. Kathleen Hall McLendon and Madeleine Hall, interview by author, tape recording, Marshall, Texas, Nov. 24, 1998;

58. Judge Patrice Barron, letter to author, Oct. 14, 1998.

60. Crews, interview.

61. Richardson, telephone interview.

62. Metzger, interview; Ernest Metzger, letter to Judge Sam B. Hall Jr., Oct. 29, 1991, Hall family files.

63. G. Hobart Miller, telephone interview by author, tape recording, June 3, 2003.

64. Hohn, letter, interview.

65. Sharon Kacmarcik, telephone interviews by author, tape recording, Aug. 2 & Sept. 13, 1999.

66. *Ibid.*

67. Kay Lynn Brumbaugh, letter to author, Aug. 31, 1998.

68. *Ibid.*

69. Jill Renfro Willis, letter to author, Aug. 10, 1998.

70. *Ibid.*

71. Katie Dukes, telephone interview by author, tape recording, July 15, 1999.

72. Sally Socia, interview by author, tape recording, Marshall, Tex., Jan. 18, 1999.

73. Hohn, interview; Smith, interview.

74. Smith, interview. Of the three cases noted, one judgment proposed a compromise to requests to extend the time allowed for discovery in a high profile case involving the Xerox Corporation, partly in order to promote efficiency of the court docket and to reduce litigation costs. The published decision included the judicial law clerk's reference (which Judge Hall allowed) to one of C. Northcote Parkinson's laws, "work expands so as to fill the time allowed for its completion," in the decision on the key issue, to adjust, but also restrict, the time allowed for pretrial discovery processes for both plaintiffs and the defendants. Another decision related to the proper jurisdiction for a case relating to the "side saddle" gas tanks on eighties-model pickups built by General Motors. The third related to the determination of "unseaworthiness" of an oil-drilling vessel in deciding an injury lawsuit. Hohn, interview; the book reference is C. Northcote Parkinson, *Parkinson's Law or the Pursuit of Progress* (London: John Murray, 1958), 4; *R&D Business Systems, et al., v. Xerox; Gemini Equipment Partners Income Fund I, et al., v. Xerox,* 150 F.R.D. 87 (1993); *Tommy Dollar, et al., v. General Motors Corporation, et al.,* 814 F. Supp. 538 (1993); *Kenneth Brown, Jr., v. Cliff's Drilling Company,* 638 F. Supp. 1009 (1986).

75. *Ibid.*

76. Hohn, interview.

77. *Ibid.*

78. Kacmarcik, interview.

79. Smith, interview.

80. Kacmarcik, interview.

81. Hohn, letter.

82. Hohn, interview.

83. Hohn, letter.

84. Smith, interview.

85. Editorial, "Supreme Court? What's wrong with Sam Hall?" *Marshall News Messenger*, July 15, 1990; on the Thomas controversy: *Marshall News Messenger*, Oct. 13, 1991.

86. Edwin P. Horner, letter to author, Apr. 13, 1999; *Marshall News Messenger*, Apr. 8, 1991.

87. "In the United States District Court for the Eastern District of Texas, Marshall Division, *Presentation of the Portrait of the Honorable Sam B. Hall, Jr.*, to the United States District Court, Eastern District of Texas by the Harrison County Bar Association and Attorneys in and for the Eastern District of Texas," November 15, 1991, in *Federal Supplement* Vol. 781 (St. Paul, Minn.: West Publishing, 1992), lxv-lxvii.

88. *Ibid.;* William Barclay, *More Prayers for the Plain Man* (London: Collins, 1959; reprint, 1981), 34-5. The working title of the present biography came from the middle line, which originally read, "We thank Thee for those in whose presence it is *easier to be good.*"

89. *Marshall News Messenger*, Sept. 17 & Oct. 2, 1992. The fund-drive committee mem-

bers were Franklin Jones Jr., chairman, Joe Lovelace, Charles Thompson, F. Scott Baldwin Sr., Rex Houston, Lloyd Taylor, William Huffman, Gilbert I. Low, Ernest F. Smith, and Frank Finn; ETBU *Hilltop* (Fall/Winter, 1992): 7.

90. Ellis concluded, saying, "Years from now, if collectively we are able to produce a product even similar to Sam B. Hall, his benefactors, supporters, friends, and peers will have considered the opportunity and their individual investment as fulfilled." Don Ellis, personal notes given to author, Sam B. Hall Professorship file, ETBU.

91. Author, personal notes, Sept. 24, 1992, Sam B. Hall Professorship File, ETBU. Summers continued, "The friends of Judge Sam B. Hall have established a professorship at East Texas Baptist University in his honor, I think, precisely because they see in him a man of integrity, faith, moral strength, and leadership. They see a man who has embraced his commitments in order to do the good. He has done commendably well as he has achieved the good. Indeed, he is a man of historical worth. . . . I trust that the Hall professorship will always be a worthy reminder of the man of faith and commitment in whose name it has been given. I pledge that this first recipient of the professorship will seek to fulfill that purpose for the Judge Sam B. Hall professorship worthily."

92. *Ibid.*

Chapter 13

1. Judge William Wayne Justice, letter to author, Aug. 11, 1998.
2. Fred C. Hall Jr., letter to author, Aug. 17, 1998.
3. Judge Howell Cobb, letter to author, Dec. 2, 1998.
4. Dwight Hartley, telephone interview by author, tape recording, July 9, 2001.
5. Becky Hall Palmer, letter to author, undated.
6. Sally Cook Socia, interview by author, tape recording, Marshall, Tex., Jan. 18, 1999.
7. Ed Merritt, telephone interview by author, tape recording, Apr. 5, 1999.
8. Ed Hohn, interview by author, tape recording, Daingerfield, Tex., Mar. 9, 1999.
9. Marguerite Ratcliff, conversation with author, Marshall, Tex., Apr. 26, 1999.
10. Becky Hall Palmer and Pinkie Palmer, interview by author, tape recording, Marshall, Tex., June 14, 1999; Richard Anderson, interview by author, tape recording, Marshall, Tex., Nov. 17, 1998.
11. Wendell Klennert, telephone interview by author, tape recording, July 11, 2000.
12. Arthur O. Wesley, telephone interview by author, tape recording, Dec. 30, 2000.
13. D. Glenn Elliott, interview by author, tape recording, Longview, Tex., June 21, 1999.
14. Richard Haynes, telephone interview with author, tape recording, July 9, 2001.
15. Palmer and Palmer, interview.
16. Klennert, interview.
17. Madeleine Hall and family, conversation with author, July 20, 1998; Hohn, interview.
18. Madeleine Hall and family, conversation.
19. Madeleine Hall and family conversation, story from Hall son-in-law Tom Wynn.
20. Bobby Johnson, letter to author, Aug. 20, 1998.
21. Audrey Kariel, letter to author, Aug. 5, 1998.
22. Ronald Ned Dennis, interview by author, tape recording, Marshall, Tex., Feb. 18, 1999.
23. Florine Miller, interview by author, Marshall, Tex., Jan. 28, 1999.
24. Madeleine Hall and family, conversation.
25. Judge William J. Cornelius, letter to author, Dec. 21, 1997.
26. Bill Bradford, telephone interview by author, tape recording, June 28, 1999.
27. Chase Palmer, letter to author, undated.
28. Rebecca Palmer, letter to author, Aug. 24, 1998.
29. Darren Bodenhamer, school essay mailed to author, Sept. 13, 1994.
30. Madelyn and Meredith Bodenhamer, letters to author, July 1998.
31. Chase Palmer, letter.
32. Ray Lawson, interview by author, tape recording, Marshall, Tex., Oct. 7, 1998.
33. Florine Miller, interview.
34. Romano L. Mazzoli, letter to author, Dec. 15, 1998.
35. Robert Wainscott, telephone conversation with author, Jan. 10, 1999.
36. Bobby Johnson, letter.
37. Videotape, Mar. 14, 1994, Madeleine Hall personal files; Madeleine Hall, interview

by author, tape recording, Marshall, Tex., June 29, 2001.

38. Letters in Madeleine Hall personal files: Michael Shappell, letter to Sam and Madeleine Hall, Feb. 11, 1994; O. Ivan White Jr., letter to Madeleine Hall, Mar. 31, 1994; Becky Hall Palmer, letter to Sam B. Hall Jr., undated; Carolyn and Bob Richardson, letter to Judge Sam B. Hall Jr., Feb. 14, 1994; Earl S. Hines, letter to Sam B. Hall Jr., Feb. 1, 1994; J. J. "Jake" Pickle to Sam and Madeleine Hall, Mar. 9, 1994; John C. Fisher, letter to Madeleine Hall, Apr. 14, 1994.

39. Libby Crawford, letter to Sam and Madeleine Hall, Feb. 21, 1994.

40. Joe Waggonner, letter to author, Feb. 26, 1998.

41. Chase Palmer, letter.

42. Amanda Hall Wynn and Tom Wynn, interview by author, tape recording, Marshall, Tex., July 15, 1999; Verta Williams, interview by author, tape recording, Marshall, Tex., July 15, 1999.

43. O. Ivan White Jr., letter to author, Feb. 19, 1998.

44. *Marshall News Messenger*, Apr. 11, 1994.

45. Patrice Barron, letter to author, Oct. 14, 1998.

46. *Cong. Rec.*, 103d Congr., 2d. sess., 140, no. 40, daily ed., (Apr. 14, 1994): S4280.

47. Madeleine S. Hall, letter to Joe W. Lovelace, May 17, 1994, copy accompanying letter to author, Mar. 3, 1998; Joe W. Lovelace, eulogy notes accompanying Hall letter to author, Mar. 3, 1998.

48. *Marshall News Messenger*, Apr. 14, 1994.

49. Wendell Klennert, telephone interview.

50. *Cong. Rec.*, 140, no. 67, daily ed. (May 25, 1994): H4081-H4084.

51. *Ibid.*

52. *Cong. Rec.*, 140, no. 65, daily ed. (May 23, 1994): H3836-H3838. The courthouse act H.R. 3840 became Public Law 103-289, *Cong. Rec.* (15 July 1994): S9134.

53. Program, *Ceremony to observe the naming of the Sam B. Hall, Jr., Federal Building and United States Courthouse*, May 29, 1995; East Texas Baptist University, Sam B. Hall Jr. Professorship Files.

54. *Marshall News Messenger*, May 30, 1995.

55. Bill Palmer, interview by author, tape recording, Marshall, Tex., Oct. 20, 1998.

56. R. Orin Littlejohn Jr., interview by author, tape recording, Marshall, Tex., Feb. 23, 1999.

57. Dwight Hartley, letter to Madeleine Hall, Apr. 14, 1994, Madeleine Hall personal files.

58. *Ibid.*

59. Sue Jordan, letter to author, May 12, 1998.

60. B. B. Boon, telephone interview by author, tape recording, Jan. 14, 1999.

61. Madeleine Hall, interview.

62. *Ibid.*

Index